Preface

The aim of this book is to provide the reader with a substantial amount of information about how adolescents grow and mature, and to indicate some of the problems encountered in this remarkably complex process.

After consulting with dozens of psychologists who specialize in human growth and development, with hundreds of university students who want to learn about adolescent psychology, and with many more hundreds of young people growing through the teen years, I culled the topics and concerns which make up this book. I think they represent the most pressing topics of adolescent psychology, although certainly not the only ones.

Professionals who work daily with adolescents, particularly school teachers, social workers, counsellors, and psychologists want to know as much as possible about how young people change during the course of the adolescent years. They want to know the differences which exist between 13-year-olds and 17-year-olds and how these differences come about. They want to know the "hows" and "wherefores" of the growth process. The entire second half of this book is devoted exclusively to this topic, and, as of this date, is one of the few books written in English to do so.

The book deals with other topics also. Chapter One deals with a fundamental issue in adolescent psychology: the extent to which the adolescent years are filled with "storm and stress." Our personal response to this basic question greatly influences our outlook towards youth, and indirectly, our outlook towards the inherent turbulence of all growth periods.

Chapters Two and Three deal with what adolescents themselves tend to view as the most vital topic of adolescent psychology: How do I know "who" or "what" I am, or will become. Chapter Two distills the basis to "normal" features within the adolescent identity process while Chapter Three overviews malfunctions within the identity process.

Chapter Four analyzes the vital issue of adolescent sexuality. Despite our society's preoccupation with sex and sexuality, knowledge about adolescent sexuality remains relatively obscure. This chapter attempts to do more than merely report the incidence of sexual behavior during the teen years, it attempts to explain the *nature of sexuality* during this time period.

Chapter Five describes the various ways in which adolescent behavior, adolescent thought and adolescent perceptions of reality are influenced by *defense mechanisms* and other devices which protect the young person from the bitter realities of what seems to many an indifferent universe.

The subject matter of this small book in no way deals with all of the exciting and vital issues of adolescent psychology. Hopefully, however, it embraces a spirit of inquiry, and a foundation of information, which will encourage the reader to learn more about this exciting field of study, and to appreciate the intrinsic complexity of the teen years.

J.J. Mitchell
University of Alberta
December, 1985

Contents

1   **The Storm and Stress Debate** **1**

Storm and Stress: Yes   2
Anna Freud's Viewpoint on Storm and Stress   5
Storm and Stress: No   7
Bandura's Viewpoint on Storm and Stress   9
Additional Perspectives   11
Postscript   12

2   **Identity Formation During Adolescence** **15**

Role Experimentation and Identity   17
Self-Importance and Identity   21
The Peer Group and Identity   23
The Role of the Future in the Formation of Identity ..   25
Constraints Upon Adolescent Identity   27
Identity in Primitive Societies   29
Postscript   30

3   **Malfunctions Within the Identity Process** **33**

Identity Crises   33
Negative Identity   34
Identity Diffusion   36
Identity Disorder   38
Alienation and Identity   38
Nihilism: The Collapse of Identity   40
Postscript   45

4   **Adolescent Sexuality** **47**

Personality Factors in Adolescent Sexuality   48
Sex Differences in Adolescent Sexuality   52
The Unconscious Desire to Become Pregnant   53
Sexual Abstinence During Adolescence   56
Intimacy and Sexuality   59
Depersonalizing Sex   61
Misperceptions About Adolescent Sexuality   64
Postscript   66

5   **Defense Mechanisms: Their Impact on Adolescent
       Behavior** **69**

The Defense Mechanisms   69
Protective Structures and the Adolescent Personality .   82
Some Further Considerations   87
Postscript   89

Section Two: The Three Ages of Adolescence

6   The Early-Adolescent Period: A General Overview **93**

The Effects of Physical Growth on the Early Adolescent   96
The Social and Private World During Early Adolescence   98
Social Outlooks during Early Adolescence   99
Home and Family During Early Adolescence 102
Moral Outlook During Early Adolescence 103
Sexual Curiosity During Early Adolescence 104
Postscript 108

7   The Early Adolescent Period: Some Specific Considerations **111**

Storm and Stress During Early Adolescence 111
Identity During Early Adolescence 113
Sexual Interests During Early Adolescence 114
Defense Mechanisms During Early Adolescence 116
Narcissism 120
Postscript 124

8   The Middle-Adolescent Period: A General Overview ... **127**

The Body During Middle Adolescence 127
The Intellect During Middle Adolescence 128
The Effects on Mental Growth on the Middle-Adolescent 132
    Personality ....
Free Will During Adolescence ....` 134
Social Living During Adolescence 135
Pathology During Middle Adolescence 137
Postscript 138

9   Middle Adolescence: Some Specific Considerations ... **141**

Storm and Stress During Adolescence 141
Identity Formation and Identity Confusion During Middle Adolescence 143
Sexuality During Middle Adolescence 145
Defense Mechanisms During Middle Adolescence 146
Non-Rational Beliefs and Irrational Perceptions 149
Postscript 154

10   The Late Adolescent Period **157**

From Adolescence Into Adulthood 157
The Body During late Adolescence 160
The Intellect During Late Adolescence 161

Psychological Makeup of the Late Adolescence 161
Intimacy During Late Adolescence 164
The Fundamental Needs of Adolescence 166
Love, Belonging and Esteem Needs During Adolescence 168
Postscript 171

11   The Late Adolescent: Further Observations **173**
Storm and Stress During Late Adolescence 173
Identity During Late Adolescence 174
Sexuality During Late Adolescence 178
Defense Mechanism During Late Adolescence 180
Hypocrisy and Prejudice 180
Adolescent Prejudice 183
Postscript 185
A Final Postscript 186

References **189**

Index **195**

1
The Storm and Stress Debate

Is adolescence a period of powerful stress and intense anxiety? Is it more painful than other ages? These questions form the basis for a debate in contemporary psychology which goes like this. *Position One*: Adolescence is a time of unusual and excessive stress which creates considerable anxiety for all adolescents. *Position Two*: Adolescence is not a time of unusual and excessive stress; therefore, it is not a period of considerable anxiety for all youth.

In this chapter a brief investigation of each viewpoint will be undertaken, with Anna Freud defending Position One, and Albert Bandura Position Two.

In recent years the phrase "storm and stress" has been used to symbolize adolescence as a period of chronic turbulence and emotional turmoil. However, the phrase is used with such diversity, and it encapsulates so many different meanings to so many different scholars, that Coleman says it is "perhaps the most ambiguous concept in all the literature on adolescence" (1980, p. 148).

For example, some psychologists who claim adolescence is a period of storm and stress really mean that it is a time when *psychiatric ailments increase* in a dramatic fashion. Since most research indicates that this increase is true, they view this as support for storm and stress. On the other hand, even though adolescence witnesses an increase in psychiatric ailments when compared with the childhood years, it does not witness as much emotional disturbance as the early adult years (ages 20-24); therefore, it is not more stressful than early adulthood.

Some psychologists do not consider adolescence an overly troublesome time because many disturbances of this age are *situational* disorders which tend to disappear with time. They feel the storm of adolescence is more of a thundershower, which is horrendous for the moment, but which in time subsides, permitting the return of normal climate.

Finally, storm and stress theorists recognize that all periods of adolescence are not equally distressful. As is documented in greater detail in the final section of this book, the *late* stage of adolescence experiences the most severe pathology, while the *early* stage is characterized by squalls but few genuine storms; the *middle* period of adolescence is between these extremes as far as psychiatric problems are concerned.

Let us now examine the two viewpoints. Storm and Stress: "Yes," and Storm and Stress: "No."

Storm and Stress: Yes

Psychologists, educators, parents, and adolescents have long observed that the teen years are a time of turbulence. St. Augustine and Jean Jacques Rousseau, separated by fourteen centuries, wrote amazingly parallel overviews of their adolescent experiences, confessing to the tension of unliberated sexuality, the pressure of social expectation, the conflict of contradictory rules, and the despair of crushed passion. Upon reading their reports of adolescent strife, one cannot escape the idea that there is something *about adolescence itself* which causes a wide range of anxiety and insecurity.

The *inherent troublesomeness* of the adolescent experience as described here by Ackerman typifies the storm and stress posture:

> The fluidity of the adolescent's self-image, his changing aims and aspirations, his sex drives, his *unstable powers of repression*, his *struggle to readapt* his childhood of right and wrong to the needs of maturity *bring into sharp focus every conflict, past and present*, that he has failed to solve. The protective coloring of the past personality is stripped off, and the deeper emotional currents are laid bare. (1958, p. 227)

Some psychologists are even more forceful, claiming that *all* adolescents experience extreme turmoil, that they toil in the relentless grip of alternating depression and ecstasy, and that their day-to-day living is an emotional battlefield.

These beliefs have been popular since 1904 when G. Stanley Hall in his two-volume classic on adolescent psychology introduced the phrase "Sturm und Drang" (storm and stress) to typify the psychological climate of the adolescent. Hall wrote that it was characteristic of youth to vacillate between the extremes of sorrow and exuberance, and to shift unexpectedly from friendly altruism to selfish hoarding. It was Hall's opinion that adolescents were capable of the most intense romantic passion and "Promethean enthusiasm." All in all, they were accorded an incredible range of emotional abilities which they roamed unpredictably.

Hall further claimed that: "The teens are emotionally unstable and pathic. It is a natural impulse to experience hot and perfervid psychic states, and the whole is characterized by emotionalism. We see here the instability and fluctuations now so characteristic. The emotions develop by contrast and reaction into the opposite" (Vol. 2, p. 74-75).

G. Stanley was one of the most prodigious scholars of North American psychology. He studied under Wilhelm Wundt, who some scholars consider the father of experimental psychology, and with William James, whose writings are included in the Great Works of the Western World. He founded Clark University, as well as the American Psychological Association. He persuaded Sigmund Freud to lecture in the United States (a remarkable feat), and was academic supervisor of Arnold Gessell, one of the most influential developmental psychologists of our era. All in all, his energy was herculean and his achievements prolific. From this man sprang the first systematic study of adolescent psychology, and with it his proclamation that adolescence is a time of "storm and stress." (I provide this information to impress upon the reader that the origins of storm and stress rest on the shoulders of one of psychology's most prominent scholars, and do not derive merely from popular images or stereotypes).

Psychotherapists, social workers, school counselors and other professionals who work with adolescents are perhaps the strongest supporters of storm and stress. They note that drug use, delinquency, and self-destruction are widespread in the adolescent community. They also claim that adolescents themselves report more trouble and stress than during childhood. This accumulated data from professionals in the field lends strong support for adolescence as a time of genuine storm and stress.

Anthony makes his point directly: "The adult in our western culture has apparently learned to expect a state of acute disequilibrium and anticipates the "storm and stress" in his adolescent child as he once anticipated the negativism of his 2-year-old." He also notes that "The expectation has been incorporated into the literature of psychological development, and it may take methodological research and many years of endeavor to remove it from the textbooks." Anthony, however, also provides this insight, which the storm and stress theorists do not usually agree with, but it is nevertheless thought-provoking: "There is, however, growing anthropological and sociological support for the concept that society gets the type of adolescent it expects and deserves . . ." (1966, p. 65).

Friedenburg argues an interesting premise. He claims that the progressive maturity of the adolescent personality *requires* conflict and confrontation with the dominant society, and that in the absence of such conflict, the adolescent does not mature into a robust and hardy adult. Friedenburg asserts:

> Must there be conflict between the adolescent and society? The point is
> that adolescence is conflict . . . protracted conflict . . . between the
> individual and society. There are cultures in which the conflict seems
> hardly to occur; but where it does not, the characteristic development of
> personality which we associate with adolescence does not occur either.
> (1959, p. 32)

Never far away, however, are the more detached assessors who claim
that no reasons dictate that there *must* be conflict between the adolescent
and society. Offer dampens Friedenberg's zeal with:

> All our data, including the psychological testing, point in the opposite
> direction. The adolescents not only adjusted well; they were also in touch
> with their feelings and developed meaningful relationships with others.
> (1969, p. 184)

Erik Erikson, the most quoted (and most prolific) of the youth experts
lends his support to the storm and stress viewpoint when he comments
"every adolescent is apt to go through *some serious struggle* at one time or
another."

Thornburg's description of adolescent complications is typical, even
though he is not a "hard line" storm and stress theorist.

> Stress in the environment may become so intense that the adolescent
> entertains the idea of escaping to drugs, committing suicide, or with-
> drawing into loneliness. Fear of being unacceptable to others often causes
> emotional panic. Such panic may result in unpredictable or undesirable
> behavior. Social stimuli may overload the mind to the point that the
> adolescent thinks his or her "head is going to explode." . . . These types
> of emotional experiences may lead to the confusions and disillusion-
> ments featured in the storm-and-stress hypothesis of adolescent emotional
> development. (p. 71)

Peter Blos believes that adolescent storm and stress is aggravated by
the trauma of *childhood*. He notes: "It is assumed here that trauma is a
universal human condition during infancy and early childhood, leaving,
even under the most favorable circumstances, a permanent residue." Adolescents strive to overcome childhood trauma, but, for the most part, they
are "unable to overcome the disequilibrizing effect of this residue . . ."
(1979, p. 183) In essence, the pain of childhood disrupts, even contami-
nates, the adolescent years. (See Laufer & Laufer, 1984, for a more
thorough analysis of this viewpoint).

It is worthy of special note that adolescent turmoil is often aggravated
by the "midlife crisis" of parents. Prosen and Toews (1981) claim that

many parents experience fears and uncertainties in their own lives, especially a fear of death, and a sense of meaninglessness about their life accomplishments. These anxieties interfere with effective parenting, and complicate the psychological climate of the household. Prosen sees it this way:

> While the middle-aged parent may experience a certain passivity and helplessness, their adolescent children tend to experience opposite feelings. They are in rebellion, actively questing for their own identity and the right to control and determine their own future in line with their own goals and dreams. They resent parental authority and control and indicate to the parents that the parents are helpless. As a result, the midlife feelings of the helplessness and passivity experienced by the parent are intensified. Added to the passivity of not being able to control one's own life is the distress of not being able to control one's own children; added to the anxiety about the uncertainty of one's own future now is the anxiety about the uncertainty of the adolescent's future. (p. 174)

Therefore, the "storm and stress" of middle age indirectly compounds the turmoil of adolescence.

This brief collage of viewpoints helps us appreciate that a wide variety of psychologists view adolescence as a period of unusual and, on occasion, profound stress. In order to construct a more thorough defense of adolescent storm and stress, we shall now overview what Anna Freud has to say on the topic.

Anna Freud's Viewpoint on Storm and Stress

As we have already mentioned, G. Stanley Hall pioneered the concept of stress, drawing heavily upon Darwin's ideas of the biological determinants of behavior. And it was Sigmund Freud who pioneered the psychodynamic theory of personality which claims that the mind is governed by biophysical determinants. However, it was the daughter of Sigmund Freud, Anna, who blended the ideas of these two great men into a cohesive statement of adolescent storm and stress.

Anna Freud began with two vital assumptions. First, she claimed that adolescence, by its very nature, is an interruption of peaceful growth. Second, "peaceful adolescence" is itself an abnormal process. In her view, genital feelings and sexual goals become the primary adolescent focus, throwing the individual into conflict with both the ego and the superego. These conflicts predispose the adolescent to two dramatic consequences: first, the new rush of sexual energy makes the id so powerful that it begins to dominate the ego, thereby replacing the ego control-centres with the amorality of the unconscious; second, and the diametric opposite of the first, the ego reacts to the invasion of sexual impulses with a defensive front which denies the new sexual "rush." Whichever reaction emerges, the adolescent experiences turmoil.

Freud further claims that during adolescence, "aggressive impulses are intensified to the point of complete unruliness, hunger becomes voracity and the naughtiness of the latency period turns into the criminal behavior of adolescence." To further bring home her message: "habits of cleanliness, laboriously acquired during the latency period, give place to pleasure in dirt and disorder, and instead of modesty and sympathy we find exhibitionistic tendencies, brutality, and cruelty to animals." Finally, ". . . in boys ideas of castration and in girls penis-envy once more become the centre of interest" (Newman, p. 18).

Anna Freud viewed suspiciously those adolescents who do not experience upheaval because, from her perspective, this signalled a defensiveness against normal growth. Youth for whom adolescence is sexually uneventful are "children who have built up excessive defense against their drive activities and are now crippled by the results, which act as barriers against the normal maturational processes of phase development." This viewpoint is not unique to Anna Freud. Laufer, for example, pens a virtually identical comment: "We know that a picture of equilibrium during adolescence is itself a sign of danger . . ." (1977, p. 69).

Anna Freud understands human behavior from definite assumptions and like all psychoanalytic writers, she is straightforward about her biases. Here are two of them to help the reader understand her viewpoints. "Our insight into *typical developments* will increase with the number of adolescents who undergo analysis." In other words, her primary source of information, and the data to which she lends most credence, derives from therapy. (Many psychologists simply do not agree with this because it precludes the vast array of knowledge which comes from investigating "normal" youth, from large population groups, from surveys, interviews, and so on).

Second, "Where adolescence is concerned, it seems easier to describe its pathological manifestations than the normal process." It stands to reason that her overall conclusions will favor the unhealthy rather than the healthy.

Extending the foregoing to its logical conclusion we understand why Freud claimed: "Adolescence constitutes *by definition* an interruption of peaceful growth which resembles in appearance a variety of other emotional upsets and structural upheavals." (A Freud, 1968)

Anna Freud is one of the most forceful defenders of the "storm and stress" philosophy. She and other psychoanalysts have been the most sophisticated promoters of adolescence-as-turmoil, and, in large measure, they are responsible for its rather widespread acceptance, in both the academic community and society-at-large.

In summary, a wide variety of specialists ranging from clinical psychologists to social workers to academics have raised a collective banner signalling adolescence as a time of distress and turbulence. As a note of historical interest, this viewpoint dominated "accepted" opinion for the most of this century. It was not until the sixties that another group of experts began to argue alternate viewpoints.

Storm and Stress: No

According to "Storm and Stress" psychologists the adolescent resembles a runaway locomotive on a collision course with whatever (or whoever) happens along the tracks. One author says: "one cannot analyze an adolescent in the middle phase, it is like running next to an express train." Another writer likens adolescence to "an active volcanic process with continuous eruptions taking place, preventing the crust from solidifying." In the clinical literature the use of terms such as "turbulence," "chaos," and "turmoil" are frequent. Blos, for example, has stated that early adolescence is a period of profound emotional reorganization "with attendant and well defined states of chaos." After reviewing these assessments of youth, Anthony insightfully notes: "Once the psychotherapist gets it into his head that he has to deal with a bomb that might explode or a volcano that might erupt or an express train that will outpace him . . . his view of youth is likely affected for the worse" (Anthony, 1969, p. 57).

Offer makes an important observation about such metaphors:"Investigators who have spent most of their professional lives studying disturbed adolescents stress the importance of a period of turmoil through which all teenagers must pass in order to grow into mature adults. On the other hand, investigators who, like us, have studied normal adolescent populations tend to minimize the extent of the turmoil." (1969, p. 180) (Michalko, 1984, provides an insightful overview of various metaphors frequently used by social scientists to "understand" adolescence).

That adolescence is not necessarily a time of unbearable stress becomes more fitting when one is not overly impressed with metaphors such as erupting volcanoes and runaway express trains. Life must be more than inconvenient or bothersome to be "stormy."Offer draws the following conclusions:

> *We have not found turmoil to be prevalent in our normal adolescent population.* The concept of adolescent turmoil should be seen as only one route for passing through adolescence, one that the majority of our subjects did not utilize. Rebellion was seen in the early adolescence of our

subjects; in all but a few cases that rebellious behavior was not a part of a total picture of turmoil but was coped with before it grew to chaotic proportions for the individuals involved. (1969, p. 179)

The Offers (1975) postulate three distinct growth patterns for adolescents. The first pattern, which they call *Continuous Growth*, typified 23% of their subjects. This group passed uneventfully through their teen years with a fairly clear picture about where they were going and what the future held in store for them. They got along rather well with their parents, and showed no unusual stress in their relations with the opposite sex. Their superegos (conscience) did not trouble them in any way resembling what psychoanalysts claim is typical for this age. The second pattern (*Surgent Growth; 35%*) was more typified by stress than the first pattern. These youngsters had lower self-esteem, longer periods of regression mingled with their growth progressions, and they struggled more with depression and anger than the first group. Interpersonal relations had more rocky moments, but, on the whole, overall adjustment was adaptive and effective. The third group (*Tumultuous Growth; 21%*) reads like G. Stanley Hall wrote their life script. Internal turmoil was the highest among the three groups, as were behavioral problems at school. The ego employed a greater range of defenses in order to cope with their considerable anxiety; as a group they mistrusted adults, and encountered numerous conflicts with them.

J.J. Conger suggests that most North American youth do not experience the turmoil attributed by clinical psychologists; neither does their behavior assume the extremes which storm and stress authors such as G. Stanley Hall or Anna Freud claimed. Conger concisely summarized his findings:

It appears that the stresses that adolescence imposes on the individual, particularly in our culture, do not for the great majority, lead to the high degree of emotional turmoil, violent mood swings and threatened loss of control suggested by clinical theorists. All of these consequences clearly characterize some adolescents, but the evidence suggests that there has been an unwarranted tendency on the part of clinicians to generalize too readily to the average adolescent findings obtained from a limited segment of the adolescent population (particularly middle to upper-middle class patients and sensitive, alienated young writers). (1973)

This observation has since been made by many "youth-watchers', and among psychologists in the '80s it is the most widely accepted viewpoint on adolescent storm and stress. However, its acceptance is not universal.

Cross cultural research has not supported the notion that adolescence is *necessarily* a time of storm and stress. We are indebted to Margaret Mead and Ruth Benedict for their insights into the cultural differences in the amount of storm and stress encountered by adolescents. Mead noted that cultures with few age-determined roles witness fewer child-to-adult transition problems than is true in North America. Likewise, cultures which ceremonialized or ritualized the young person's entrance into the adult world seemed to ease the "growing pains" so evident in our culture.

Based upon her research with girls in the Samoan culture, Mead drew these conclusions:

> Adolescence represented no period of crisis or stress, but was instead an orderly developing of a set of slowly maturing interests and activities. The girls' minds were perplexed by no conflicts, troubled by no philosophical inquiries, beset by no remote ambitions. To live as a girl with many lovers as long as possible and then to marry in one's own village and have many children, these were uniform and satisfying ambitions. (1928, p. 120)

Mead supports the idea that it is not adolescent growth unto itself which causes storm and stress; equally at cause are the discontinuities and expectations of the culture in which the adolescent lives.

Bandura's Viewpoint on Storm and Stress

An early and influential critic of the storm and stress viewpoint was Albert Bandura, a social-learning theorist who investigated adolescent boys, their parents, and the interaction between them, and from this investigation concluded that storm and stress was not nearly as troublesome as Freud, Hall, or any of the storm and stress theorists claim.

Storm and stress theorists emphasize that the combination of internal adolescent growth and external societal restraint percolates high anxiety within the adolescent (and the society which houses them). In particular, parental restrictiveness, dependence-independence conflicts, and parent-peer group conflicts enhance the misery of adolescent existence. Bandura's research contradicted all three categories. "At adolescence, parents supposedly become more controlling and prohibitive. We found the very opposite to be true." Bandura claims that by the time adolescence arrives most boys have already internalized most of their parents' values and standards of behavior, and as a result restrictions and external controls have actually been lessened rather than intensified. With regard to dependence-independence conflicts, Bandura reports: "The view that adolescents are engaged in a struggle to emancipate themselves from their parents also receives little support from our study." For most boys independence training began during childhood, and in many respects, was "largely accomplished by the time of adolescence." Finally, the touted struggle between parents and their adolescent children's peer group turned out to be not such a struggle after all. Many teens, Bandura claims, choose friends who share similar values not only with themselves but also with their parents. Consequently, "the peer group often served to reinforce and to uphold parental norms and standards of behavior . . ."

Bandura claims that there is a variety of reasons why we misperceive the nature of adolescents, all of which cast insight into why we understand youth in our culture as we do.

First, *Overinterpretation of superficial signs of nonconformity*. Adults make too much of youthful fads and eccentricities, and overestimate the extent to which these peculiarities are a function of age. Bandura personalizes this viewpoint with the following anecdote:

> At a recent cocktail party the present writer was cornered by an inquiring lady who expressed considerable puzzlement over adolescents' fascination for unusual and bizarre styles. The lady herself was draped with a sack, wearing a preposterous object on her head, and spiked high heel shoes that are more likely to land one in an orthopedic clinic, than to transport one across the room to the olives.

Second, *Mass media sensationalism*. The media hypes what sells. Excitement and sensationalism beat out their opposites. The popular audience, and the media specialists who make their living catering to it, have had a field day with the storm and stress image of youth. James Dean's classic rendition of volcanic youth in *Rebel Without a Cause*, and Salinger's portrayal of William Caufield as the perplexed and bewildered adolescent in *Catcher in the Rye* are considered honest reflections of adolescent chaos by the mass audience. As Offer's research indicates, however, these literary prototypes represent only a limited segment of youth, and in many respects these images are projections of adult misconceptions more than accurate portrayals of the adolescent experience.

Third, *Generalization from samples of deviant adolescents*. Our knowledge of what makes adolescents tick is overly biased with data from psychiatrically or behaviorally disturbed youngsters. These data are vital to understanding adolescent disturbances; however, they are not a reliable source of knowledge about normal, or healthy, youngsters.

Fourth, *Overemphasis on the biological determination of heterosexual behavior*. Adolescence is viewed as a time when the individual is encumbered with a sudden and powerful urge for sexual involvement. Bandura counters: "In contrast to this widely accepted biological drive theory, evidence from studies of cross-species and cross-cultural sexual behavior reveals that human sexuality is governed primarily by social conditions, rather than endocrinal stimulation."

The adolescent as a seething cauldron of sexuality is one of the more firmly entrenched stereotypes in our culture. Researchers who investigate the daily habits of adolescents, however, provide little support for this point of view. Interestingly, adolescents themselves, when interviewed about their sexual drives and impulses, rarely rate them as highly as do adults who describe the same youths.

Fifth, *Stage theories of development*. The proliferation of stage theories has conditioned the public to believe that adolescence occurs suddenly, on an established timetable, with a series of tendencies and desires that are somewhat out of control. One parcel within this package, according to some stage theorists, is storm and stress. In other words, adolescence is perceived as a stage of development which is unavoidably filled with turbulence.

Sixth, *Self-fulfilling prophecy*. Bandura claims that much "unacceptable" adolescent behavior is little more than self-fulfilling prophecy. That is, if society labels its teenagers as wild and free-wheeling, expects them to be rebellious and defiant, sloppy and recalcitrant, and if this image is reinforced by television, by literature, and by the newspapers, then it is quite possible that these series of expectations force adolescents into roles that, in all probability, would not otherwise have been natural to them.

Bandura is not a spokesman for those who oppose the storm and stress doctrine of adolescent development. However, his writing shows a clarity which frequently eludes the topic; and his arguments are representative of a larger cluster, the nuclear idea of which is that adolescence, though a difficult time of life, is not *inherently* turbulent.

Additional Perspectives

To understand adolescent storm and stress it is important to keep in mind that a traumatic experience is *not inherently destructive*. As Maslow says: "a traumatic situation *may* be psychologically threatening but it does not *have* to be. It may be educative and strengthening if well handled." (1970, p. 110) This observation merits special attention because we sometimes see trauma where it does not exist. Equally troublesome, we sometimes confuse ordinary life pain with trauma — an error which makes the pain of youth appear more disastrous than it really is.

F. Barron reminds us that it is not "pressure" or "strain" *per se*, which weakens the adolescent personality. Equally important is the degree to which *the character* of the individual has been nurtured to handle disappointment and hardship. He comments:

> Everyone alive has troubles and problems and, as we learned from our studies of especially "sound" individuals, the most important consideration in determining personal effectiveness is not the amount of trouble

or misfortune (within limits) a person encounters, but *how he responds to the vicissitudes and challenges of life*. This capacity to meet problems without being dismayed or overwhelmed, to endure suffering and face great loss without foundering is an aspect of psychological strength and vitality that deserves special study. (Barron, 1969, p. 121)

Barron's concluding phrase is timely because adolescent character and internal strength is something we know little about — further study definitely is needed!

Finally, Gordon Allport reminds us that all youth struggle with adversity, and incorporate this struggle into their normal growth plan. He also claims that youth are busy with "gradual learning and quiet coping, and the extension of selfhood, with noncritical failures and successes, with developing . . . a personal style of life." As a final reminder of the durability of adolescence, Allport says:

Even in the throes of crisis, he seeks in *undramatic ways to consolidate his* gains and continue on the path of *becoming*. Crises in normal personality development are important, but so too is the slow growth of each youth's unique style of life. (1964, p. 241)

Postscript

Adolescence, more so than childhood, is embroiled in controversy concerning the subjective nature of its existence. The controversy is complicated by the fact that adolescents, like adults, have different temperaments and styles, which makes universal statements about them impossible.

The purpose of this chapter is to point out the diversity of thought concerning adolescent psychology, and to indicate that all youth do not follow the same path. In other chapters we will note similar controversies.

The focus of this book is adolescence in North America. However, we must note that *culture* influences the adolescent experience in profound ways; therefore, although it is unfair to think of adolescent psychology only as the cultural anthropology of youth, it is equally unfair not to view it in its cultural context.

Also, we are left with the inescapable fact that not all *groups* of youth are equally likely to encounter storm and stress. As is true for adults, the more one reaps the benefits of society, the less stormy life is *likely* to be. The talented, the gifted, the socially astute, the privileged, and the educated, while facing the universal dilemmas of growth and maturation, encounter fewer obstacles from society, and therefore, in a cumulative sense, incur less overall storm and stress. Erikson has summarized well the differences between the "haves" and "have-nots" as far as life struggle is concerned:

> Adolescence, therefore, is least "stormy" in that segment of youth which is gifted and well trained in the pursuit of expanding technological trends, and thus able to identify with new roles of competency and invention and to accept a more implicit ideological outlook. . . . On the other hand, should a young person feel that the environment tries to deprive him too radically of all forms of self expression which permit him to develop and integrate the next step, he may resist with all the wild strength encountered in animals who are suddenly forced to defend their lives. For, indeed, in the social jungle of human existence there is no feeling of being alive without a sense of identity. (1968, pp. 129-130)

Finally, a healthy respect for individual differences is in order. After all, we do not observe complete uniformity during childhood, or adulthood; therefore, we do not expect adolescence to yield a uniformity of personal experience not found elsewhere in the human growth cycle.

In the next chapter we shall take a look at some of the problems surrounding the search for identity during adolescence. The attentive reader will note that the path toward identity is greatly influenced by the storm and stress the individual experiences, and as well, by the pressures, both internal and external, to which he is exposed.

2
Identity Formation During Adolescence

Identity:

"Identity" does not have an existence of its own awaiting discovery. Rather, it is a gradual and consistently changing appraisal of oneself anchored in the core of experience, guided by the facts of personal history, and destined by the hopefulness of the future. Except in unusual instances of foreclosure, identity remains fluid and expansive as the adolescent becomes increasingly aware of the widening circle of people who are significant to him and to whom he is significant.

The nuclear components of identity are: (1) a sense of personal importance; (2) continuity of experience; and (3) a solidarity with family, community and society. It is the task of the adolescent to somehow integrate these diverse components into a cohesive unity. This, however, which proves extremely challenging to most youth, and for good reasons. First, the sense of *personal importance essential to a wholesome identity eludes many youth because they are not valued as important by other people and in their daily lives they do not do* much of importance. Second, for many youngsters daily life is *not* characterized by a *continuity of experience*; rather it is filled with unexpected failures and disappointments. Third, many adolescents do not have a sense of solidarity with their family or their community — if anything, they have a sense of hostility toward them.

Identity is established within a social context. Parents, friends, teachers, coaches, brothers and sisters form the backbone of day-to-day interactions, and they, in large measure, foster the specialness, uniqueness, and esteem vital to identity. Not surprisingly, therefore, the quality of our human contacts greatly determines the quality of our identity. A personal identity means knowing myself in relation to "me" *and* in relation to others.

Adolescence as the Age of Identity

Identity is not finalized during adolescence; however, it is the age when it progressively solidifies. Identity cannot emerge until the individual begins to envision himself within the panorama of an unfolding future. This unique sense of "me-ness" begins when the adolescent places himself in what Erikson calls "ego-space-time', a unified reconciliation of past history, present realities, and future possibilities. In the life span, adolescence is the first period when these requirements can be met. It is not the *only* period — it is merely the first period.

The complexities of personal identity cannot be negotiated without a highly developed ego. In order to attain a *convincing* sense of our own self, we must be able to distinguish how we are like other people, like some other people, and like no other person. We must be able to see ourselves in terms of family and society, in terms of group affiliations, but within these configurations, isolate our own uniqueness and privacy. We must be able to make decisions about aspects of our character we want to expand, about limitations we want to improve, about deficiencies we want to eradicate. These evaluations require intellectual dexterity and substance. In Piagetian terms, they require *formal thought* which is an adolescent reality. (It is, in most instances, a middle and late-adolescent phenomenon.)

Identity requires an assessment of one's abilities and a vision of how these abilities can be synthesized with society. It demands not only that we make judgements, but also that we judge people who are judging us. Erikson put it this way:

> . . . identity formation employs a process of simultaneous reflection and observation, a process taking place on all levels of mental functioning, by which the individual judges himself in the light of what he perceives to be the way in which others judge him in comparison to themselves and to a typology significant to them; while he judges their way of judging him in the light of how he perceives himself in comparison to them and to types that have become relevant to him. (1968, pp. 22-23)

An adult identity cannot be established without an adult body. The emergence of the adult body does not *create* an adult identity, but it forces the adolescent to envision himself in terms of adultness. Likewise with sexual desires and ambitions. By societal decree, these realities carry adult responsibilities and confer a certain amount of adult status.

In essence, the combined vitality of expanding intelligence and the unfolding body makes adolescence the "age of identity" not only in our era but in all eras of recorded history.

The emotional makeup of adolescents complicates their quest for identity. For example, identity requires a sense of personal uniqueness, and this is *encouraged* by egocentrism and narcissism. However, the diversity of experiences which adolescents encounter, plus their uncertainty about the future interferes with their need for *continuity of experience*. An increased ability to criticize society sometimes leads to a greater allegiance with it, but equally true, it sometimes leads to alienation from it. Therefore, the quest for identity is not uniformly propelled by the adolescent character; rather, it is both pushed and pulled in something of a psychic tug-of-war where the adolescent is simultaneously the participant and the spectator.

The core of the identity problem for the adolescent is selecting an occupation or other life goal. "The future, he knows, must follow a *plan*, and in this respect his sense of self-hood takes on a dimension entirely lacking in childhood" (Allport, 1961, p. 126). As we shall see, this "entirely new dimension" poses considerable problems, sometimes crises.

Personal identity includes positive as well as negative elements: "Mixed in with the positive identity, there is a negative identity which is composed of what he has been shamed for, what he has been punished for, and what he feels guilty about . . . Identity means an integration of all previous identifications and self images, including the negative ones." (Evans, p. 36)

Therefore, before we begin a more thorough assessment of identity and its relationship to the adolescent we must recognize that it requires a complicated blending of one's past, present and future, as well as an integration of self with society. The attainment of identity is beyond the scope of childhood and, as we shall discover, frequently beyond adolescence. Nevertheless, in our culture, adolescence is the "age of identity."

The scope of this chapter:

In this chapter we shall overview the factors which contribute to normal adolescent identity. Special emphasis is placed upon *role experimentation* and the sampling of identities. This chapter draws heavily upon the insights of Erik Erikson, especially his concepts of *foreclosure*, *fidelity*, and *the moratorium*. The role of *self-importance* in the formation of identity as well as the role of the *peer group* will also be discussed.

Role Experimentation and Identity

In some respects the adolescent is similar to the pre-school child who, upon encountering a world beyond mother, grapples with new roles, expectations, and rules. The adolescent replays the sandbox drama to learn afresh the roles and rules of adolescence. Identities which served well during childhood (son, daughter, "good boy," "good girl,") no longer suffice. Adolescent identity demands that the individual have some idea *who* he is, *what* he is, and *why* he is, all of which require sampling and experimenting. How, for example, can an adolescent girl establish a sense of femininity without interacting in a wide variety of ways with other girls and boys? How is the adolescent boy to establish a sense of masculinity without testing himself in numerous and varied social settings? How can any adolescent cultivate a sense of personhood without experimenting with activities which have the potential to produce feelings of worthwhileness? *Identity demands experimentation*, and adolescence is the time when a good deal of it takes place.

Role experimentation is particularly important in four general areas: (1) gender roles, (2) competence roles, (3) social roles and, (4) independence roles. *Gender roles* refer to the patterns of behavior which suit the adolescent's concept of appropriate sex behavior. Girls learn to express what they consider feminine behavior (adolescent girls change their viewpoints about feminity as a result of sampling different roles, discovering that some of their ideas are fictitious or, at least, unrealistic); boys learn patterns which permit expression of their "manliness." Gender ideas are absorbed from the outside culture; thus, one of the primary developmental tasks for youngsters of this age is sorting out cultural stereotypes which are inappropriate for them as individuals. *Competence roles* are those which permit the exercise of skills the adolescent is attempting to master; athletics, drama, debating, etc., are provided by the school system on the assumption that these activities promote skills while offering social exchange and self-expression. *Social roles* represent patterns of interaction which allow the individual to discover how it feels to express different aspects of his own personality in a social setting. For example, he may play a dominant, assertive role in one situation and a tender, compassionate role in another, or first wax antagonistic or whiny and later supportive and affirmative. During the adolescent years the teenager learns the give and take of social exchange, but he can give and take only within his range of social competence. *Independence roles* relate to actions which the individual decides for himself he shall do with full realization that the price for doing so is accountability.

In effect, youth is a time when identities proliferate and a time when the things (or people) one has always wanted to be are given a trial run. It is a proving ground for self-doubt as well as something of an experimental laboratory for conflicting passions. (For special emphasis on the important topic of sex role identity — which is given very little attention in this book — see J. H. Block, 1984).

Adulthood, as defined in our society, could not exist without the freedom to sample identities during the adolescent moratorium. In this respect, it is as much a need of adulthood as of adolescence.

The Moratorium

Erikson believes that a period of time should be set aside for experimenting with different roles and exploring one's personality. This "moratorium" is essential for two reasons: first, the adolescent cannot make important decisions without a range of experiences to base them upon; second, most adolescents are not mature enough to assume adult roles, therefore they require additional time for growth and expansion.

A moratorium is a period of delay granted to someone who is not quite ready to meet an obligation. More precisely:

> By psychological moratorium, then, we mean a delay of adult commitments, and yet it is not only a delay. It is a period that is characterized by a selective permissiveness on the part of society and of provocative playfulness on the part of the youth, and yet it also often leads to deep, if often transitory, commitment on the part of youth, and ends in a more or less ceremonial confirmation of commitment on the part of society. (1968, p. 157)

In essence, the moratorium is a time for role experimentation, for sampling identities, and for learning some of the hard lessons of life without having to suffer excessively while doing so.

Foreclosure

Despite the significance of the moratorium, for some youth it is wasted because they foreclose upon their identity before they have had the opportunity to explore it. Foreclosure is identity without experimentation — deciding upon an occupation, a role, or self definition without examining alternatives. Foreclosure is especially common in cultures where traditional roles are blindly adhered to, and where few options are available. However, it is also widely observed in complex, technological cultures, such as our own.

Unto itself, foreclosure does not forebode bad news. Some young people are very clear about their ambitions, their purpose and their future. They make firm decisions and do not waver from them. Foreclosure, however, also stems from *fear* of breaking away from the expected path, or from fear of failure. Some youth have never been encouraged to diversify, or to branch out. In this regard, it is important to remember that many youngsters are so conventional that it simply does not occur to them to be anything other than what they are or what they are expected to be — they are what Murphy calls "obedient traditionalists." Foreclosure increases life stress in some ways, and decreases it in others. For example, the serious ailments of *negative identity* and *identity diffusion* are rarely observed among youth who choose early their identity, or who precisely map out their future. Likewise, cynicism, resignation, or despair are rare among those with identity foreclosure. In this regard, it is a positive reaction to the demands of identity. There is another side to the coin, however. The most specific hazard is that the identity foreclosed upon proves to be totally inappropriate to one's emotional needs. Or, that the identity requires skills or abilities the young person thinks he possesses, but does not. In these instances foreclosure, rather than enhancing identity, results in a *failure* of identity. Foreclosure is even more complicated when it entails commitments from which it is difficult to extricate oneself: early marriage, early parenting, and early withdrawal from school are foreclosures which, in our culture, frequently backfire.

The popular wisdom of our era proclaims that identity foreclosure yields more negative than positive results. In fairness, however, there is no way to be certain of this. Many youngsters regret their early choices and commitments and sometimes require therapy to overcome them. However, we know virtually nothing about young people whose identity is formed early and *who show no ill effects from it*. Our culture places such a heavy premium on "freedom" and "choice" that we find it hard to accept foreclosure as a realistic way to cope with identity formation. It should not escape our awareness that some cultures in which identity foreclosure is universally adhered to have existed for hundreds of generations. Current research suggests that certain religious communities (especially the Hutterites) which pressure their young into identity foreclosure have less individual pathology and less social pathology than society in general. On the other hand, foreclosure tends to impede the formation of intimacy bonds. As Stevens-Long reports ". . . foreclosed individuals seem far more likely to have *stereotyped or pseudo-intimate* relationships than do other subjects." (1983, p. 309) Therefore, in certain circumstances, foreclosure is an asset whereas in others, a liability.

In conclusion, we may surmise that while adolescence is generally acknowledged by our society to be a special time for role experimentation and the sampling of diverse identities, it is not used in this manner by all adolescents. Individuals who foreclose upon their identity, and thereby cancel the moratorium, do not follow a universal path into adulthood. Some regret their foreclosure; others do not. For some the decision was conscious and premeditated; for others it was defensive and unconscious. The fact remains, however, that in our culture, foreclosure is not mandatory; therefore, role experimentation is chosen by most young people.

Fidelity

One of the most intriguing concepts in adolescent psychology is what Erikson calls "fidelity." This concept has direct implications for the search for identity because it influences the kinds of people and the types of activities to which the adolescent attaches himself. Every adolescent, according to Erikson, possesses a desire to give his allegiance and dedication to someone or something. Every adolescent has, so to speak, a desire to attach himself to something he thinks is equal to, or greater than, himself.

In essence, fidelity is a *predisposition to faithfulness and commitment.* Therefore, ". . . When you reach a certain age you can and must *learn to be faithful* to some ideological view . . . without the development for a capacity for fidelity the individual will either have what we call a weak ego, or look for a deviant group to be faithful to" (Evans, p. 30).

Fidelity is a mixed blessing because it is frequently directed towards people or institutions which prove unworthy of it: ". . . the delinquent adolescent, too, is looking for the chance to conform to some subculture, to be loyal to some leader, and to display and develop some kind of fidelity" (p. 40, Evans). The *predisposition to fidelity* increases one's susceptibility to manipulation and exploitation. It inclines youth to overestimate the worth of those who are the recipients of their allegiance, and it also makes them easy prey for charlatans: ". . . the adolescent is vulnerable to fake ideas, he can put an enormous amount of energy and loyalty at the disposal *of any convincing system*" (p. 34).

On the positive side, fidelity encourages loyalty and perseverance. It promotes allegiance to the dominant society *when it appears worthy of allegiance.* Fidelity increases the capacity to *sustain* love relationships; it discourages egocentrism by focussing one's interest outside oneself; it facilitates long-range planning. Fidelity exists as a predisposition and requires only an object *perceived as worthy* to blossom.

When the adolescent is unable to attach his fidelity to someone or something, it creates feelings of aimlessness and disconnectedness. These feelings sometime create panic, or foster the belief that nothing in life is worth attaching oneself to. For many youth the empty aimlessness of ungratified fidelity is their most powerful anxiety.

Self-Importance and Identity

All youth are filled with a desire for self-importance so intense that it assumes the characteristics of a need, and this need for self-importance exerts as much influence on the quest for identity as any other single factor. To be important means to be essential, to be thought highly of, and to be missed when away. It also means to do things of relevance, contribute to the significant events in one's peer group and family, and achieve accomplishments thought important by oneself and one's close associates.

Self-importance rarely is experienced in a conscious, rational way. That is, rarely do youth actually say, "I am important," or, "I feel important today," or even, "I wish I felt more important." As with all subjective needs, satisfaction may or may not become the object of rational thought and the pleasure of its gratification may or may not be abstractly experienced.

The search for self-importance is a dominant theme of youth fantasy. It motivates much of their daily striving and usually represents the object of their ambition. Few things stir the adolescent with more fervor than feelings of prominence, distinction, and substantiveness — that is, self-importance.

Self-importance is crucial to identity for several reasons. First, it provides the personal confidence required to investigate the environment — the absence of which stalls identity. Second, self-importance creates a *reserve of psychological strength* which allows youth to cope with tension, anxiety, and frustration. Third, a sense of self-importance makes unnecessary the constant appraisal of new people or novel situations as threatening. Fourth, and in many ways the most important, self-importance means that the young person is not always at the mercy of contrived rituals designed by peers to *prove* one's importance. Self-importance makes the adolescent less reliant upon the opinions and judgments of others, especially when they contradict his self-definition. Self-importance opposes the kinds of conformism which derive from the desire to attain importance at the expense of individualism.

Certain *actions* create self-importance. Such actions include building useful products, asserting one's values, and establishing intimacy relationships. Certain *reactions from others* create self-importance, such as being thought capable of making sound judgments or having one's opinion carry social weight. From the foregoing we deduce that self-importance derives primarily from the reactions we receive from others and from the behavior we carry out.

For the majority of youth, little opportunity exists to do things which generate self-importance. Little opportunity arises to build useful products; little opportunity exists to assert oneself in a positive manner because the areas where youth truly make a difference are minimal; some opportunity exists for love and intimacy (and, for many, this represents the most feasible way to attain self-importance). However, adolescent romance tends not to be stable or consistent and cannot be counted upon as a primary source of self-importance.

Because the social formulae governing adolescent action opposes importance derived from *actual* work or *real* love, most youth turn to their peer society for personal importance. This, in turn, makes them highly preoccupied with their agemates and imprints within them the tendency to *pursue importance in terms of how it is defined within the peer group.*

One does not have to be an astute social critic to observe that many youth show poor discretion in deciding what determines self-importance.

As we know, some adolescents consider membership in a motorcycle gang, using drugs, stealing clothes, or defacing property to be measures of self-importance. For others, outsmarting school authorities, tricking policemen, and double-talking unsuspecting strangers are indicators of importance and intelligence. For still others, sexual conquests, alcohol consumption, or flashy automobiles are symbols of prowess. Further examples of the adolescent capacity for distorted images are not needed to make the point that youth in our society have a poor batting average when it comes to formulating ideas about what it means to be important. A significant point is this: youth so desperately need to feel important that they are easily duped into pursuing absurd and self-defeating approaches. The foolish extravagance of youth comes as no surprise to anyone who perceives how we exclude young people from worthwhile pastimes and herd them into arenas where only Saturday matinee theatrics are permitted. Their intemperance should not deceive us about their true motives, nor should it lead us to faulty conclusions about the kinds of behavior most suited to their personality dispositions. In fact, youth crave self-importance, a craving optimally satisfied when they are allowed to *do* important work and when they *receive* special esteem from their peers. Thus far, we have successfully tapped the second means of achieving importance, but we have made virtually no progress with regard to the first. Because of this, the formation of a mature identity during adolescence is infrequent in our culture.

The Peer Group and Identity

As a general rule (to which we note many exceptions), the peer group exerts greatest control during the early adolescent years, yields to greater personal autonomy during middle adolescence, and exerts the least influence during the final two or three years before early adulthood. This trend is sometimes contradicted by university students who find that late adolescence brings the greatest peer pressure they have ever experienced, especially those living in fraternities and sororities. For the most part, however, peer control is conversely related to age, thus, as age increases, peer control decreases.

What brings adolescents together? What causes them to hang around with one another? What impels them to pursue companionship even at the risk of ridicule and belittlement? What need is frustrated when the adolescent does not interact with people of like age?

Most explanations of adolescent behavior emphasize reward and punishment, or imitation and modelling. Such explanations account for portions of their behavior but certainly not all of it. For example, adolescents daily engage in behavior which leans considerably closer to punishment than reward. They associate with peers who ridicule or exploit them; they commonly endure the pain of parental rejection in order to hang out with peers they do not like all that much in the first place; they volunteer their time and energy for group projects which not only are exhausting but deprive them of money they could earn elsewhere. Without question, much adolescent behavior is motivated by factors beyond either pleasure or pain.

Neither can we understand adolescent behavior by viewing it only as the result of imitation or modelling because adolescents define themselves partly in terms of their ability to *defy* what is expected, to *contradict* the roles prescribed for them, and to *negate* those models most highly praised and rewarded (negative identity — discussed in the next chapter — is a striking example of this). The teenager is not exempt from the influence of imitation and modelling, but in no way is his behavior comprehensively explained by these concepts.

Fitting In: Identity and Compliance

The adolescent is constructing an identity, but for the most part, he is not sure what the building blocks of that identity are or what the final product will be. The range of activities and experiences demanding experimentation are almost beyond numeration. The personality, with all its complex parts, demands expression; the hostile as well as the gentle requires ventilation; sexual experiences must be sampled, relationships with parents altered. The net consequence is that the adolescent is never really one person; rather, in a manner of speech, he is a series of persons, roles and personalities.

Not *any* identity will do. It must be loose enough to nurture a growing personality but firm enough to lend security. Cautious exploration (punctuated by occasional boldness or an intemperate outburst) is the guiding principle. Efforts must be made to ensure that others do not exploit or belittle. Even more importantly, care must be taken that the fragile parts of one's inner self are not trampled. Until these conditions are met, the quest for identity is usually protective and cautious.

Self-definition and self-esteem are unalterably linked with peer acceptance; therefore, not fitting in is, in many respects, not to be.

Despite this, everyone does not have a clear idea what it is that he wants to fit into. He simply does not know enough about himself — his social strengths or his psychological weaknesses. The adolescent puts himself on the open market, awaiting appraisal of his "material." Many teenagers are shocked to discover that peers consider them interesting, attractive, influential, or fun to be with; others are dismayed to learn that peers find them unimpressive, easily outwitted, and impressionable.

It surprises adults to learn that young people do not always want to "be themselves." Even though they say that they want to let their "real self" shine forth, many adolescents simply do not know what their "real self" is. Especially during early and middle adolescence, they do not know what to think of their "self." Frequently, they wish they were more like a best friend than like themselves. It is unfair to think that adolescents "know" themselves in a comprehensive sense because their selves are not fully formed, and thus are not completely knowable.

Adolescents protect themselves against what others think by pretending that opinions do not matter. Despite this protection, they tend to worry a great deal about what others think of them.

> The adolescent is also afraid of revealing a view of self that is believed to be uninviting. The adolescent is mildly paranoic in his belief that others will discover his frailties, and enormous psychic energy is assigned to the task of disguising what is impossible to hide. The flight to secrecy is not unlike the schizophrenic's bizarre speech, for in both instances to be understood is to be known and to be known is to be vulnerable to the mind of the knower. (Kagan, 1972, p. 337)

On the whole, we may conclude that youth not only worry about what their peers expect of them, they also worry about themselves because they often do not know *what to expect from themselves.* Such uncertainty about oneself, even though it is typical among adolescents, is a stumbling block to the formation of identity and is one additional reason why a mature sense of identity rarely is formed during the adolescent years.

The Role of the Future in the Formation of Identity

Youth do not, and cannot, live entirely in the present. They visualize and anticipate their future, assessing in their own minds what it holds for them. This assessment of the future, which is an intrinsic and inevitable consequence of human intelligence, is one of the most important factors in the formation of identity among young people.

The ability to cope with stress or to endure anxiety is related to where one is going. The more optimistic the future, the greater is the ability to cope with adversity in the present; the more negatively one views the future, the more overpowering is present pain. When the future is painted brightly, filled with promise and high expectation, the turmoil and anxiety of everyday living is reduced and placed in perspective; when the future is perceived as holding little promise for personal growth or self-assertion, the anxiety of present time becomes the central fact of life.

Youth are pulled toward the future by their *biology*. They are growing, unfolding and expanding; therefore, to know oneself as an adolescent is to know that the future is essential for completion of the bodily self. Youth are biologically incomplete and they know it; the future holds their biological maturity and this fact is acknowledged by preparing for it.

Youth are pulled toward the future by their *psychology*. The need for intimacy increases during late adolescence; thus, the search for an intimacy partner is essential for psychological fulfillment. "I-ness" is gradually being replaced with "we-ness'; until the transaction takes place, the self is not complete. Youth are pulled toward the future because without it they are only partly actualized.

Youth are pulled toward the future by their *morality*. As they shed the moral dogmatism of childhood, they search for viable explanations and viewpoints; uncertain as to what is right and what is wrong, they formulate moral codes which balance impulses and justify actions in order to keep their own equilibrium. Youth tire in their search for moral guidelines and lapse into periods of comparative amorality, but they inevitably come around and realize that amoral existence is self-defeating and self-debasing. The pull of the future is the only hope for reconciling moral dilemmas; therefore, if morality is to exist in a meaningful way, youth must look to the future.

Do not misread the message. Youth are not overpowered by the future; they do not spend every waking moment in its anticipation or calculate every step in terms of where it leads. The message here is more moderate but, nevertheless, crucial. Future time is an essential parcel in the adolescent package; optimal growth cannot take place when the future is feared or when it is thought to be unworthwhile. Youth need to be convinced that the future will not deny them intimacy, productive work, acceptance, esteem and love. When the future is perceived as holding only chains but never keys, the growth of adolescence sputters. The present acquires unnatural power because it has been stripped of the only thing which lends it clemency — the future.

Future pull is not a dominant fact in all stages of the growth cycle. For infants it exerts negligible influence; for young children its presence is felt more so, but remains embryonic; for middle-years children, future pull becomes stronger but lags behind other growth requirements; with early and middle adolescence the role of the future is dramatic, exerting greater influence than ever before. However, in late adolescence and early adulthood, future pull reaches its peak. It can be mistreated during childhood and even during early adolescence without serious effect; with late adolescence no such latitude exists. More than ever before in the life cycle the future is central to ambition, purpose and identity.

A malevolent person, bent upon destroying the energy and enthusiasm of youth, would have only to destroy their future because vices of self-destruction proliferate when the future is cancelled. The great tyrants of our century have known the principle well. The slave labor camps of Soviet Russia and the concentration camps of Nazi Germany operated on the same maxim: force prisoners to live a day-to-day existence and deny them their future; ergo, their will to resist will decay in the misery of present pain.

Constraints Upon Adolescent Identity

To what extent is the adolescent *able* to form an identity?

Adolescence is a period in which limitations exist alongside strengths. It is the limitations, however, which constrain the capacity to form an identity. With regard to the intellect it is widely assumed that the late-adolescent has attained most of his "raw intelligence." However, limited experience with the outside culture and limited opportunity to employ one's intelligence (except in school) prevents the adolescent from possessing the *range* of intellect or the "wisdom" of more experienced adults. The emotional centres are well developed, but the full range of human emotionality rarely blesses the adolescent personality. Moral development is also advanced, but it has had little opportunity for genuine exercise. Even the youthful virtues of fidelity and dedication, though amply displayed, have not been tempered with time, nor thoroughly evaluated by experience.

The cumulative effect of the foregoing is that identity is not finalized during adolescence. A foundation is established, but the final product awaits the adult years. Blos, to whom we are indebted for many insights pertaining to the growth process, has this to say on the topic:

> At the close of adolescence, as I have remarked earlier, conflicts are by no means resolved, but they are rendered specific; and certain conflicts become integrated into the realm of the ego as life tasks. This was described as the achievement of late adolescence. *It remains the task of postadolescence to create the specific avenues, through which these tasks are implemented in the external world.* (1964, p. 150)

Erikson supports Blos in this matter: "I would say that you could speak of a fully mature ego only *after* adolescence, which means, after all, becoming an adult" (Evans, p. 31).

Fear as a Constraint

To appreciate the factors which impede identity we must acknowledge the fearful atmosphere in which many adolescents live. Fear impedes identity because it prevents investigation of the outside world and promotes egocentric self-immersion. Fearful adolescence is not a time of outgoing experimentation, rather it is a period of self-protection.

All youth fear some aspects of their world, and this fear is reconciled with the search for identity in the following way:

1. Adolescents continually defend themselves from fearful encounters, and, if possible, they deny their existence;

2. As a result, their interpersonal world is viewed as a potential threat;

3. Thus, interpersonal relationships, the words and behavior of other people are experienced as threatening even though they were not intended that way;

4. Words and behavior of others are attacked because they represent or resemble the feared experiences;

5. There is then no real understanding of others as separate individuals, since they are *perceived primarily in terms of their threat or nonthreat to the adolescent's self*;

6. However, when all experiences are integrated into the self, and when perceived (real and imagined) threat lessens, there is less need to defend and less need to attack;

7. When there is no need to attack, other people are perceived for what they really are and do not have to be dealt with behind a defensive cloak.

The fearful facts of one's own personality and the frightening obstacles of the environment are not the only constraints imposed upon adolescent identity. Equally powerful is the *fear of the future* because one's identity can attain viability only when it is envisioned within a viable future. When the future presents itself as tortured, identity is replaced with "survival." The interdependence of future time and present identity has been emphasized elsewhere in this book and, therefore, shall not be discussed further at this point. Instead, we shall draw upon Cottle to summarize the substance of the message:

> When realistic prospects for the future are bleak, the span of future time that may be integrated into present experiences will be affected. An unhappy adolescent, aged 14 or 15, is now likely to restrict his perspective to the surer rewards available in his present surroundings in an effort to avoid the discomfort generated by anticipations of an unpropitious future. (1974, p. 98)

In summary, fear of oneself, fear of the environment, and fear of the future must be overcome before an effective identity can be established. Most youngsters overcome these fears but many do not, and the formation of their identity is reduced as a result.

Identity in Primitive Societies

In this last section, a brief digression is undertaken to discuss youth in "primitive societies" in an attempt to offset a prevailing stereotype which claims that identity confusion is a modern phenomenon which did not exist in previous centuries and does not exist in the twentieth century among "primitive" cultures.

Images we conjure of primitive societies are often distorted and unrealistic. Primitive societies are in fact riddled with strife between the generations, with confrontations over who shall hold the balance of power, and with arguments over how daily routine shall be governed.

Youth in primitive societies do not always accommodate passively to the rules of their tribal units. As with North American youth, their socialization process begins in the earliest months of life and carries through the pre-adult growth cycle. Also, as with North American youth, for a certain number the socialization messages do not take hold. It is not easy, no matter what the historical custom, to convince a 14-year-old boy that he is ready for the 'fire ceremony,' where he is required to lie down for several minutes on green boughs laid over an open fire and then kneel on the coals of a small fire. Not all Arunta youth look forward to the fire ceremony, no matter that some anthropologists claim that they do. To some of them the idea seems absurd; to others, it is a painful but acceptable inconvenience; to others, it is welcome. As with most social customs, the Arunta fire ceremony is resisted by some, rejected by some, and accommodated by most.

Primitive societies place tremendous pressure on their youth because the premium upon conformity is greater in small societies than in larger units. Small tribal groups cannot survive if even a small number of their young defect or become anarchists. Survival rests upon all group members giving their allegiance, contributing their share, and carrying their portion of societal burdens. Youthful rebellion, like many of nature's idiosyncracies, is beyond the coping resources of small social groups. Therefore, early in life the rules are laid down and their violation brings severe censure. The smaller the group, the more each member must conform because in primitive societies, group needs invariably take priority over individual needs. The code of survival is based upon the inherent supremacy of the group over the individual.

We glamorize primitive life with the myth that youth "naturally" (or at least, easily) adapt to the rules of their society. Such is not the case. Youth eventually acquire the habits and values expected of them, but rarely is this done easily or naturally. Quite frequently youth are cajoled, bribed, or simply overpowered by the socializing agents. Frequently, youth adopt the customs of their elders simply because no other customs are available to them. Arunta boys of Australia do not on their own think of celebrating puberty by slitting open the shaft of their penis and inserting foreign objects into it. They do, interestingly enough, submit to this time-tested tribal custom. Those who believe that submitting to this custom comes easily or naturally fail to recognize both the universal human tendency to avoid unnecessary pain and the universal adolescent tendency to oppose inconvenient social customs which do not yield immediate returns.

Unquestionably, many youth believe that it is better to obey custom than to oppose it. A few youth, however, in any given society, *never so conclude.* Primitive societies are more severe than urban societies in their methods of keeping youth in line because in the latter defiance can be absorbed by the diversity and immensity of the culture, but in the former it cannot.

Primitive societies, popular sentiment to the contrary, are as obsessed with material goods, ownership, showmanship, and conspicuous consumption as their industrialized brothers. Group status in a primitive tribe can be significantly altered by acquiring a new possession or inheriting a valued piece of property. Some boys and girls are highly valued because of what their parents own. Some boys and girls are permanently locked out of the sexual or matrimonial marketplace because of birth defects, lack of social alertness, or the universally chastised habit of being continuously outsmarted by peers. In primitive societies, we observe monopolies on good land, good water, good jobs, good animals, and good marriage partners.

From the foregoing it may be concluded that the problems facing youth are characterized by some universal similarities. All youth encounter the perplexity of mapping their future, of coping with sexual conflicts within the guidelines of culture, and with generational conflicts within the guidelines of family. Primitive cultures, which anthropologists for decades have glamorized and distorted, have their own demands which their youth must cope with in their quest for a personal identity.

Postscript

The quest for a solid and cohesive identity is one of the fundamental demands of the adolescent years. It is a task which consumes vast sums of energy for all youngsters and which entails considerable pain and discomfort for about one-third of them.

In an elementary sense, "identity" is the way one defines oneself. However, a comprehensive identity permits one to envision himself in terms of family, and culture, past time and future time, and actuality and potentiality. Identity assumes its general outlines during adolescence, and from these outlines eventually emerges the adult personality.

The "search" for identity is not merely metaphorical. That is, searching, experimenting, and testing are actual facts of daily routine. Identities are sampled and tested; many are rejected, some are shelved and others eventually become "me." The four- or five-year period during which experimentation and sampling takes place is called "the moratorim" by Erik Erikson. Some youngsters, however, foreclose upon their identity and forego experimentation. Foreclosure usually backfires when the identity chosen is not appropriate; in other instances, however, it gives the adolescent a head start on an adult identity, engenders both clarity and purpose, and serves the youngster well.

The building blocks of identity are competence, positive self esteem, and integrity. As they prosper and as they suffer, so also does identity. Many commentators have observed that in our culture it is difficult for adolescents to attain adult competencies, and therefore, it is difficult for them to hold a sense of self-esteem based on legitimate accomplishment.

Identity cannot be separated from self-importance, and, as a rule, self-importance is the connective tissue which binds competence, self-esteem and integrity. Adolescents crave importance and suffer painfully when it is not attained. Youth who lack importance tend also to lack direction, purpose, and confidence — all of which impede a dignified sense of identity and, even more damaging, promote identity confusion and identity disorders.

Adolescents not only construct their own identity, they also attach themselves to the identity of others. This propensity is prompted by *fidelity*, the intrinsic tendency toward dedication and faithfulness, in which adolescent allegiance, affiliation, and love are grounded.

The peer group attains startling significance during adolescence, although its power is neither automatic nor blind. The group is the context in which the young person acts out his search for identity; however, it is not the author of it. From the peer group the the young person learns about himself and gains insight into what is desired and despised. From this insight a small segment of identity is formed, and from it a large segment of one's assessment of the group is formed. Within this mutually evaluative context the group judges the person and the person judges the group, and from these evaluations emerge two vital ingredients to personal identity: the group's assessment of the individual's importance and the individual's assessment of the group's importance.

3
Malfunctions Within
the Identity Process

The struggle for identity is not without pitfalls. The chaos, the bewilderment, and the seeming disconnectedness of the social universe leaves many youth in a state of panic and confusion. Identity requires clarity and when it is not attained the end result is confusion — about identity, within identity, and confusion as to whether identity can ever be achieved.

In this chapter we shall describe some of the most widely recognized forms of identity confusion in order to clarify their abnormal as well as their normal properties. All forms of identity confusion do not produce equally profound ailments, and they do not all derive from the same causes.

Identity Crises

Identity *crises* occur when the adolescent cannot find someone (or something) to believe in, or to attach himself to. Erikson, in a now-classic example, portrays an image of such a crisis.

> For the moment, we will accept Biff's formulation in Arthur Miller's *Death of a Salesman*: "I just can't take hold, Mom, I can't take hold of some kind of a life." Where such a dilemma is based on a strong previous doubt of one's ethnic and sexual identity, or where role confusion joins a hopelessness of long standing, delinquent and "borderline" psychotic episodes are not uncommon. Youth after youth, bewildered by the incapacity to assume a role forced on him by the inexorable standardization of American adolescence, runs away in one form or another, dropping out of school, leaving jobs, staying out all night, or withdrawing into bizarre and inaccessible moods. (1968, p. 131)

Typical of identity crises is an *over*identification with movie stars, athletic heroes, or music sensations and a simultaneous surface rejection of parents and parental values.

The image projected by "Storm & Stress" theorists of the helter-skelter, bewildered youth confusedly treadmilling into oblivion is, in reality, not a portrayal of normal adolescence, but of an identity crisis. Such a crisis is only one reaction to the pain of adolescent identity.

Identity crises have long been associated with youth. The inability to know "what it's all about," the perplexity of the "meaning of life," as well as the narcissistic fascination with "who am I" are inevitable youth struggles. Some experts believe that identity crisis is a profound problem and should be minimized whenever possible. Other experts, who now represent the majority opinion, consider identity crises to be an acceptable, though troublesome, characteristic of the identity process.

To maintain our perspective, however, it is important to remember that a significant percentage of young people simply do not experience identity crises. In fact their path to identity is fairly uneventful. Manaster maintains that many youth have neither the time, nor the inclination, for the complicated mental operations required by identity crises. And, in many respects, dwelling upon one's identity is a luxury that comes from an extended moratorium, from not having to work every day for a living, or from a narcissistic fascination with oneself that not all youngsters possess. As Manaster points out:

> But not every adolescent by any means is granted this time, or possesses these capabilities. The majority of adolescents come to the end of their schooling with, at most, a high school diploma, and maybe even an additional technical training course of some type. They are pressed into the adult world. They need to find a job. They want to get married and move out of their parents' home. The question for psychologists, teachers, and counselors is whether these adolescents experience an identity crisis, and whether there is any need for them to do so. (1977, p. 123)

It is reasonable, therefore, to conclude that many adolescents do not experience identity crises. Equally certain, however, is the fact that many *do*, and it is they who are our immediate concern. It also seems likely that adolescents who experience identity crises are more likely to be portrayed on T.V., in newspapers, and on documentaries. As a result, in the minds of many adults, adolescence is mistakenly perceived as a time in which all young people suffer through identity crises. Such is not the case.

Negative Identity

For some young people the messages of socialization simply do not take hold. In fact, among them one observes "a scornful and snobbish hostility towards the roles offered as proper and desirable in one's family or immediate community." Either part or the entirety of what is expected is met with refusal and rejection. The adolescent becomes consumed with the belief that nothing in the immediate environment is worth emulating or assimilating, however, that which is distant or unattainable appears attractive, even "fantastic."

Negative identity, however, is not merely rejection; it also is doing *the opposite of what is expected.* It is a strategy for youth who have had ideals paraded before them which seem unattainable, or equally important, for youth who believe that others have already attained these ideals with such a high level of superiority that they themselves could never equal them. (For further elaboration of this idea, see W. McBroom, 1985).

In regard to the foregoing, Rollo May draws an interesting parallel, which pertains directly to adolescence — especially angry and anti-social youth. He comments: "No human being can exist for long without some sense of his own significance. Whether he gets it by shooting a haphazard victim on the street, . . . or by rebellion, or by psychotic demands in a hospital, or by Walter Mitty fantasies, he must be able to feel this I-count-for-something and be able to *live out* that felt significance" (1972, p. 37). Among youth admitted for psychiatric care we note that their negative identity closely resembles a "cry for significance" and their behavior, defiant though it may be, is a plea for recognition and importance. They are engaged in a desperate attempt to attain significance in a life situation where positive identity has either been rejected or cancelled. And, as Erikson comments, for some young people it is *easier* to "derive a sense of identity out of total identification with that which one is *least* supposed to be, than to struggle for a feeling of reality in acceptable roles which are unattainable . . ."

The concept of negative identity has received wide audience in recent years and, as a consequence, the term has acquired a broader usage since some experts now use the term to refer to a *normal adolescent tendency to defy convention or authority.* This watered-down version should not be confused with the clinically more profound reaction which Erikson described.

Nevertheless, the less technical definition is of assistance. For example, some youngsters raised in a household with no noticeable psychopathology sometimes reject, or run away from, expected roles. These youngsters show no desire for the roles their parents want them to fulfill, no matter how richly rewarded or how severely punished. Social learning theorists claim these adolescents were inadequately socialized. This seems doubtful, however, because refusal occurs too frequently within healthy youngsters living in emotionally healthy families. In other words, negative identity, unto itself, does not indicate a disturbance within the adolescent personality, nor a disturbance within his family life. Most psychologists agree, however, that prolonged and consistent patterns of negative identity are more frequently associated with a disturbed personality than with a healthy personality.

Many young people feel that they are expected to blindly follow the paths established by parents without their own feelings considered. As Hendin (1975) observed: "They believe their parents want them to look nice, do well, and achieve in ways their parents and their parents' friends can measure. At the same time they think their parents do not care about what they feel or what kind of people they really are." Under these circumstances it is not surprising that ". . . student rebelliousness takes the form of getting back at their parents through their clothes, their hair, and their marks." For many adolescents negative identity, when all is said and done, is primarily an attempt to strike back against their parents. As early adulthood approaches, and a more liberated perspective toward their parents is attained, the behavior associated with negative identity — as well as the motivations which gave birth to it — tend to gradually disappear.

Many adolescents simply *do not want* to achieve the roles expected of them. These roles nourish more anxiety than they reduce and pose more problems than they solve. Once the negation of these roles has begun, the adolescent must defend and justify his actions with extra zeal, and thus negation (and the defense of this negation) becomes part of his identity, part of "me," part of "the way I am."

Negative identity and identity crises are the most "typical" forms of adolescent identity confusion; they are usually the shortest in duration; and they frequently elicit stereotypic behavior. Nevertheless, either of them *may* alter the course of adolescent growth and may exert tremendous influence on emotional stability.

Identity Diffusion

Some adolescents are incapable of attaining a systematic self-definition or of maintaining themselves with any consistent style. As a result, their personality is a diffuse mixture of depression, acting out, and bewilderment — a syndrome Erikson calls "identity diffusion." Identity diffusion is a far more serious phenomenon than the two problems previously discussed. Identity diffusion is associated with a general deterioration of the personality and an overall lack of ego strength. It is not part of what can be thought of as "the normal adolescent process." It is, without doubt, a more serious malfunction within the process of identity formation.

If the adolescent avoids normal growth "difficulties" such as intimacy or important occupational choices, he may not experience major difficulties while living through identity diffusion. However, as adulthood approaches, or as the youngster moves away to university, or leaves the parental home to establish his own household, he discovers that he cannot handle these responsibilities with an impoverished, juvenile identity. As a result, *normal growth demands* trigger an emotional breakdown, or a depressive withdrawal. Usually, however, all important life decisions are simply avoided: "The person with identity diffusion is undecided and unconcerned about an occupation and uninterested or indiscriminating in regard to ideological matters" (Weiner, p. 46).

Intimacy is virtually impossible during identity diffusion, and in those rare instances when it does occur, the partner usually is equally troubled, or, at the very least, chronically lonely. *Genuine* intimacy is too demanding for identity diffusion because when a serious attempt is made to become intimate, *pre-existing weaknesses* sabotage the links which connect the intimacy partners. As a result, "*Pseudo-intimacy may instead be practiced* by a series of group participations or happenings which give a spurious reassurance of intimacy" (Malmquist, p. 386).

In a state of identity diffusion, the youngster will reject any person or any experience which threatens the self. Such universal repudiation is not necessary for ordinary youngsters because they can handle threat without the ego fearing its own destruction. In identity diffusion, the strength engendered by a positive self-definition is lacking; therefore, every threat is perceived as a total threat, and the person mobilizes for a fight to the bitter end. It is worthy of special mention that some adolescents who are essentially "normal" in their personality development have *temporary* bouts of identity diffusion. Most typically this occurs during periods of exhaustion or fatigue, or after long periods of rejection or discouragement. Among young people of adequate personality strength, as contrasted with young people experiencing identity diffusion, these behaviors tend to be abandoned after a few days or sometimes even after a few hours. This tendency to "backslide," that is, to show a temporary deterioration in ego strength, occurs with sufficient frequency during the adolescent period that it can be considered normal, which is not the same as healthy. "Normal" means that it occurs with considerable frequency. "Healthy" means that it is good for you.

The key experience of identity diffusion is *shame*. Its presence creates feelings of worthlessness and self-hatred and nurtures habits which alienate the young person even further from friends and family.

Because identity-diffused youth doubt their own significance and are immersed in shame, they desperately require the approval of others in order to receive *some sense* of worthwhileness. Ironically, the recognition they so desperately crave usually is repudiated, because the youngster so mistrusts his own worth that he believes that anyone who praises him or likes him can only be an empty fool.

Identity diffusion also produces *time confusion* and as a result the "loss of time" typical of normal youngsters exaggerates into a more chronic time disassociation; consequently, identity-diffused youth may experience bizarre "time flights" and bewildering time lapses.

How are we able to differentiate pathological from non-pathological identity diffusion? In general, when *three or more* of the following symptoms appear, identity diffusion has gone beyond "normal disturbance" and indicates serious disturbance.

1. Incapacity for personal intimacy, with resulting isolation, stereotyped interpersonal relationships, and frenzied quests for intimacy with improbable partners.

2. Diffusion of time perspective, with disbelief in the possibility that time may bring change.

3. Diffusion of industry, with inability to concentrate, self-destructive preoccupation with narrow activities, and an abhorrence of com pet - itiveness.

4. The choice of a negative identity, expressed through utter disdain for community standards of desirability and propriety.

Identity Disorder

The essential feature of *identity disorder* is high anxiety about establishing a coherent and acceptable sense of self. The symptoms associated with it last several months and result in impairment of social, academic, and occupational functioning. Uncertainty regarding long-term goals is expressed as an inability to choose a life pattern, a career, or even friends. Bursts of impulsive experimentation are typical. Family relationships deteriorate, and dignified friendship disappears. Relationships with other identity-distressed youth may increase, although, for the most part, these are not rewarding friendships. Drug abuse may increase, and it usually is accompanied by episodes of despondency, apathy, or depression.

Identity disorder is not part of the normal growth process — it is a *pathological exaggeration of an identity crisis,* and it usually indicates a personality which remains troubled through the adult years.

Alienation and Identity

In the general vocabulary of the layman as well as the technical terminology of the expert, alienation is the opposite of identity.

Harry Stack Sullivan viewed alienation as isolation or estrangement from "significant others." Kenneth Keniston claimed that alienation among the young takes the form of rejection of cultural values, a distrust of others, and a pessimistic world view similar to psychogenic nihilism. Alienated youth usually hold contempt for the "mass man;" and even though they themselves are sometimes members of a recognized subculture, they rarely think of themselves as such.

Adolescent alienation manifests itself through the experiences of *meaninglessness, powerlessness,* or *isolation.* Each of these experiences causes problems for the person struggling to reconcile the demands of the external world with the perplexities of the internal world. Interestingly, many "normal" adolescents experience meaninglessness, powerlessness, or isolation; therefore, the mere presence of these painful realities does not confirm alienation.

Youth whose alienation manifests itself as meaninglessness perceive the future as empty, and view their actions as having no significance. Generally, they subscribe to the premise that *all* life is meaningless. Since meaninglessness cancels the significance of values, a state of *valuelessness* characterizes this type of alienation.

Alienation manifested as *powerlessness* (which earmarks the '80s in the way meaninglessness characterized the '70s) inclines youth to conclude that they have no control over their environment, that they are pawns on a chessboard they did not create, manipulated by players they did not choose. Often they feel inferior to their parents, and usually they believe that all important decisions are made by others. They are not "rugged individualists" and are never surprised at the failure of those who struggle against institutional bureaucracy or impersonal bigness.

Alienation experienced as *isolation* may manifest itself either as estrangement from society-at-large (which represents the classic definition of alienation) or as estrangement from one self. Alienated youth, as Sullivan points out, are disconnected from significant others, and frequently lack the skills or social attractiveness to draw others to them. Their feelings of isolation make interaction with others problematic; they are inclined to employ protective structures such as *insulation* or *excessive control* (see the chapter on adolescent defense mechanisms for further elaboration of these terms) to regulate their day-to-day actions. Although this helps them maintain equilibrium, it magnifies their isolation by keeping others at a distance.

There is no consensus as to whether alienation is a healthy or unhealthy condition because this requires a judgment on what the person is *alienated from.* Essentially, four viewpoints concerning alienation and mental health are to be found. The first views alienation *as disturbance* and emphasizes that alienation derives from weaknesses within the personality, the family structure, or the socialization process. It views alienation as a defect which we should *strive* to overcome. The second viewpoint asserts that alienation is *normal in the statistical sense,* because of its commonness. Adherents of this viewpoint believe that alienation derives from a combination of intellectual perplexities, emotional dislocations, and the inability to meaningfully read the future. This view also claims that *normal* conditions of adolescence (especially rapid intellectual growth and emotional upheaval) contribute to feelings of meaninglessness, powerlessness, and isolation. Therefore, alienation is a reasonable by-product of normal adolescent metamorphosis. The third viewpoint claims that "adolescent alienation is basically a normal and necessary developmental phenomenon *that has pathological forms*" (Cambor, 1973, p. 101). This viewpoint is widely accepted by therapists (especially psychiatrists), because of the preponderance of young people who manifest "traditional" psychological ailments such as phobias, obsessions, parent hatred, etc., *in addition to* their alienated traits. Among these youngsters, emotional disorders encourage their alienation. Even though it is widely agreed that psychological disturbance spurs alienation, few psychologists believe that *all* forms of alienation are *caused* by it. Finally, alienation is understood by some experts *as a form of identity*. They claim that for some youth their sense of estrangement becomes part of their self-definition. This kind of alienation is not merely negative identity, rather it is an identity based upon an ideology of distance and separateness. The individual for whom alienation *is* an identity is not emotionally paralyzed or even excessively anxious about estrangement; quite the contrary, this type of identity often promotes a sense of heroic individuality. Alienation-as-identity is most frequently observed among early adults and late adolescents. It is rarely seen among middle or early adolescents.

The nature of alienation is greatly influenced by the *mental skills* which evaluate reality and the *emotional processes* which enrich subjectivity. Broadly speaking, whether alienation is viewed as deviant or normal, it is *more frequent* and *more profound* during the later years of adolescence. Furthermore, for most alienated youth, the first years of early adulthood bring little change.

Nihilism: The Collapse of Identity

Nihilism is a doctrine which denies the existence of any objective ground for knowing the rightness or wrongness of one's personal actions. In its extreme form it declares that present conditions are so bad that their destruction can be justified, even though no alternate plan of reform or rebuilding is held by those who participate in the destruction; for the nihilist things cannot get worse. Nihilism presupposes that the universe is meaningless and that it is devoid of purpose. Man, being part of the indifferent universe, is also without purpose or meaning. The purpose here is not to investigate nihilism comprehensively, but rather to indicate some of the ways in which it cripples identity formation during the adolescent years. For the nihilistic adolescent every encounter with defeat or ridicule fuels feelings of inferiority; every national scandal confirms the absurdity of power; every act of warfare proves that peacefulness turns to violence. The nihilistic attitude is easily intensified when alternative views are not available or when the adolescent receives no adult guidance or assurance.

Adolescents challenge their identity when they consider that "I" am nobody. To those for whom this thought becomes an obsession it eventually occurs that nobody is anybody. The idea that "nobody is anybody" is discouraging as a general abstraction; however, *it is reassuring to a person who considers that he is nobody*. Thus, one response to nothingness is identical to the grand thesis of nihilism: everything is nothing, therefore, nothingness is that natural order of things. This conclusion helps to dull the pain of a growing self and holds considerable appeal to adolescents for whom meaningful beliefs seem impossible to come by and for whom the pain of emptiness seems impossible to shake.

In a clinical sense, several similarities exist between nihilism and what Erikson calls "identity diffusion." In identity diffusion, youth cannot establish any firm identity and are incapable of maintaining themselves in "their own style," or with dignified continuity. They frequently maintain a facade of reserved coolness which distances others (although in some subcultures coolness is socially attractive); and, as a rule, they hold skeptical and cynical attitudes toward society at large.

Young people never accept gracefully the idea of their own insignificance. They are too egocentric and too narcissistic; they surrender their centredness only after being assaulted year after year with the evidence of their impotence. Accepting one's insignificance cannot be achieved without psychic insulation and without distorting the assessment of self or the universe.

Protective conclusions emerge: "If I am meaningless, so then is the whole society. If 'I' am insignificant, so are those people who treat me with disdain. If I cannot change things, nothing is worth changing." Psychogenic nihilism proves to the adolescent that if he is meaningless, so then is the entire world.

The price paid for such proof is staggering. Anxiety is intense, loss of belief is spiritually defeating; and the loss of future ambition forces an obsessive anchoring onto the present. Most painful of all, the entire scheme works only when the adolescent admits to his own worthlessness.

The adolescent gripped by nihilism resembles what Dennis (1982) called "jaded" youth. These youngsters simply have no reference points, no moral anchors, and invariably develop profound behavioral problems.

Cynicism is the dominant attitude of nihilistic youth and this becomes a significant part of their overall word view. Cynicism is far more than merely a critical outlook — it is a form of emotional protectionism which manipulates that ego solely to reduce anxiety. Bischof explains its psychological significance in the following passage, and its relevance to adolescence is unmistakable.

> The cynic plays it safe by not believing in anything with an ethical or moral structure. If he follows a pattern of total disbelief, he is then disappointed in nothing. Because he believes in nothing, he avoids the heartaches that come from having believed in something that ends in failure. The device he uses is to deprecate any value which seems to hold forth hope. Probably growing from a background of repeated failure, his decision is never to believe in a value system again. In this way he avoids the failures of the past. (1970, p. 225)

The resources that oppose anxiety are missing in youthful nihilists. They do not believe in themselves; therefore, they do not offer firm resistance to ego destruction. They do not believe in others; therefore, needs satisfied only by companions or confidants go unmet. They do not believe in the future; therefore, they are condemned to an empty present. All these factors make them incapable of coping with life, with themselves, and most assuredly, with a positive identity.

Symptoms of Psychogenic Nihilism

The *intellectual* components of psychogenic nihilism include a world view of meaninglessness and refusal to acknowledge anything as having truth, validity, or universality; this in turn, contributes to the adolescent's perception of human events as absurd, artificial, or unreal.

The *emotional* components of psychogenic nihilism are blandness and boredom with intermittent periods of depression. The long periods of compulsive apathy which fill their victim's days and weeks require extensive use of emotional insulation. Quite rare are affectional states common to the healthy personality, such as zestfulness, robustness, joviality, and unconditional merriment.

Activities are not directly chosen; behavior responds to the pressure of currents and countercurrents and lacks the self-directed firmness characteristic of the healthy adolescent. The prime criterion for selecting behavior is minimal expenditure of effort and decision-making. The cognitive view of meaninglessness, coupled with apathy, produces a youngster in whom ambition, future plans, and commitment are radically absent.

The overall scenario of the nihilistic population is described well in the following passage:

> This is the story of a bored, jaded generation which never learned how to dream the grand dreams. By their 10th birthdays, they have seen it

all, these children whom affluence has warped like welfare in reverse, creating an enormous listlessness, a weary sense of *deja vu.* Unlike their parents, who earned privileges by degrees, they seem to have it all at once; they need never learn patience or yearning . . . Some of them drink a lot. Some of them run away. But by their own admission and according to the testimony of the people whose lives touch theirs on a daily basis, a lot of these kids don't do very much of anything. They have trouble, they say, thinking of what there is to do. (Dennis, 1982)

To summarize, psychogenic nihilism emerges when a person has nothing to believe in, nothing to strive toward, and nothing to commit oneself to. By definition it is the opposite of positive identity. It manifests itself in the following profile:

1. A world view of meaninglessness which in turn encourages cynicism, pessimism, and fatalism, and which inclines the adolescent to think of himself and the people near him as purposeless.

2. An emotional state of monotony, apathy, and nonselectivity, which prevents the adolescent from becoming involved in relationships (or activities) that counter the perception that he is worthless.

3. "Drift" behavior where actions are unpredictable and boundaries nonspecific, making it impossible to predict turns in behavior.

4. Absence of enthusiasm, supported by defense mechanisms which claim that zestfulness is stupid or self-defeating.

5. Absence of belief in the worth of self. This should not be overlooked because the individual who does not believe in any form of higher values has nothing that can establish his own personal validity, and, consequently, comes to define himself with the same sense of neutral equivalence by which he defines the rest of the world. Therefore, what we call poor self-image, low self-concept, and feelings of insignificance are basic to psychogenic nihilism.

6. Persistent use of defense mechanisms that insure survival of the defensive attitudes required to maintain nihilism. The defense mechanisms best suited are repression, rationalization, intellectualization, emotional insulation, and denial.

Aimlessness and Identity Confusion

The failure to have direction is one of the most significant impediments to adolescent identity. Adler claims that goals are the most vital ingredient in our psychic lives:

If we look at the matter more closely, we shall find the following law holding in the development of all psychic happenings: We cannot think, feel, will, or act without the perception of some goal . . . . Every psychic phenomenon, if it is so to give us any understanding of a person, can only be grasped and understood if regarded as a preparation for some goal (Adler, p. 68-69).

Aimlessness is a fact of life for adolescents who have nothing to believe in, because belief, in essence, provides direction to life. The aimlessness of psychogenic nihilism is *not* that of the youth who leaves time open so that he can pursue important events when they present themselves. Rather, it is an aimlessness in which nothing at all is important except those events powerful enough to temporarily overrule the lack of direction which fills the day. The adolescent may present a front of "openness" or "spontaneity" to disguise aimlessness, but the inevitable symptoms of boredom (which always accompany aimlessness) cannot be kept underground. When boredom surfaces, it combines with aimlessness to form a personality which grows further each day from its own centre and which progressively loses sight of itself.

One antidote to boredom is euphoria. Therefore, chemicals which induce temporary episodes of high sensation are sought by adolescents whose lives are void of meaningful beliefs. Chemically induced euphoria, unto itself, is not pathological nor indicative of an impoverished personality. However, when nihilism is added to the equation, many comparatively harmless chemicals become personality cripplers. The normal adolescent takes the drug experience. The drug experience takes the nihilistic adolescent. Roszak observed this fact before most psychologists because of his early exposure to nihilistic drug adventurers.

> Some minds are too small and too young for such psychic adventures, and a failure to recognize this is the beginning of disaster. There is nothing whatever in common between a man of Huxley's experience and intellectual discipline sampling mescaline, and a 15-year-old tripper whiffing airplane glue until his brain turns to oatmeal. The prospect held forth by drug experimentation — that of conscious expansion — has proved abortive at the *level of disaffiliated adolescence*. Dropped into amorphous and alienated personalities, dope has precisely the reverse effect; it diminishes consciousness by way of fixation. (1969, p. 159)

From here, he goes on to note that alienated and purposeless youth rarely benefit from drug use.

> Perhaps the drug experience bears significant fruit when rooted in the soil of a mature and cultivated mind. But the experience has, all of a sudden, been laid hold of by a generation of youngsters who are pathetically acultural and who often bring nothing to the experience but a vacuous yearning. They have, in adolescent rebellion, thrown off the

corrupted culture of their elders . . . at best, in favor of an introspective chaos in which the 17 or 18 years of their own unformed lives float like atoms in a void. (*ibid.*)

When speaking with nihilistic youth, one is struck not so much by their rhetoric of despair, but rather, with the behavioral proof that despair is the dominant fact of their existence. The adolescent who does not work, who does not care, who does not involve himself with anything except trivial games becomes trapped in a self-destructive lifestyle with virtually no awareness of its destructive nature.

Factors Which Contribute to Psychogenic Nihilism

The most conspicuous characteristic of the adolescent nihilist is a fragmented sense of identity. The adolescent who perceives himself mainly in terms of the social roles he carries out and the biological needs which sustain his physical existence is more susceptible to perceiving himself as worthless than is the youngster who possesses a higher belief system. Such an identity leads the person to consider himself nothing more than a player of social roles and an embodiment of physical needs. He does not possess a self-concept upon which self-pride, self-love, or self-confidence can be built. A fragmented sense of personal identity usually is projected outwards; therefore, other people are perceived in the same limited, mechanical manner as oneself. This projection prevents meaningful social relationships and "justifies" the expedient, sometimes ruthless, treatment of others.

Because he defines himself as a player of social roles, he validates his self in terms of these achievements, erroneously thinking that the more perfectly social roles are carried out, the more self-satisfying life will be. Thus, one of the more obvious personality characteristics of the psychogenic nihilist is an overly concrete and fragmented sense of identity which encourages viewing others in an impersonal, or mechanical fashion. This, in turn, makes intimate personal relationships virtually impossible, and thereby prevents an identity based upon mutual affection.

Postscript

During the adolescent years the search for identity often results in a variety of "identity confusions" or "identity malfunctions." In no way is it fair to claim that all adolescents experience these, but, without doubt, a great many do.

The most common complications of the adolescent identity process are *identity crises*, and *negative identity*. These occur with enough frequency that they can be considered "normal" in the statistical sense; however, they should not be taken lightly because they hold the potential to deteriorate into far more serious identity problems.

Identity diffusion and *identity disorder* are more profound malfunctions within the identity process. They are less likely to "go away with time," and much more frequently predict a troubled or disturbed future. As a rule, identity diffusion and identity disorder are more likely to be associated with a troubled childhood and with a history of interpersonal failures. Despite their serious nature, we often observe "normal" adolescents going through episodes which highly resemble identity diffusion or identity disorder, but which tend not to be as lasting or as emotionally devastating as the real thing. This tendency to acquire short-term behaviors which resemble more serious malfunctions make it difficult to diagnose adolescent problems.

Alienation merits special attention in this chapter because it is a unique complication within the identity process. Certain forms of alienation are consistently associated with immature personality development or deficiencies within the personality. Other forms, however, have neither of these characteristics, and therefore, can be more honestly assessed as alternate life styles or, simply, unconventional deviance. Thus, alienation per se does not tell us too much about the psychological health of a young person. However, when it is accompanied by traditional indicators of psychiatric malfunction, such as extensive use of defense mechanisms or consistent non-satisfaction of basic needs, the probability increases that alienation will deteriorate into a psychiatric disorder of some kind.

A special section in this chapter covered a relatively new phenomenon in the adolescent area — *nihilism* — which is viewed as a general collapse of identity at the emotional *and* the intellectual level. The primary consequences of nihilism are meaninglessness, a loss of future directedness, and a sense of despair and futility. It is a more serious condition than alienation, more closely resembling identity confusion. It is durable because it tends to be encased within a philosophical outlook which justifies its despairing world view.

4
Adolescent Sexuality

In an earlier chapter we investigated the inherent stressfulness of adolescence; the reader will recall that a debate wages in academic circles as to how filled with "storm and stress" adolescence really is. A similar debate exists concerning *the power of sexual impulses during adolescence.* As with the first debate, one side claims that adolescents are emotionally charged and highly sexual, while the other side admits that adolescents are sexual creatures in a certain sense, but that they are nevertheless moderate in their impulses, their ambitions, and their actions. A second parallel also holds true between these two debates: the most passionate literature on the topic claims that youth themselves are highly passionate, while the most persuasive empirical evidence suggests that youth, like their parents, are moderate and conservative in their sexual activities.

The most significant thinker in the history of personality theory, Sigmund Freud, is given little emphasis in this chapter because there are few areas where his brilliant mind was less productive or where it entrenched more misunderstanding than in sexuality. It is important to recognize that very few modern psychologists attribute to sexuality the intense fears and anxieties which Freud believed typified it. He was radical in his day for the high premium he placed upon sexuality in the formation of the personality. And though time has seen many converts, even today his emphasis on sexual trauma remains an extremist point of view. Freud claimed that children held terrifying fears about sex because they believed that the father was brutalizing the mother during the sexual act. He also believed that young boys genuinely feared they could be castrated for masturbation or for feeling hostile toward their fathers; further, Freud believed that feminine psychology was distorted by young girls' impression that their lack of a penis left them sexually incomplete. These powerful childhood fears and misconceptions, according to Freud, are repressed and become part of the unconscious, but they forever influence the sexual experience. These Freudian viewpoints encourage an outlook which many psychologists consider scientifically unconfirmable and morally vacant. Equally important as far as adolescent sexuality is concerned, they suggest sexual and emotional realities observed in, and reported by, very few adolescents.

Our concern in this chapter is with the following topics, although not exclusively:

(a)   personality factors which encourage adolescent sexuality;
(b)   the unconscious desire to become pregnent;
(c)   personality factors which discourage sexual behavior during adolescence;
(d)   the interrelationship between intimacy and adolescent sexuality;
(e)   desacralizing (de-humanizing) sexuality;
(f)   some misconceptions of adolescent sexuality.

Before proceeding, it is only fair to remind the reader that one of the pitfalls involved in the study of youth and sex is the tendency for adults to project their personal anxieties (and fantasies) onto their younger subjects. And as a result, healthy skepticism is in order when adults claim to know exactly how young people experience their sexual desires and ambitions.

The realization that our understanding of adolescent behavior is subject to the limitations and deficiencies of the adult personality is not new. Paul Goodman and Edgar Friedenburg have both written intelligently about this phenomenon and its implications for youth-watching. So has Thomas Cottle:

> There is, however, a curious turn about the young, or of any group which because of its peculiar nature the rest of us tend to sequester or grant a semi-citizenship. It has to do with the fact that at some point in our relationships with other groups we project onto these groups the traits, drives, and maybe too the ambitions and animus we despise or at least find uncomfortable in ourselves and in our groups. (1967, p. 319)

Admittedly this insight creates more mysteries than it resolves; however it is worthy of mention because it provides a check against our own defense mechanisms, and helps us recognize that a completely objective assessment of adolescent sexuality is a very difficult task indeed.

Personality Factors in Adolescent Sexuality

The adolescent does not engage in sexual behavior merely because of the impulses brought into existence by puberty. Sexual behavior is greatly influenced by personality factors, sometimes to such a degree that they outweigh biological factors. On occasion, sexual behavior among the young is little more than an attempt to gratify emotional needs.

In this section several personality factors which contribute to adolescent sexuality will be discussed.

1. *Intimacy.* Harry Stack Sullivan was among the first psychologists to stress the need for intimacy. Although definitions of "intimacy" vary, most include the need for a close personal relationship, or the need for closeness with someone or something meaningful. Intimacy can also be understood in terms of what it is not. It is the opposite of isolation, of estrangement, of alienation, and is characterized by closeness rather than distance, by intensity rather than neutrality, by fusion rather than mere nearness. Embracing, holding, and hugging are physical components; closeness and self-surrender are emotional components.

The need for intimacy begins to manifest itself in pre-adolescence where the desire for a personal confidant first becomes central. With the partial disintegration of the peer group as well as the tendency toward heterosexual pairing, the intimacy need is accentuated. Most adolescents find it difficult to make it through their daily existence without having someone in whom they can confide and articulate their most pressing problems.

Intimacy nurtures love, and love nurtures sexuality. This holds true for adolescents as well as adults. Perhaps the strongest indicator of sexual intimacy during adolescence shows when the partners proclaim that they are "in love." One expert stated it this way: "Most high school girls believe that intercourse and love go together. If they have sex at all, it is usually with a boy they love. Their relationship will either endure or collapse as time goes by, but while it lasts the girl and often the boy as well are in love." (Paine, 1975).

In sum, the emotional need for intimacy nurtures physical sexuality.

2. *Belonging* is among the most powerful human needs. Maslow includes it in his hierarchy, Murray in his listing of psychological needs (he calls it affiliation), and all neo-Freudians acknowledge it as a basic psychological reality. Sociologists, more than psychologists, emphasize the human significance of belonging and participation. Although Maslow distinguishes between belonging needs and esteem needs, it is not uncommon in general theory for them to be grouped together. The need to belong implies a sense of membership in, or participation with, another person or group. It differs from intimacy in that it does not have to be experienced directly to be gratified. That is, the need for belonging can be satisfied when one is separated from that to which one belongs. Intimacy, in some aspects, can be understood as the experiential component of a belonging need which has been satisfied.

A twofold relationship exists between sexuality and the need for belonging. (1) The need for belonging impels adolescents toward one another, and even though they congregate without initial sexual attraction, in the course of being brought together a sense of relatedness emerges which increases the probability that sexual behavior will ensue. In this respect group affiliation indirectly encourages sexual interaction. (2) The female acquiesces to the sexual demands of her partner because her sense of belonging is threatened if she refuses. This practical consideration influences adolescent pairings because it is usually the girl who determines the degree of sexual activity, and when it will occur.

3. *Dominance and Submissiveness.* Although it is doubtful that dominance is a *need*, it nevertheless plays an important role in sexuality. Dominance is generally understood to mean control or mastery. It doesn't imply tyrannical or dictatorial manipulation.

Submissiveness likewise plays a role in adolescent sexuality in that sexual submissiveness often permits indirect gratification of the need for intimacy, relatedness and sexual expression.

Because our society condones female submissiveness more than male submissiveness, it is more prevalent among girls. One might observe, however, that strong forces are at work in our culture counterbalancing feminine submissiveness.

A unique form of submissiveness is what Erich Fromm calls *idolatrous love.* He describes it this way: "If a person has not reached the level where he has a sense of identity, of I-ness, rooted in the productive unfolding of his own powers, he tends to 'idolize' the loved person. He is alienated from his own powers and projects them into the loved person, who is worshipped as the *summum bonum*, the bearer of all love, all light, all bliss. In this process he deprives himself of all sense of strength, loses himself in the loved one instead of finding himself." This submissive collapse which typifies idolatrous love is most likely to occur among youth who have not established a firm identity, or who have no person or object to which they may dedicate their fidelity.

Since no person can, in the long run, live up to the expectations of her (or his) idolatrous worshipper, disappointment is bound to occur, and as a remedy a new idol is sought, then in turn another, in an unending circle. "What is characteristic for this type of idolatrous love is, at the beginning, the intensity and suddenness of the love experience. This idolatrous love is often described as the true, great love; but while it is meant to portray the intensity and depth of love, *it only demonstrates the hunger and despair of the idolator*" (p. 99).

The adolescent is particularly susceptible to idolatrous love, as described by Fromm, for several reasons, the two most important being that they overly glamorize the "substance" of their loved one; and, they tend to believe that their experience of love is far more profound than any one else's experience of love. (For further elaboration of the latter idea see *personal fable*).

In the submissive act one's sense of worthwhileness is verified when the partner concentrates all energy and affection in a dominant and total manner. In this way submission is experienced as genuine relatedness. Therefore, while it facilitates sexuality, submissiveness also contains elements which may lead to emotional defeat rather than emotional fulfillment.

4. *Curiosity and Competence.* Robert White defines competence as "an organism's capacity to interact effectively with its environment." In the adolescent subculture, sexual interaction is a vital ingredient of daily living. In this respect, sexual behavior is part of a reality in which competency can be achieved only by exploration. For most adolescents sexual behavior is novel, exciting, and stimulating, possessing the thrill of newness which accompanies "first-time" behavior. Competence motives expedite sexual involvement because experimentation is the only means by which competence can be achieved.

It should be noted that exploratory behavior in sexual activity does not mean that it is pursued in a cold-blooded manner. Most adolescents require that specific conditions be met before sexual activity occurs, especially friendship, a certain amount of respect, a period of psychological intimacy, and sexual passion at the moment of sexual involvement. These conditions hold true especially for girls.

In summary, one cannot learn (whether child, adolescent, or adult) without tampering, exploring, investigating that which one is learning about. Sexual behavior is no exception. Speaking in purely statistical terms, the incidence of sexual behavior would increase during adolescence if for no other reason than that there is no other way to obtain first-hand knowledge about it.

5. *Passion and Intensity.* What Freud calls "libidinal force," or what Fromm labels "erotic love," reaches considerable intensity during adolescence — especially late adolescence. Allport claims: "We should face the fact that at least in the early years of college life, crises in the sexual sphere are for the most part frankly genital in their preference. The biological drive is so powerful that the youth is concerned with it almost by itself." He supplements this with a further comment about sexuality and the adolescent personality: "Its integration into mature love, into marriage, into career plans, into an embracing philosophy of life, exceeds his present capacity." For final emphasis: "He is likely to think that genitality by itself is maturity. Sexual gratification is frankly the aim, often with devastating consequences. At this stage of development, the students have much to say about sex and little to say about mature love" (1969, p. 240).

Sexual passion, for many adolescents, is the most profound element in their emotional lives. The passion of sexuality confirms that one is desired, perhaps even loved. In few areas of human interaction is the self acknowledged as ardently as in sexual passion, and as a result, passion is valued not only for its physical pleasure, but also for its confirmation power.

6. *Rebelliousness and Negative Identity.* Some adolescents engage in sexual behavior because of contempt for their parents. "Negative identity" refers to satisfaction obtained from doing the opposite of what is expected. It is more than mere stubbornness because the adolescent actually gains a sense of meaning and purpose as a result of the negative behavior. (For a more thorough overview of negative identity, refer to Chapter Two).

Although most adolescents do not engage in sexual behavior *primarily* because of negative identity, this can be a fragment of their motivation (especially among youth with intense parent conflicts). Of special interest is the observation that hostility towards parents is commonly reported by girls pregnant out of wedlock. These girls often admit to a strong hostility, even hatred, for their parents, voicing a desire to get even with them or to cause them anguish, and their pregnancy serves these purposes.

Sex Differences in Adolescent Sexuality

During adolescence noticeable differences in male and female sexuality begin to show consistent trends. For example, the masturbation fantasies of males tend to portray them as aggressive and dominant whereas female fantasies tend to be passive and compliant. Adolescent girls, however, have only slight aggressive element in their sexual fantasies, preferring instead emotional and romantic scenarios. Interestingly, girls frequently play passive roles in their own sexual fantasies whereas males rarely do. Although neither sex talks freely about their private fantasies, males tend to talk more about their sexual involvements, and appear to receive more status from their peers as a result of sexual exploits than do girls (Berger, 1975).

Other differences also exist. Males, for example, frequently describe their sexual encounters as having only mild emotional significance, and describe them in surface terms. Girls, on the other hand, attribute greater emotional significance, and greater romantic involvement, to their sexual activities. It is worthy of brief mention that lack of sensitivity on the part of the male appears in later life as one of the pressing matters in marriage counselling, and also contributes immeasurably to what Maslow calls the "desacralizing" of sexuality.

A corollary of the masculine propensity to claim that intercourse holds less emotional significance is the frequency with which they report that their first sexual encounter was with a casual date, a pick-up, or someone with whom they had only minimal emotional attachment. Females rarely report that their first sexual experience occurred under these conditions.

Although sex researchers know that adolescents are not the most reliable subjects, the male-female differences are too consistent to overlook.

Females, as a group, view sexuality in a more romantic way, although not universally, and not in all circumstances. Males tend to invoke a greater objectivity on their sexual experiences, although not universally and not in all circumstances. Therefore, it seems fair to conclude that the effects of personality not only vary from person to person as far as sexuality is concerned, but also exert their influence upon males and females in different ways.

It is apparent that adolescent sexuality is both a biological and a psychological phenomenon. The extent to which one is dominant over the other is a function of one's theoretical understanding of sexuality. The impulse for sexuality is primarily a biological phenomenon; however, more than most biologically-based phenomena, it blends with psychological factors, so that it often is impossible to distinguish one from the other in adolescent sexuality.

Important issues of adolescent sexuality, such as frequency and partner selectivity, are regulated by psychological factors. Most adolescents have specific preferences for the person(s) with whom they are willing to engage in sexual behavior, and also demand a particular psychological climate. Sexuality is regulated by individual conscience and social sanction, and each of these is of critical importance in the ways sexuality manifests itself.

Parents tend to underestimate the emotional significance of adolescent sexuality because they perceive adolescent sexuality as *solely* a biological reality. If this were the case, parental demand for abstinence would have a more realistic foundation. In fact, the biological component is sometimes incidental. Probably at no other time in the life cycle is the individual so predisposed towards sexual behavior in order to satisfy as many diverse and unrelated needs.

This overlap of sexual and emotional needs is hard to delineate precisely because adolescent needs are influenced by their egocentrism, by their pursuit of identity, by their desire for affiliation, and by their craving for intensity. And if this is not enough, their need structure is encapsulated within a biological organism which itself is undergoing a revolution of growth, design, and experience.

The Unconscious Desire to Become Pregnant

Intriguing objects of study are adolescent girls who understand the ovulation cycle but who nevertheless engage in sexual intercourse when the probability of pregnancy is high. To some researchers it appears they intentionally try to become pregnant.

Some experts conclude that by becoming pregnant, girls satisfy unconscious desires or unconscious needs. Jense, for example, states: "Whereas it may appear at first glance that most adolescent pregnancies are the result of accident of contraception or misinformation, repeated studies have shown that *the great majority of teenage girls get pregnant because they want to.*" He further extrapolates: "Generally, the motivation for pregnancy is unconscious, although some girls readily admit that they want to become pregnant."

The most common reasons, according to Jense, for wanting to become pregnant include:

a.   to prove that she is a woman and that her body works the way it should;
b.   to have someone, the baby, to love;
c.   to please a man who wanted to impregnate her;
d.   to get back at her parents for hassling her about her sexual behavior;
e.   to get away from her rejecting home environment, her boring school, and the "awful town" she lives in;
f.   to satisfy her parents' covert wish for her to get pregnant and have the baby;
g.   to get a man to marry her; and
h.   to relieve loneliness and depression. (1976, p. 148)

Ironically, teenagers who become pregnant find that their pregnancy *rarely* satisfies any of these needs or wishes. On this point, experts agree, whether or not they believe in unconscious motivations. (C. F. Olsen, 1984, and L. Simkins, 1984, both provide interesting research and documentation on this issue).

Social workers and youth workers tend not to agree with this theory. They claim that most girls, from the moment they discover they are pregnant, wish it were not so. Girls who become pregnant usually do not need to prove that they are able to bear a child, to get even with their parents, or to satisfy the desire of a boyfriend. With the increased availability of medical abortions, more teenagers are electing to terminate their pregnancies. This would indicate that their desire to become pregnant (or at least to remain pregnant) is not strong.

Gordon claims that research which indicates girls are unconsciously motivated to become pregnant is weak, and after the fact. "However, the evidence shows that the only trait pregnant teenagers share, besides sexual experience, is a lack of knowledge about the reproductive process and birth control." Pregnancy among teenagers is best explained not by the unconscious desire to become pregnant, but rather, from the lack of information about preventing pregnancy (1973, p. 37).

Elkind makes an interesting observation about the relationship between pregnancy and egocentric thought. He notes: ". . . many young girls become pregnant because, in part at least, their personal fable convinces them that pregnancy will happen to others but never to them *and so they need not take precautions*" (1967, p. 1030).

Some research indicates that teenagers who become pregnant have weak self-concepts. Zongker (1977) studied a group of teenage mothers to compare their self-concept with that of adolescent girls who never had been pregnant. Several findings highlighted this research, including:

a. the pregnant adolescents exhibited a decidedly low self-concept in most areas;
b. the pregnant girls were extraordinarily low in self-identity, family, and social relationships;
c. pregnant girls held a low opinion of themselves but had accepted the presence of these feelings;
d. about 60 percent of the school age mothers were without fathers or stepfathers in their home as compared to 18 percent of the control group.
e. school age mothers were older but at a lower grade level than the control group;
f. pregnant adolescents were dissatisfied with their looks, bodies and physical performance.

All researchers do not portray such a negative picture of the pregnant adolescent. Some critics claim this study was overly influenced by socio-economic factors. Nevertheless, the information is thought-provoking when cast in the perspective of personality variables which influence adolescent sexuality.

Even when the object of study is the *normal* adolescent, one cannot underestimate the power of irrational motives in sexual behavior. There-fore, even though an unconscious desire to become pregnant does not seem to explain most teenage pregnancy, we cannot overlook the numerous per-sonality limitations which increase the probability of pregnancy.

For example, among some girls the need for reassurance, affection, acknowledgement is so powerful that, even at the risk of pregnancy, they will attempt to gratify them through sexual intercourse. Other teenage girls are overly impressionable and easily manipulated. Some girls have such low self-concepts that they will do whatever brings praise. Others cannot handle rejection of any kind, and sexually submit at any hint of it. All of these traits, within the sexual context, incline girls toward decisions (and actions) which increase the chance of an unwanted pregnancy.

Sexual Abstinence During Adolescence

Just as it is not precisely understood why adolescents engage in sexual intercourse, neither is it clearly understood why they do not. Most youth are biologically capable of sexual relations by middle adolescence and virtually all are ready by late adolescence. If sexual desire is "natural" why don't more youth engage in sexual intercourse?

Several factors contribute to sexual abstinence, the most important of which are: (a) moral reasons; (b) fears and anxieties; and (c) partner availability. By briefly overviewing these factors, we obtain a more comprehensive picture of adolescent sexuality; and we also recognize that personality factors sometimes hinder rather than encourage sexual expression.

Moral reasons: Many adolescents believe that sexual behavior before marriage is morally improper. Generally speaking, three types of moral objections characterize adolescent thought. First come beliefs and convictions learned from adults, especially parents. Youngsters who have been taught that sexuality is bad, unhealthy or evil often incorporate this teaching into their own outlook. Second come beliefs acquired from a religion or philosophy. This is a better example of a "moral reason" for opposing sexual intercourse than the first, which is more an example of social learning.

Many adolescents subscribe to the Puritan belief that sexual pleasure is unto itself bad; others adhere to the Stoic belief that all desires (including the sexual) should be held in check; others believe in the Buddhist maxim that no desire means no disappointments. Therefore, to not desire sex is to never be disappointed by it.

The third moral objection to sexual involvement is founded upon beliefs and convictions derived from personal experience. Some youth learn that sexual involvements are emotionally strenuous, and create more problems than they solve. They conclude — for the moment at least — that sexual involvement is not for them. Closely related is the widespread belief that sexual behavior is acceptable only when couples are "in love."

Age trends are evident in these matters. Early adolescents are likely oppose sexual involvements merely because abstinence is the viewpoint of their parents, their church or their friends. Middle adolescents are inclined to give greater weight to philosophical and moral principles, but they remain greatly influenced by upbringing. Late adolescents are more impressed by personal experience than either of the two younger ages, and are also more likely to think of sexuality as a personal matter which must be worked out on an individual basis.

Fears and anxieties: Adolescents, like most young adults, harbor fears and anxieties about sexuality. Some fears are social, such as the fear that sexual intercourse will foster a bad reputation. Some youth are opposed to intercourse because they know it will offend their parents, or cause them anguish if they are found out. Sorenson, however, reports that couples who *strongly desire* sexual relations rarely avoid intercourse only because of parental disapproval.

Virtually all adolescents are body-conscious and some are so shy that they refuse to expose their bodies. They are fearful because they do not know if they are attractive, or if they will be laughed at. (Unlike adults, especially middle-class adults, some adolescents have intercourse with most of their clothes on). Closely related to body-shyness is the anguish that they will not be "any good at it," a fear which frequently lasts through early adulthood. Some youth are also simply frightened of the unknown and refuse to venture into it.

Among the most significant inhibitors of adolescent sex is guilt. Why sex creates guilt is not agreed upon. The most accepted viewpoint is that youngsters are taught that sex is bad, unhealthy or unclean — a teaching which is incorporated into their world view and carries into adolescence. Some teenagers "lose" this teaching rather quickly and experience no guilt from their sexual episodes. Others, however, find that the teaching lingers forcefully in the form of conscience pangs, guilt feelings, and a free-floating fear of sexuality. Based upon the evidence garnered from interviews with young people, from psychiatric therapy and from developmental know-ledge, there is no doubt that guilt is a *major* inhibitor of adolescent sexuality.

Partner availability: Adolescents take sex seriously. Little recreational sex (in the "swinger" sense) takes place. A certain amount of sexual adventuring is found, but it is not widespread. Almost all girls, and most boys, agree that sexual intercourse should be reserved for couples who are "in love," or who have some kind of commitment to one another. Most girls are offended when they think they are "being used," or when their sexual acts are made light of.

An "appropriate" partner for most young people is one who shares personal intimacies, who shows respect for personal vulnerabilities, and who, at the same time, is a desired sexual companion. Most adolescents have difficulty finding a partner who fits these conditions, yet they generally do not engage in sexual intercourse *until* these conditions are met. (Ishiyama, 1984, presents thought-provoking ideas on the relationship between shyness and partner availability).

The closely supervised lifestyle of youth (especially early and middle adolescents) also makes sexual intercourse awkward. Often it is difficult to find an acceptable location (most adolescent sexual activity takes place in the home of the boy's parents). These factors constrict sexual activity.

Partner availability is compounded by the fact that sexuality is a complex experience made even more troublesome by egocentrism. Sexual fondling, for example, among adolescents sometimes resembles a mixture of wrestling, debate, and persistence because a certain component of adolescent sexuality is more "selfish" and "self-searching" than anything else. In this matter Erikson notes: ". . . much of sexual life is of the self-seeking, identity-hungry kind; each partner is really trying to reach himself. Or it remains a kind of genital combat in which each tries to defeat the other" (1968, p. 137).

Elias and Elias (1975) report that girls who did not engage in petting gave the following reasons: (1) it is wrong or immoral; (2) they were uncertain they could control their partner; (3) they never met a boy they wanted to do it with; (4) fear of parental disapproval; (5) too shy.

With regards to youth who have not experienced sexual intercourse Elias and Elias report the following reasons (in order of importance) as contributing to avoidance of sexual intercourse.

1.   the fear of pregnancy;
2.   the belief that it is wrong or immoral;
3.   the partner was unwilling to go along;
4.   never met a boy/girl I wanted to do it with;
5.   lack of opportunity;
6.   fear of parental disapproval

As Mussen, *et al*, have pointed out in their investigation of adolescent sexual habits and attitudes, a genuinely conservative tone typifies their style and their perspective:

> It should be noted that in no study available to us did a majority of the students approve of premarital sexual relations for couples who are not in love or engaged, and in most studies, less than 50 percent approved even where there was a formal engagement . . . Contrary to popular adult stereotype, it appears reasonably clear that promiscuity is widely disapproved of by both adolescent boys and girls of all ages. (1969, pp. 641-642)

Even though the above information was written in 1969, little, if any, research conducted during the '80s suggests that the main ideas are less appropriate today.

It is apparent that not all of the forces acting upon youth propel them *toward* sexual activity. In many instances, the opposite is true. Nor can we conclude that sexual abstinence occurs only because of *strengths* within the personality. Personality *deficiencies* also inhibit sexual expression. Some adolescents, for example, never establish the kind of interpersonal relationships in which sex is possible. Others feel gravely threatened by their sexual desires and repress them. Others have such poor social or physical characteristics that no one wants them for a sexual partner. Still others hold such a weak self-concept that they shun social settings, and especially avoid dating. Finally, some youth possess such an overriding fear of belittlement that they lack the confidence for any kind of intimacy, social or physical.

For the vast majority of youngsters who possess these deficiencies, sexual abstinence is the rule, and will continue to be until the limitations of their personality permit a greater range of behavior. For most youth this liberation occurs during late adolescence or early adulthood.

Intimacy and Sexuality

The impulse for emotional intimacy eventually becomes interwoven with the impulse for sexual expression. It is difficult to imagine otherwise because the body, in the midst of its great sexual unfolding, fills the adolescent with sensations which demand a partner to reach their natural fruition. The closeness of sexual contact nourishes emotional intimacy and with equal certainty, the richness of emotional intimacy kindles sexual desire.

> If one knows, grasps, the internal reality of someone, he grasps the intimus, the inmost character of the person . . . When I am in touch with the intimum of another, I know that which is ordinarily hidden from public view yet revealed in the closeness and vulnerability of the relationship. When I am aware that someone else is in touch with my own intimum I know I have been reached at the deeper levels of my consciousness. (Oden, 1974)

The trait most essential to intimacy is *honesty* because intimacy offers little opportunity for deceptive camouflage. It is too powerful an experience to risk with a person who is not honest. Intimacy, therefore, usually lessens when either partner is dishonest with the other.

On the other hand, some youngsters are frightened of being too "honest" in their expressions of intimacy and love. Here is how one 16-year-old girl summarized it:

> When I love someone and want to know him better, I am afraid to tell him of my feelings for fear that his reaction will disappoint me. He may not love me back. This would shatter all the fantasies I had while loving this person. So, I may stifle my feelings of love because I don't want to handle the disappointment of being refused the real love that I would eventually ask for. (DeVaron, 1972, p. 342)

The distancing games devised to protect against rejection frequently backfire. Youth sometimes become so proficient at keeping their distance that they lose the ability to be intimate when the situation is right; for some, the distinction between real-self and pretend-self becomes so confused that they do not know when they are being honest and when they are merely acting out an image.

Friendships encourage intimacy, and therefore, are vital to forming love bonds; they help correct the narrowness of patterns established with parents; and, they also provide opportunities to learn about other people, their inner workings and their unique features.

Friendship undergoes a significant qualitative progression during adolescence. Pre-adolescent friendships link youngsters with one another at a fairly surface level. "Pals" is a good term for such friendships. These embryonic friendships, however, encourage intimate relationships during late adolescence, which, in turn nurture the capacity for reciprocity with an intimate lover.

Genuine intimacy rarely takes hold in an insecure or immature personality because it requires more than receiving affection. It also demands selfless giving. Although moments of intimacy are experienced during middle and early adolescence, it is not until late adolescence and early adulthood that durable intimacy usually occurs. Erik Erikson, one of the few psychologists to closely inspect the phenomenon of youthful intimacy, comments:

> Only as a person begins to feel more secure in his identity is he able to establish intimacy with himself and with others, both in friendships and eventually in a love based, mutually satisfying sexual relationship with a member of the opposite sex. A person who cannot enter wholly into an intimate relationship because of fear of losing identity may develop a deep sense of isolation. (1965,p. 328)

Of special significance with regard to the foregoing is that it is possible for young adults to live out their day-to-day routine without genuine attachment or commitment, but the very act of doing so is apt to create a "severe character problem" which lasts through the adult years. Once again we shall draw upon the insight of Erik Erikson:

> . . . where a youth does not accomplish such intimate relationships with others in late adolescence or early adulthood, he may settle for highly stereotyped interpersonal relations and come to retain a deep sense of isolation. If the times favor an impersonal kind of interpersonal pattern, a man can go far in life and yet harbor a severe character problem doubly painful because he will never feel really himself, although everyone says he is "somebody." (1969, p. 135)

The subtle intertwine between the childhood need for security, caress and affection, and the adult need for mature love, is connected in the life cycle by the adolescent need for intimacy. Harry Stack Sullivan, perhaps more clearly than anyone, emphasized the link between these three life stages and these three forms of human affection. He offers these comments on adolescence, intimacy and love:

> And added to all these important integrating tendencies, there comes in pre-adolescence the need for *intimate* exchange, for friendship, or for . . . in its high refinement . . . the love of another person . . . This becomes, in early adolescence, the same need for intimacy, friendship, acceptance, intimate exchange, and in its more refined form, the *need for a loving relationship, with a member of the other sex*. Now this is the great structure which is finally consolidated, made meaningful, as the need for intimacy as it characterizes late adolescence and the rest of life. (1953, pp. 290-291)

In Sullivan's theory, the adolescent need for intimacy, and the impulse for sexuality, are part of a chain of experiences which eventually produce an adult capable of what Erikson, Freud, and Fromm call "mature love."
Although the foregoing comments have been presented in rather loose form, a number of relationships have been hinted at, which are of immediate concern to the topic of sexuality. The foremost of these relationships is that the quest for emotional intimacy directly promotes physical intimacy; and, conversely, the sexual desire encourages the emergence of emotional intimacy. Either of these basic needs may nurture the other into existence, and either may exist fully on its own. However, because emotional intimacy and physical sexuality are *inherent complements* to each other, in the adolescent, they tend to go together.
The need for intimacy increases gradually with age, and the ability to effectively satisfy it also increases gradually with age. Intimacy *may* occur among younger adolescents, but, as a rule, the immaturity of early or middle adolescence conspires against it. "Adolescents are certainly capable of loving, but in the sexual context the mid-adolescent . . . generally remains too self-involved to undertake the mature responsibility of deeply caring for another peer" (Sondheimer, p. 224).

Depersonalization is the opposite of intimacy but it also exerts influence on adolescent sexuality.

Depersonalizing Sex

It is difficult to discuss depersonalized sex within the context of adolescent psychology because it is unquestionably more of an adult phenomenon. Nevertheless, there is no doubt that depersonalized sex is part of adolescent sexuality. Like many topics of interest to the student of adolescent psychology, this one is not widespread within the adolescent community, but it is sufficiently prevalent that it merits investigation.

In its most elementary usage, depersonalized sex refers to sexual activity in which the partner is not treated with respect, or is not taken seriously. It is superficial and short-term. It is not restricted to one sex, although males appear more inclined towards it.

In many respects the immaturity and lack of experience of adolescence contributes to depersonalized sex; so also does egocentrism and narcissism. Another contributing factor is that much adolescent sexuality is experimentation carried out to learn about oneself, about sexual experience, and lastly, about one's partner. For whatever reasons, depersonalized sex influences, to a certain degree, adolescent sexuality.

With increasing frequency clinical psychologists are reporting that sexual activity is being overly objectified, and being made into an experience which deprives it of its symbolic qualities. The factors which depersonalize sexuality are subtle. Perhaps it is a subset of a larger trend towards desacralizing life in general — the tendency towards greater aloofness and detachment. For some young people the ideal sexual encounter is where intimacy (in reality pseudo-intimacy) and love (pseudo-love) can be achieved without risk or emotional hurt for either partner.

The depersonalizing of sexuality produces several emotional effects, the chief of which is a sense of meaninglessness (or emptiness) about sexuality itself. It prohibits truly intimate sexuality. As one adolescent boy put it, "having intercourse is like masturbating with someone else." Even for those who have never experienced integration which potentially accompanies sexuality, there is a realization that something is missing.

Although the desacralizing of sexuality is not unique to adolescents, its existence during adolescence may in the long run prove to be more problematic than the same experience during adulthood.

Rollo May is of the impression that the mechanization of sexual behavior contributes to the general emptiness which pervades contemporary society. Deprived of the spiritual rebuilding inherent in ideal sexuality, modern man flounders — searching for meaningful sexuality while frightened of it. As May articulates: "The technologically efficient lover, defeated in the contradiction which is copulation without eros, is ultimately the impotent one."

Quite obviously, all adolescent sex is not ideal. Youth are subject to the same limitations which leads to exploitation and dehumanization in adult sexuality. Not infrequently adolescent girls are used by their partners only as sexual playthings, or as compensatory devices for the personality limitations of their male companions. For many girls this results in degradation of their self-concept, and an overall desacralizing of sexuality. Girls in this situation understand what it means to be "used," and they may warn a new boyfriend "You better not use me." But a week or a month later they admit to a friend or a counselor, "I was used." Although the consequences of this kind of sexual relationship are not necessarily pathological, rarely does anything *good* come from it.

> A young girl caught in this pattern dislikes herself because other people, especially her parents, seem to dislike her. Almost everything she says about herself and about life in general is negative, and her obsessive despair feeds on itself, growing with time into ever more despondent moods. She is overwhelmed if she finds a friend, particularly a male friend, who likes her "for herself," but rarely meets anyone like that because she has come to suspect everyone. She believes that one has to perform in order to get approval, and she is often right about this if you look at the people around her. (Paine, 1975)

Promiscuity, especially when motivated by unmet needs, or when fueled by the flight from boredom, reduces the emotional significance of sexuality. The following observation was made during the sixties, but it rings true for the 80s:

> I have interviewed a number of sexually promiscuous girls from comfortable suburban families, including a number . . . of girls who marry in their early teens because they are pregnant. Talking to these girls . . . one quickly sees that sex, for them, is not sex at all. They have not even begun to experience a sexual response, much less "fulfillment." They use sex — pseudo-sex — to erase their lack of identity: it seldom matters who the boy is; the girl almost literally does not "see" him when she has as yet no sense of herself. Nor will she ever have a sense of herself if she uses the early rationalizations . . . to evade in sex-seeking the efforts that lead to identity.

In this instance, sexuality is used not for the pleasure inherent to it, but rather to compensate for a lack of personal identity, or to nurture an artificial identity which denies authentic investment in another person.

Many youth learn important lessons from their superficial relationships, and recognize the inherent futility of narcissistic relatedness. As with many phenomena effected by developmental transformation, desacralized sexuality may disappear altogether, it may become an entrenched part of the personality, or it may become progressively more profound.

Personality variables influence whether dehumanized relationships lessen with age. Youth whose personalities are anti-social or narcissistic often develop patterns of detached objectivity in interpersonal relationships — including their sexual involvements. Likewise, youth who consistently use rationalization, denial, and projection usually lack insight into the inner workings of their partner. Finally, individuals to whom emotional insulation

and elusiveness are important *protective structures* are increasingly susceptible to "spiritual-less" sexual relationships.

Misperceptions About Adolescent Sexuality

The beliefs that adolescents are sexually vigorous, that they are able to
find a willing partner at a moment's notice, and that they experience powerful sexual arousal are myths which have found considerable audience
among the adult population. As with most myths or stereotypes, they hold
a particle of truth but in no way embrace the whole truth. Several factors
contribute to the perpetuation of the myth, some based upon the sensual
and open nature of youth gatherings, and others upon the unconscious projections of envious adults.

The *behavior* of adolescents is sufficient to destroy the myth that they
are sexually adventurous. By virtually every criterion, adolescents are less
sexually active, less easily aroused, less abstract and calculating, and less
effective in their sexual ambitions than are adults.

Very few adolescents could be described as sexually carefree because
sex is a serious matter not easily separated from their sense of personhood;
youth are considerably less able to partake in recreational or impersonal
sexual escapades than are young adults, and they are more likely to be
crushed when a sexual partner does not take them seriously. In essence,
"adolescents tend to see sexuality as an expression of love, not as a form of
pleasure that is sought for its own sake" (Newman & Newman, p. 260).

Adolescent boys demonstrate only a nodding acquaintance with sexual
technique. They tend not to understand the frame of reference of their
partner, and appear singularly preoccupied with themselves. They are not
attuned to their partner in a detached, or "chivalrous" manner. Their partner is primarily an extension of their own passion. In a phrase, adolescent
sexuality is egocentric, concrete, and tentative.

Nothing shatters the myth of adolescent sexual vitality more convinc-
ingly than the fact that only about one-half of all girls between the ages of
15 and 19 have ever had sexual intercourse (Zelnick,1977). This acquires
additional impact when one realizes that most of the girls who have *not* had
sexual intercourse have been in a situation where it was possible ('even
sensible," as one teenage girl said) but have refused. The consuming passion for sexual intercourse that some people attribute to adolescents simply
is not there. For the majority of youth, the conditions, the circumstances
and the partner are more important than the sexual activity itself.

The myth of the sexually promiscuous adolescent is ignited further by
belief that the automobile allows young people to travel unsupervised around
the countryside in a portable bedroom. The evidence does not indicate that

the sexual habits of young people are determined by the automobile. For example, in one research study it was found that between 40 and 50 percent of the sexually active girls had either their first or their most recent sexual experience in the homes of their partners. Only about nine percent had their first intercourse in a car, and less than six percent had their most recent intercourse in an automobile. Only five percent had either their first date or their most recent coitus in a hotel or motel. Although mobility increases the opportunity for sexual experience, sexual coupling in motels or automobiles is infrequent, while the home of the partner remains the most likely location for the sexual rendezvous.

Other data indicate that adolescent girls are not sexually adventurous. For example, only about 20 percent of all 15-year-olds and about 25 percent of the 16-year-olds *have ever* had sexual intercourse. Zelnick and Kantner investigated the sexual habits of girls age 15-19 and found that among those who were sexually active over 60 percent *had not had intercourse within the month previous to their research interview.* Among the sexually experienced girls of this age over 60 percent have had only one sexual partner, whereas only 25 percent have had either two or three partners in their sexual lives. (See Polit-O'Hara, 1985, for a more thorough discussion of sexual behavior among adolescent couples).

Virtually all research conducted during the past thirty years indicates that few adolescents are promiscuous, and that most of them are responsible in their attitudes and behavior. Neither has the birth control pill encouraged excessive sexual involvements among the young. One researcher summed it up this way:

> The majority of young people currently involved in a sexual relationship were having sex with someone they had been going out with for more than six months, and there was no evidence that the pill was encouraging casual relationships since most of the girls who were taking the pill at the time of the interview had known their partners for more than six months . . . This overall picture of teenage use of birth control gives the lie to the image of careless and casual teenage sex often promoted by the media. Although there are gaps in birth control use particularly at the initial stages of sexual experience, the majority of teenagers held responsible attitudes to sex before marriage. (Farrell, 1978, p. 219)

Sexual passion, as adults experience it, begins during the adolescent period. It appears a year or two after the onset of puberty, usually during middle adolescence. Sexual passion is not merely a by-product of physical maturity; it also requires maturity within the emotional structure. Sexual passion comes into existence during the first half of adolescence, but it does not acquire force or vitality until the latter half; although popular stereotype holds that young people reach the peak of their sexual drive during adolescence, it is much more likely to peak during the early adult years.

Many youngsters do not possess powerful and clearly defined sexual impulses. The desire for sex, or an interest in it, is universal; however, for many it is no more powerful than their need for acceptance, for achievement, or for a code of morality. Only a limited percentage of adolescents experience sexuality as an overpowering urge which requires a major effort to keep under control.

Adler and Freud debated the importance of sexuality in the life of the young adult, with Freud holding that sexuality was such a powerful force until mastered, it virtually ruled the personality; Adler claimed that the sexual impulses are subsumed under more important *social needs*, and rarely are they powerful enough to overrule the personality. To Freud sexual impulses have the person; to Adler the person has sexual impulses. As far as the adolescent personality is concerned, Adler seems to have been the more accurate of the two by a considerable margin.

In summary, even though adolescents give an image of outward sensuality, and even though they appear to the adult observer as sexually adventurous, the evidence indicates that this is not an accurate portrayal. The data indicate that most early- and middle-adolescent youth have not as yet experienced sexual intercourse. Youth are less likely than adults to engage in "recreational" sex or to clearly differentiate a casual sexual escapade from a serious personal encounter.

On the whole, adolescents are not nearly as sexually active as young adults and they view sexuality as a serious theme in their personal lives. They tend to be "monogamous" and they place considerable importance on partner fidelity. The belief that they are casual about sex, promiscuous, or sexually adventurous is, for the most part, a myth.

Postscript

Adolescent sexuality, in both its experiential and behavioral manifestations, is a complex topic. In this chapter a special effort has been made to integrate adolescent personality with adolescent biology to attain a unified assessment of sexuality.

Youth are impelled toward sexual involvements by psychic imperatives, and they likewise avoid sexual involvements because of psychic imperatives. The needs for belonging, intimacy, submission, as well as passion and intensity all contribute to sexual desire. Counterbalancing these are forces which encourage abstinence, particularly moral viewpoints, fears, and partner availability.

The unconscious desire to become pregnant motivates some girls. However, no reason exists to consider it a *major* factor in pregnancy during the teen years. On the other hand, adolescents possess an abundance of personality limitations which contribute to their sexual activity, and add to it an irrational dimension which even the adult community cannot equal.

Intimacy becomes a life force during adolescence, exerting tremendous impact on all phases of interpersonal existence, including sexuality. The need for intimacy, when bonded with eroticism, creates a powerful sexual imperative. Integrating these two life forces is one of the paramount tasks of late adolescence and early adulthood.

Adolescent sexuality, like adult sexuality, is susceptible to spiritual deterioration. It is aggravated by egocentric and narcissistic elements within the growing personality, by social hypocrisy, and by the naivete of youthful sexual partners.

In terms of behavior, however, adolescence (especially early and middle) is a time of low sexual involvement. The belief that most adolescents are sexually active, sexually aroused, and sexually available is unquestionably a myth manufactured by the adult mind, and occurs with just sufficient frequency for the myth to be perpetuated.

5
Defense Mechanisms: Their Impact on Adolescent Behavior

In personality theory wherever one finds the importance of self one also finds the importance of *defending* the self. Whether it takes the form of defense mechanisms as described by Freud, the protective reactions detailed by Karen Horney, or the compensatory reactions elucidated by Adler, the self cannot be described with cogency until the means by which it defends itself are also described. Because of the effect defense mechanisms exert on perception, and because of their power to manipulate thought, they are among the most significant determinants of adolescent behavior. In this chapter we shall highlight the premise that adolescents, while dominated by the need to assert themselves, are, with equal measure, required to *defend* themselves from both real and imagined threats. We shall also take note of the fact that, in many instances, young people expend vast sums of their energy protecting themselves against what they consider to be "major assaults" on their personhood. We shall also note that sometimes they are correct in this perception and sometimes they are not.

The Defense Mechanisms

A defense mechanism is a psychological mechanism which defends the ego from anxiety or other forms of injury, pain, or disintegration. Its primary function is to reduce anxiety.

Defense mechanisms cause the adolescent to deny or turn away from reality. They are problematic because they fail to deal with the *real* causes — they ease symptoms but do not cure causes. They are an anesthetic which soothes painful aspects of interpersonal relationships.

Defense mechanisms are given special attention in the psychology of adolescence because of their significance in day-to-day living. Indiscriminate use leads to vicious circles which increase anxiety; when they are employed over a long period of time they cause maladaptive behaviors and prevent the individual from confronting reality.

The most critical function of any defense mechanism is to distort anxiety-producing events. The degree to which this end is served is the degree to which the defense mechanism is executing its purpose. However, the more a defense mechanism distorts reality the greater the probability that negative consequences will emerge.

Defense mechanisms are most likely to be used when a the young person strongly desires something but is convinced that it is unattainable. This predicament can be resolved in three general ways as far as defense mechanisms are concerned. First, it is possible *to deny the desire*: this is most effectively carried out by repression or denial of the desire, or by reversing the desire to its opposite (reaction formation). Second, it is possible to admit to the desire but to *devalue its object*: this is most effectively carried out by rationalization ("I must have been out of my mind to want to date her; she is such a scatterbrain"). Third, by *emotionally blunting*, that is, deadening one's emotional state.

Adolescents frequently experience desires which they are convinced can never be satisfied. This belief, perhaps as much as any other, calls into existence a vast array of defense mechanisms which leave their imprint on both attitudes and behavior. Individuals with low self-esteem, or with low interpersonal competence, are most likely to believe that their desires will never be satisfied, and as a result they rely more upon defense mechanisms than do youngsters with adequate levels of esteem and competence.

Our assessment of defense mechanisms is based on pragmatic grounds; therefore when they reduce anxiety, when they make the individual more effective in day-to-day activities, and when they permit a more stable psychological balance, they are thought to be "good." On the other hand, if they increase anxiety, make interpersonal relationships more difficult, or alienate us from loved ones, they are thought to be ineffective or "bad" mechanisms. In this spirit, Glasser (1970, p. 35) says: "There are two important categories of specific ego defenses. These are the good ego defenses . . . and the poor ego defenses . . ."

It is instructive to note that defense mechanisms tend to follow three general paths. First, the defense mechanism *may weaken or disappear* as the individual eliminates the anxiety which requires control. From the viewpoint of psychological health, this is the ideal outcome. Second, the defense mechanism *may become more powerful*, bringing into it additional forms of distortion (such as projection or reaction formation) if it is not, unto itself, effective in reducing anxiety. Third, and perhaps most typical during the adolescent years, the initial defense mechanism *may be replaced by another mechanism which is less distortional*. This most frequently occurs when the individual has made some progress in reducing anxiety, but not enough to get along completely without the assistance of some defense mechanisms. This final option is frequently observed among youth who during early and middle adolescence have considerable difficulty coping with daily stress, and therefore, deploy many defense mechanisms; as their coping skills increase they are better able to resolve their conflicts. Therefore, instead of totally denying their sexual impulses (repression) they may, for example, channel sexual energy into work or sports (sublimation). In essence, they replace a powerful mechanism (which was necessary when they had virtually no coping skills) with a weaker mechanism (now that they have attained some coping skills). For many youngsters, this gradual weakening of their defensive approach to life problems is among their most significant growth advances.

In summary, defense mechanisms distort reality in order to shelter the personality. They are employed by all adolescents whether neurotic or healthy, and they become more serious the longer they are used. Even when defense mechanisms prove effective in reducing anxiety they are less adaptive than rationally-based solutions. Most psychologists subscribe to the following descriptions of defense mechanisms:

1. They are involuntary reactions.
2. They have a heavy unconscious bias but nevertheless can be understood by the conscious mind.
3. They attempt to reduce anxiety or soothe pain.
4. They are self-deceptive; they distort the ego's perception of reality.
5. Although they can be understood by the conscious mind, they are not *controlled* by it; they cannot be reasoned out of existence.

Freud's theory of defense mechanisms is the most influential, but as Gordon Allport points out "It is not necessary to accept Freud's theory of motivation and of the unconscious in order to appreciate his brilliant account of the protective strategies we all employ in order to guard our self-esteem" (p. 155).

Freud viewed the personality as composed of stratified layers with consciousness at the top; directly beneath is the preconscious stratum, and beneath that the unconscious layer which is the seat of our instinctual impulses, and the depository of our repressed memories and buried anxieties. Not all theorists agree with Freud's specific formulations, but all psychodynamic theories adhere to the notion of "layers" or "strata" of the human psyche. Implicit to understanding defense mechanisms is the image of a fluid personality in which the energy of each system flows back and forth, and with this flow each stratum weakens or strengthens depending upon whether energy is entering or leaving it.

The Scope of this chapter:

Our primary concern is to assess how defense mechanisms manifest themselves during adolescence, and to evaluate their consequences. Those defense mechanisms most frequently observed in the adolescent population will be our focus, with further commentary directed to their "normal" and "abnormal" properties.

The specific defense mechanisms discussed are: repression, projection, rationalization, reaction formation, identification, regression, and insulation. In addition, we shall overview several *protective structures* (as defined by Karen Horney) which mold adolescent behavior specifically: blind spots, compartments, excessive self-control, arbitrary rightness, elusiveness, and cynicism.

Repression

Repression is the most vital of the defense mechanisms. Freud referred to it as the "cornerstone" on which the entire structure of psychoanalysis rests. Repression, according to Freud, is the process by which a mental act is forced into the unconscious system. Its primary function is to reduce anxiety by rendering the ego unaware of a particular thought, wish, or memory which causes anxiety.

Repression is done without awareness. When confronted by a friend (or a therapist) with evidence that he has "repressed" a source of anxiety, the adolescent is genuinely befuddled — so total is the ego's imperviousness to the repression.

Suppression is a milder form of anxiety displacement which refers to those instances when we actively keep an unpleasant thought or idea "out of mind." Suppression is an act of the conscious mind; therefore, even though it yields a consequence similar to repression, it does so by a conscious rather than an unconscious process. Allport succinctly summarizes the issue this way: "Repression, then, is the process of excluding from consciousness all or part of a conflict situation. (If the process is deliberate. . . we speak of *suppression*; if not deliberate, of *repression*) (p. 158).

The concept of repression is important to our understanding of the adolescent for several reasons. First, it demonstrates that the rational portion of our personality is susceptible to manipulation by mechanisms of which it is unaware. Second, repression is the foundation for more complicated defense mechanisms. Third, when an idea, wish or memory is repressed into the unconscious it *continues to seek expression* and, therefore, periodically manifests itself in dreams, fantasies, and fears. For all of these reasons repression is considered the most significant and influential of the defense mechanisms.

The fearful anxieties of sexuality, the guilt from violating rules (or even being tempted to do so), or the embarrassment of making a fool of oneself, are all susceptible to repression. It is assumed by psychotherapists that all youngsters repress; therefore, repression alone does not betoken pathology. However, the unconscious cannot retain an infinite number of repressions, and when it is overburdened, anxiety resurfaces, flooding the ego with anxiety made even more powerful by its unexpectedness and by the individual's inability to understand where it came from.

The ego expends its own energy to prevent repressions from coming back into consciousness. Individuals with weak ego find this energy depletion a major loss. Even though repression is universal, some adolescents overuse it, pushing every frustrating desire, or fantasy, out of awareness. As a result: "They use so much of their energy in maintaining their far-flung repressions that they do not have very much left over for pleasurable and productive interactions . . . with other people" (Hall, 1979, p. 86).

Behavioral implications: On the negative side, repression causes unrealistic denial of experiences and emotions; this prevents the ego from being aware of realities. Repression encourages projection *and* reaction formation, and it also requires the adolescent to devote energy to keep repressed images out of consciousness.

On the positive side, it minimizes anxiety; it reduces the chances of being overwhelmed by fear and it eradicates painful memories, all of which make life easier to cope with.

Projection

Projection is the belief that another person has motives, feelings, or desires similar to one's own. Freud observed that his patients assigned their own anxieties to the outside world. Since his original observations, projection has become accepted as basic to the normal personality, although, like all defense mechanisms, it can become destructive.

Projection typically takes the form of reversal; therefore "I hate you" is converted to "You hate me." Or, in a similar vein, a youngster who hates and punishes himself says: "You hate me." In most instances the purpose of projection is to substitute an external cause for internal anxiety.

Projection permits the adolescent to unleash hostile elements within his own personality under the pretense of defending something or someone else. "A person who believes he is hated or persecuted may use this belief as a justification for attacking his imaginary enemy. By using the pretext of defending himself against his enemies he is able to gain satisfaction for his hostile impulses" (Hall, p. 90). This particular form of projection is extremely common in the adolescent population. It is observed, on one extreme, by gang members who vindictively injure "outsiders," and, on the other extreme, by an anxious student who launches an academic attack against the sexual vileness of Shakespeare.

Two separate kinds of projection are most frequently observed during adolescence. The first ascribes desires and wishes to others *which one knows are characteristic of oneself.* The shoplifter says "Everyone does it," or "Everyone will steal if they have the chance." Here the shoplifter attributes his own behavior to others — this is known as *assimilative projection.* The second type occurs when individuals assume that other people possess motives or feelings which they themselves have repressed and, therefore, are not aware of. This is called *disowning projection* because the attempt is to disown one's feelings by projecting them to someone else.

One might suspect disowning projection: (a) when the motives imputed to others are derogatory and immoral, (b) when these motives are vigorously denied in oneself, (c) when little evidence supports the belief that other people possess these motives and, when, (d) the person who is projecting seems to possess these imputed motives.

Projection is universally observed in adolescents primarily because it allows them to blame someone else for their unwanted feelings and their personal shortcomings.

One should not underestimate the "value" of projection during the adolescent years. The turmoil induced by growth often proves too much for the youthful personality, and when realistic solutions seem unattainable, the ego is grateful for the relief afforded by this anxiety-reducing mechanism.

Behavioral implications: Projection, perhaps more than any other defense mechanism, allows the adolescent to scapegoat personal insecurities onto others. It also alleviates the burden of perfection which many adolescents place upon themselves by making others appear inferior or stupid. For most youngsters, when tension increases, so also does projection.

Projection distorts the adolescent's perceptions of the world because is based upon denial of personal feelings, and because it causes a false assessment of other people's motives. By attributing the worst within oneself to others, projection also encourages hypocrisy, prejudice and discrimination.

Rationalization

Of all the defense mechanisms rationalization is the most widely used, typically is the least harmful, and is so widely understood by the average citizen that the core of its definition is part of our folk knowledge. It was Freud's famed biographer, Ernest Jones, who introduced the term "rationalization."By it he meant that we find acceptable and rational reasons to justify an action which was motivated by something completely different — and usually less noble. In general usage, rationalization refers to protecting our self-esteem by finding socially accepted reasons for our behavior and to the tendency to cushion failure or disappointment with a platitude.

The adolescent population makes considerable use of rationalization and even though Erich Fromm was not referring to adolescents in this quote, he easily could have been:

> However unreasonable or immoral an action may be, man has an insuperable urge to rationalize it, that is, to prove to himself and to others that his action is determined by reason, common sense, or at least conventional morality. He has little difficulty in acting irrationally, but it is almost impossible for him not to give his action the appearance of reasonable motivation.

The word is deceptive because its "rational" prefix inclines us to think it is an analytic process. It is not. Sound reasoning *discovers real* reasons whereas rationalization *invents good* reasons for what we do. The teenage boy who takes his daily run on bikini beach because "sand is the best running surface" rather than at the school track (which is five miles closer) gives us reason to suspect rationalization. So also does the teacher who formerly opposed extra-curricular activities because they are "juvenile," but now that they bring extra pay, believes they mature students in ways the classroom cannot.

Rationalizations provide *acceptable* explanations which pass for truth, but which actually exist only to justify the irrational. They are easily induced because we all have been taught to provide explanations for what we do, and we enjoy hearing ourselves give them. We have a strong desire to justify what we do — especially when we are uncertain of it in the first place.

Rationalization, because it assumes the pretense of rationality, must endure questioning from doubters. If I claim that attendance in my university class is high because I am an excellent lecturer, and a student retorts "it's because you grade on attendance," my rationalization has lost credibility and doesn't stack up very well. Because rationalizations are challenged, verbally fluent and conceptually organized individuals are most able to execute them effectively.

Two common rationalizations are "sweet lemon" and "sour grapes," and most readers have heard examples of each since breakfast. Sweet lemon is when one concludes that "what I've got is what I want'; sour grapes is when one concludes that "what I missed out on wasn't worth getting." The adolescent community with its unfulfilled hopes, unrealized ambitions, and shackled fantasies is filled with both of these rationalizations.

The normal adolescent thought process is laced with rationalizations. This, at first glance, seems a contradiction because adolescence is a period of intense mental growth and, therefore, it seems that a thought *distortion*, such as rationalization, would be rare. However, the purpose of rationalization is to reduce *anxiety*, and the ideas, thoughts and conclusions which the rational mind delivers to the adolescent are often extremely anxiety-producing. The upsurge in intellectual development is, ironically, an awesome source of adolescent anxiety, from which the adolescent requires protection.

The act of rationalization is made easier by the fact that most behavior has several motivations, not merely one, so that we have "good" as well as "bad" reasons for any given action. For the adolescent, rationalization points out to oneself and to others the good reasons while pushing into the background the bad reasons. Few individuals are better at this skill than adolescents, and those adolescents who are highly egocentric are its masters.

Behavioral implications: Rationalization pervades all facets of adolescent thought, but its greatest influence occurs when the person must justify himself. Most youth are ignorant of to their rationalizations because their mental apparatus cannot objectively analyze itself, and their need for "good news" overrules good thinking.

Rationalization encourages intellectual distortions of all kinds, especially lying. It allows the adolescent to "justify" everything, and it prevents the ego from honestly evaluating its own conclusions. Rationalization is an especially destructive mechanism when the adolescent is anti-social, narcissistic, or psychopathic.

Reaction Formation

Repression causes an anxiety-producing wish, memory, or fantasy to be pushed into the unconscious, where it either remains dormant or returns to consciousness. *Reaction formation* is more complicated because following repression, the threatening anxiety is replaced in consciousness with its *opposite*. Thus, a young man whose rage has been repressed substitutes "love for every person" in its place; the woman who repressed her sexual desires replaces them with a pledge to abstinence; the mother who repressed resentment of her children dedicates all her free time to a day care centre.

Reversals of this nature prove especially successful when peers (or superiors) approve of the opposite reaction, and for this reason reaction formation is not rare in the teen culture. The adolescent whose low body-image breeds such intense anxiety that he spends all free time sculpting a new "body beautiful" usually receives praise from comrades; the adolescent who fears rejection because of her unattractiveness may react with sexual promiscuity — which always attracts attention. The same girl, with the same fears, could take another approach, and renounce her sexuality totally, as in what Anna Freud termed "adolescent asceticism."

Typically associated with reaction formation is extreme dedication (detached observers use the term "fanatic"), and intolerance or hatred of those who give expression to the repressed fear. Since Freud it has been assumed that most examples of fanatical narrowmindedness have their foundation in reaction formation. Most psychoanalytic therapists agree with Hall's statement: "Whenever there is exaggerated and rigid conformity to any set of rules, one can be fairly certain that the conformity is a reaction formation, and that behind the mask of conformity the person is *really* driven by rebellion and antagonism" (1979, p. 93).

Freud informed us how reaction formation protects the ego from sexual impulses and aggressive urges. However, subsequent therapists have pointed out that reaction formation also protects us *from the pain of everyday experiences*. For example, a young girl who has undergone a religious experience may be frightened by its unexpected power. Being unable to comprehend her experience, she represses it and in its place substitutes a cynical rejection of religion.

Elsewhere in this book adolescent hypocrisy is described. Reaction formation should not be thought of as merely a form of hypocrisy. When one *pretends* to be the opposite of what he is, that person is being hypocritical. In reaction formation there is no pretense because the person, having repressed the original fear or impulse, is genuinely unaware of its existence. Therefore, reaction formation is an unconscious response to anxiety while hypocrisy is a conscious effort to create a false impression.

Behavioral implications: Reaction formation is more profound than other defense mechanisms discussed thus far because it involves not only the repression of an uncontrolled fear, but also because it brings into existence its opposite.

Reaction formation in adolescents most frequently takes the form of sexual prudery (a reaction against sexual fears), or passive withdrawal (a reaction against competition or aggression). When it occurs in a highly repressed or extremely fearful youngster (as it usually does) it is highly resistant to change.

Unlike rationalization or projection, which yield both positive and negative dividends, reaction formation is primarily a negative mechanism which usually indicates a troubled personality and even though it temporarily masks fears and anxieties it rarely contributes to the solution of the conflicts which *cause* fear and anxiety.

Identification

The process of incorporating into one's self (or one's self-image) the traits, characteristics or properties of another person is called *identification*. This mechanism brightens our assessment of ourselves by attaching the greatness of another onto ourselves. Freud described identification as "the assimilation of one ego to another one, as a result of which the first ego behaves like the second . . ."

The identification process is observed throughout the life cycle: it is characteristic of the child who identifies with parents and teachers; of the early adolescent who identifies with, and takes as his own, the splendor of sports heroes and entertainment heroes; of the late adolescent who identifies with the prowess of a politician or the brilliance of a literary figure. Identification interferes with growth when it prevents the individual from formulating a personal self-concept, or when it takes the form of negative identity.

As a point of historical interest, Freud believed that young boys identify with their fathers partly because of the positive reasons already mentioned, and partly because the child fears retaliation (castration) from the father. Adler, who humanized the early history of psychodynamic theory, countered that children identify with their parents because of love, and for the most part, parents as well as children believe him rather than Freud.

Like all defense mechanisms, identification is employed most during periods of stress. It requires little use of repression, and except for rationalization, is the most widely used and least destructive of the defense mechanisms. Everyday examples include the student identifying with the teacher, the assembly line worker identifying with the company product, and the sports fan identifying with the local team — especially when it is winning. With regard to youth, there is no doubt that positive identifications ease identity crises and promote images of adulthood which make its arrival a cause for joy rather than sorrow.

Behavioral implications: The most important variable is *with whom*, or *with what*, the adolescent identifies. Most youngsters identify with symbols of strength, and with individuals of competence. However, not all adolescents exhibit mature judgment of what constitutes "strength," or in the competence they prize. Early adolescents are inclined to identify with surface symbols, or with individuals who appear more competent than they really are. For the most part, these identifications are gradually discarded as the thought process becomes more sophisticated and as interpersonal relationships expand. Late adolescents identify with people (or symbols) more in accord with adult tastes, and this is one of many reasons why these two ages are fairly compatible.

Submissive and passive adolescents are inclined to identify with power; therefore, alliances between them and assertive youth are not unusual. Often this alliance is outgrown, but just as frequently it sets a trend for life-long affiliation patterns.

Regression

This defense mechanism brings into existence actions which were appropriate for a younger age, but are inappropriate for one's present age. It is most likely to occur when the adolescent is frustrated or when he is being defiant or recalcitrant.

The return to bed-wetting by a 6-year-old, the throwing of temper tantrums by a 10-year-old, rekindling of thumb-sucking in a preschooler are examples of childhood regressions.

Regressive behavior may last only a few minutes as when a person experiences a sudden shock or disappointment; or it may last many years as in certain forms of illness. Regression is situational; when the situation is left behind so is the regressive behavior.

A typical problem presented school teachers is the regressive behavior displayed in the classroom when students are frustrated, bored, or seeking attention. Adolescents sometimes ridicule themselves by acting below their age, then challenge adults to interpret this regression. When the adult over-reacts or misreads the young person's motives he is snared in the trap of the mocking youth. Teachers who do not decode this ploy are short-lived in their profession.

Regressive behavior is encouraged by fatigue, by oversatiation, and by sickness. However, among adolescents, the most frequent cause is high tension.

Regression of *behavior* is not always accompanied by regression of *emotional state*. Sometimes regression is only behavioral, and accordingly, when behavior improves, no enduring problem exists. On other occasions, deterioration in emotional level occurs, creating a far more serious disturbance, because it leaves the youngster ill-equipped to handle the struggles of normal adolescent existence.

Behavioral implications: Regression brings censure from parents and teachers. Youngsters low in social status suffer most because their peers ridicule such juvenile conduct. Leaders of the pack, however, are usually immune from ridicule, and their elevated status may allow them to get away with this defense mechanism.

Regression is most common in youngsters who cannot handle pressure, or who have been overprotected during childhood. Essentially, however, it is a safety-valve device and one of the least harmful of the defense mechanisms.

Insulation

Emotional insulation is not usually considered one of the classic defense mechanisms; however, owing to its prevalence in the adolescent community, and because of recent trends in the media to lend dignity to this impoverished state, it is included in this section.

Insulation is a form of emotional blunting where the individual protects against disappointment or rejection by not caring, or by distancing himself from the objects of fear. It encourages a posture of detached "objectivity," and fosters shallow interpersonal relationships which specialize in dealing with the surface, but not the depths, of companions and acquaintances. Insulation turns emotional neutrality into a virtue because normal emotions cause anxiety which many youngsters cannot handle. In other words, normal emotion, rather than being pleasurable and desired, is painful and feared. Therefore, the person insulates against it.

This defense mechanism shelters the ego from the emotional roller coaster of interpersonal realities, and shuts painful parts of the world out of consciousness. Most adolescents draw upon emotional insulation to maintain their equilibrium, and to protect themselves from emotional wear and tear.

Emotional insulation has attained prominence in recent years because many subcultures accept it as a legitimate style. Hendin summarizes a finding reported by hundreds of specialists during the past decade:

> Young people in our culture are creating new ideal men and women who can resist each other's impact. The emotion-free, the controlled, the impenetrable, the invulnerable are praised as having characters geared for survival in the modern emotional jungle. *Students who have achieved maximal detachment from feeling are admired as unshakable.* (1977, p. 20)

This type of psychic insulation is by no means universal, nor is it found equally among all youth; however, it is sufficiently widespread that we cannot understand adolescent behavior without taking note of it.

Emotional insulation impedes love relationships and profound friendship by sealing off the deeper recesses of the personality. It lessens emotional depth and encourages surface interchange. Even though insulation rarely results in full-blown neuroses, it produces what Maslow called "stunted" and "impoverished" individuals who never experience the full range of their personhood.

The parallel between the colloquialism "cool" and the psychiatric term "insulated" is too significant to bypass. The cool person *is* insulated. "Friends" rarely touch deeply, and ordinary human emotions are not respected. The media hype of the cool personality (in which women are now embraced) finds a spellbound audience among adolescents, who see this aloofness as the best of all possible worlds. Here is a person whom everyone craves, who by merit of arriving, has instant admirers. Yet the person does not have to *earn* the affection of others, does not have to *give* anything in return for the slavish submission of others. "Cool" is tailor-made for the narcissistic element within the adolescent personality, and through the personal fable it permits fake knights to continue performing fake exploits.

Behavioral implications: Emotional insulation is a mechanism which interferes with several developmental progressions. Most significantly, it impedes the formation of intimacy bonds and encourages the egocentric elements within the personality.

On the positive side, emotional insulation helps to keep the hurricane of adolescent emotion within manageable limits. Many young people would collapse under the weight of their own emotions if they were not afforded some protection from them. In essence, some youngsters are better off being insulated from their emotions than totally exposed to them. On the other hand, when emotional insulation becomes part of one's lifestyle, or is incorporated into one's identity, it perpetuates itself through the adult years and infects one with permanent adult narcissism.

Parental defense mechanisms: A comprehensive knowledge of the adolescent requires an understanding of how they employ defense mechanisms in order to shelter themselves from guilt and anxiety. However, adolescents are also influenced by the defense mechanisms *which adults hold in relation to them*, especially the defense mechanisms of parents. For example, when *projection* is a major mechanism in the personality of a parent the adolescent is viewed as vicious, destructive, or mercenary, and may be perceived as a threat to family stability. When *rationalization* or *intellectualization* is channeled toward the adolescent the parent may conclude that whatever punishment the youngster receives is deserved, and whatever limitations may exist in the parent-child relationship are caused by the adolescent. *Identification* may result in the parent joining the youth in breaking the law, in overpermissiveness, in failure to enforce any kind of discipline, or in joining the adolescent in an alliance to oppose those authority figures which the youngster opposes. *Reaction formation* in a parent causes a severe distortion in how the sexual activities of adolescents are perceived. Not infrequently the parent believes the youth to be promiscuous and sexually adventurous when this is not true. In essence, the entire array of life pressures which beset the parent *may* be projected, rationalized, or displaced onto the adolescent.

Glasser provides an interesting example of how parental defense mechanisms influence the adolescent. If, for example, a mother feels sexually frustrated and cannot satisfy her needs for sexuality or intimacy she may experience strong discomfort and anxiety:

> If she has a daughter, however, she may transmit to her, at a level beneath the daughter's awareness, the fact that she cannot fulfill her own needs. She also transmits the thought, "If you, my daughter, will fulfill these needs for me, I will be happy," in much the same way that she might transmit the thought that if the daughter did well in school she would be happy. The sexual needs, however, pose a problem. Satisfying them is far different from the need for daughter to do well in school, because consciously the mother says, "Be good, and lead a respectable sexual life like me," while unconsciously the mother transmits, "Go ahead and have sexual relations so that I can enjoy them vicariously, which for me will be better than my present sex life." To both daughter and mother this may become a confusing, even tragic, state of affairs. (1970, p. 54)

The extent to which parental anxiety causes frustration for their adolescent children is being reported ever more frequently. Elkind, in his influential book on the ways our culture artificially hurries growth during childhood and adolescence, points out that when parents are under stress they become egocentric (like their adolescent children) and lose the ability to view their children, or their children's problems, objectively. "Such parents tend to treat their offspring as symbols upon which to project their fear, anxieties and desires . . . So we handle our stress by putting stress on our children" (Elkind, 1981).

In sum, the defense mechanisms which hinder and complicate life for adolescents are not all of their own doing.

Protective Structures and the Adolescent Personality

The personality has means of protection in addition to the defense mechanisms discovered by Sigmund Freud. Karen Horney described a series of mental devices which she called "protective structures." Our understanding of the adolescent personality is indebted to her elucidation of these protective structures, which are given brief overview here.

Blind spots. In common usage a blind spot refers to area of discernment where one exercises poor judgment. Horney observed that many individuals *simply do not perceive* interpersonal realities which contradict their vested interests, or which oppose their self-esteem. Blind spots require further defense mechanisms such as rationalization or denial, because others do not share the same blind spots; therefore, they do not distort reality in the same way as the person whose perception is so contaminated.

This protective device is more prevalent among adults than adolescents because its existence is perpetuated by lifelong values or beliefs which are contradicted by facts which the mind's eye blocks them out. Also, our culture is more tolerant of blind spots among the elderly.

Behavioral implications: Blind spots almost always occur in an area of insecurity or anxiety. They prevent awareness of personal weaknesses (such as poor academic performance), or behavioral defects (such as regressive outbursts). Blind spots impede youngsters from recognizing their own hypocrisy, or from facing up to their personal limitations. They are more serious than most forms of rationalization because they do not merely "touch up" an unwanted reality — they completely block it out. As a rule, however, adolescents face up to their blind spots when they are pointed out to them by their peers, or by non-threatening adults. In fact, some of the most important growth advances come about because of "seeing" and dealing with blind spots — frequently during middle adolescence.

Compartments. When people adhere to rigid rules, or absolute values, they encounter anxiety. To resolve this they create "compartments" where rules are unswervingly adhered to, and other "compartments" where they are set aside. The tax consultant who insists that every bureaucratic form be followed precisely, and every legal regulation be rigorously defended, but who simultaneously refuses to follow the rules and regulations of, say, the postal system, is employing compartments. He simply behaves differently in different settings.

Chekhov and Dostoyevski have written brilliant narratives on the compartmented person, of which the rigid bureaucrat is one prototype. However, Kafka's synopsis also rings true: "Officials are highly educated, but one-sided; in his own department an official can grasp whole trains of thought from a single word, but let him have something from another department explained to him by the hour, he may nod politely, but he won't understand a word of it."

The use of compartments is widespread among adolescents because much of their life is censored. When in the presence of parents, or teachers, they behave in a compartmentalized way to avoid punishment or to earn praise. However, let the parent or teacher depart, and so also does the compartmentalized behavior. This greatly increases hypocrisy and deception in the teen world.

As is true for most defense mechanisms, one of the prime functions of compartmentalization is to help the adolescent *keep the world within manageable limits*. All of the energy of youth is not spent learning, growing or advancing: much of it is consumed keeping the conflicting elements of the personality in tolerable equilibrium. The anxieties associated with dating, schooling, and an uncertain future combine to present a formidable challenge. These day-to-day complexities do not, as a rule, paralyze the adolescent; nor should they be thought of as *major* crises. However, their severity is sufficient that many youngsters cannot keep the world within manageable limits without protective structures such as *compartmentalization*.

Behavioral implications: Compartmentalization proves useful because our culture rewards the ability to behave differently in different contexts. Thus, the doctor who behaves differently at home than at the office is thought to be effectively compartmentalized, just as is the adolescent who behaves differently in the classroom than in the gym. On the negative side, this partitioning encourages a Janus mask which permits hypocrisy to flourish, and which sometimes splits the person into irreconcilable compartments. It is especially damaging to the adolescent whose family unit and peer group oppose each other, causing him to falsify important realities of one while in the presence of the other.

Excessive self-control. All of us learn self-control is a prized asset in a complex culture and, as Freud indicated, it is the prime motive underlying socialization of the young. Horney, however, in her role as therapist, observed individuals who held a slavish rigidity, and a merciless narrowness in their self-control. They encountered panic when they "let themselves go"; their antidote: *control yourself so rigorously that letting go is impossible.* They are proof of what St. Augustine long ago noted: "To many, total abstinence is easier than moderation."

Excessive control typifies the adolescent community because young people fear the unknown dimensions of their personality, (therefore they let themselves "go" at considerable peril), and because adults reward restraint of all types (particularly when adolescents restrain an aspect of their personality which adults themselves struggle to keep under wraps, such as sexuality or aggression).

Anna Freud describes a similar reaction which she calls *asceticism*. Ascetic youngsters are overwhelmed by their impulses; rather than indulge them, they try to exterminate them. "Total war is waged against the pursuit of pleasure . . ." and as a result "most of the normal processes of instinct and need satisfaction are interfered with and become paralyzed." (Freud, 1968).

Ascetic adolescents fight natural appetites. They mistrust enjoyment in general, and when they find themselves beginning to enjoy an event or an experience their emotions freeze up and their playfulness converts to sullenness or resentment. As Anna Freud points out, they do not trust their "instincts."

Every time the instinct says, "I will," the ego retorts, "Thou shalt not," much after the manner of strict parents in the early training of little children. This adolescent mistrust of instinct has a dangerous tendency to spread; it may begin with instinctual wishes proper and extend to the most ordinary physical needs. We have all met young people who severely renounced any impulses which savored of sexuality and who avoided the society of those their own age, declined to join in any entertainment, and, in true puritanical fashion, refused to have anything to do with the theatre, music or dancing. (1936, p. 154)

However, as Anna Freud observed, ascetic denial is not confined only to sexual pleasure or interpersonal play. It also includes a morbid refusal to look after ordinary creature comforts:

But we begin to be disquieted when the renunciation is extended to things which are harmless and necessary, as, for instance, when a young person denies himself the most ordinary protection against cold, mortifies the flesh in every possible way, and exposes his health to unnecessary risks, when he not only gives up particular kinds of oral enjoyment but 'on principle' reduces his daily food to a minimum, when, from having enjoyed long nights of sound sleep, he forces himself to get up early, when he is reluctant to laugh or smile, or when, in extreme cases, he defers defecation and urination as long as possible, on the grounds that one ought not immediately to give way to all one's physical needs. (1936, pp. 154-155)

Ascetic reactions often become obsessive and may include refusing food (which results in the illness called *anorexia nervosa*). For some youngsters, asceticism actually is *pleasurable* and among them exists a fascination for self-denial, masochism, and sadism. (For further information on anorexia nervosa as a form of adolescent asceticism, see E. H. Gilbert, 1984).

Behavioral implications: Excessive control is an extremist approach to impulse management. It usually begins as a reaction against sexual desires, but ends up as much more. When an entire philosophy of life is spun upon it we invariably note behavioral problems.

Arbitrary rightness. The human personality resists ambiguity. Clarity, even at the expense of accuracy, is desired by most people most of the time. Unfortunately, the adolescent is living a phase of life when uncertainty, not clarity, is the prevailing experience. One way that the adolescent copes with uncertainty is with the protective device of *arbitrary rightness*. He simply proclaims, *ex cathedra,* that this is right and that is wrong. Once proclaimed, he does not worry about it; it has been dealt with. If the youngster is clever, and decorates his proclamations with rationalizations, he may appear to friends and teachers as "committed," or as "knowing his own mind." However, certainty of outlook among adolescents often derives more from arbitrary rightness than from thorough examination of an issue.

Interestingly, many late adolescents find themselves sorting through the consequences of their gestures of "arbitrary rightness" from earlier adolescent periods. Experience brings the realization that there is more arbitrariness than rightness to many youthful proclamations.

Behavioral implications: Arbitrary rightness renders decision-making easier, but not necessarily more accurate. It increases dogmatic thinking, outright condemnation, and "proves" personal rationalizations. It is especially active among the highly authoritarian, and among youth whose guilt requires the salve that only certainty can bring. It also encourages projection because much arbitrary rightness is mere scapegoating.

Elusiveness. Arbitrary rightness shields anxiety by cancelling options. Elusiveness operates from the opposite premise: by never making up my mind I can never be wrong. The anxiety of error is eliminated, but at the expense of decision-making. The uncommitted, wishy-washy anti-hero of the contemporary cinema typifies elusiveness.

Behavioral implications: Elusiveness encourages procrastination and discourages decision-making. It impedes identity formation. It interferes with assertiveness. Essentially, elusiveness is a protective mechanism which allows the individual to remain in the background, to avoid confrontations, and to attain anonymity. It is disastrous for individuals who aspire to an outgoing, affirmative lifestyle. However, for individuals geared toward passivity it poses fewer problems. A practical drawback to elusiveness is that it renders the individual susceptible to exploitation by aggressive or domineering peers who capitalize on their inability to make decisions.

Cynicism. Cynicism is among the most effective mechanisms to shield the personality from the relentless probing of the intellect. By constant fault-finding and endless criticism, cynicism cancels the need for further understanding or greater self-extension. The cynic concludes "Why bother — it's not worth it." In a world of uncertain worth, it is an effective buffer. (See "Nihilism" for greater elaboration of this concept).

A cynic in modern times is not what the Greeks meant by the word. For them, the cynic was a critic of contemporary culture whose tools were reason and natural law; he was revolutionary in thought and avante garde in style. Modern cynics possess no such moral or academic substance — they do not follow anybody or anything. Tillich notes: "They have no belief in reason, no criterion of truth, no set of values, no answer to the question of meaning. They try to undermine every norm put before them." Tillich elsewhere notes: "The cynics are lonely although they need company in order to show their loneliness. They are empty of both preliminary meanings and an ultimate meaning, and therefore easy victims of neurotic anxiety" (1952, p. 150).

Behavioral implications: Cynicism impedes normal curiosity; it encourages lethargy and resignation; and, it encourages the adolescent to give up on long-term projects. Because it may mushroom into nihilism, it is potentially one of the most destructive adolescent protective structures. It is one of the few mechanisms which has virtually no redeeming features. It is widespread among normal as well as disturbed youth; however, most adolescents outgrow it, or at least replace it with reserved caution.

Each of the above protective structures operates within adults as well as adolescents, but their manifestations are profound, and without doubt, they contribute immeasurably to behavior we daily observe in the adolescent arena.

Some Further Considerations

Keeping the world within manageable limits:

To properly assess the normal adolescent we must evaluate the capacity to maintain the world "within manageable limits." The two most significant variables pertaining to this are: (1) the overall personality strength of a given individual, and (2) the stressfulness of the environment in which the individual lives. Both of these contribute significantly to adolescent normalcy *and* adolescent disturbance.

Most youngsters possess sufficient ego strength to cope with day-to-day living. However, few of them possess so much that maintaining their world poses *no* difficulties. For a considerable percentage of adolescents ego strength is *barely adequate* to negotiate the demands of daily living. For these youngsters, keeping their world within manageable limits is an all-consuming task which is mastered only with continuous assistance and advice from their friends. The effective management of their daily "mini-crises" consumes most of their psychic energy.

A smaller percentage of youth simply cannot handle life stress. They cannot control their anxiety, their interpersonal relationships are fragile, their basic needs for love, belonging and esteem are not well gratified. These young people often become psychiatric casualties who require therapy to establish themselves within the community of peers.

The quality of one's interpersonal environment determines how much strength *is required* for survival. An environment which provides few obstacles, which praises more than it punishes requires a less powerful personality. On the other hand, an environment in which the adolescent is constantly defending against threats to his physical or emotional well-being, or in which little success is experienced, or in which love relationships are nonexistent, requires a far more durable (and well-defended) ego which expends a far greater share of its resources simply coping with its hostile environment.

Individuals of average or below average ego strength often find that the demands of a hostile environment exceed their coping abilities, and for them keeping the world within manageable limits *becomes a primary life goal.* Although psychological ailments and behavior disturbances do not typify adolescents in general, youth with below average ego strength who live in a hostile environment are highly susceptible to a dramatic range of neurotic disorders. Conversely, individuals with above average ego strength, living within an emotionally supportive environment, are remarkably healthy.

Defensive devaluation:

This occurs when the person diverts attention away from himself by drawing attention to the faults of others. This is an attempt to deny personal deficiencies by focusing all of one's attention on the limitations of others. It is expressed by constant griping about the ineffectiveness of teachers, by incessant belittling of important people, and by nagging or complaining. Defensive devaluation is rarely constructive, in fact, its entire purpose is to escape personal insecurities by focusing on the actions of others. Early adolescents are perhaps the world's "best" at this, not only because they (by adolescent standards) possess fewest skills, but also because they have never held positions of responsibility so they have no first-hand knowledge of what is involved in teaching, coaching, parenting, etc. With increased maturity their detraction of others becomes less blatant. An *early* adolescent might say: "Mr. Smith is the worst teacher in the school. I don't know how he keeps his job." A *late* adolescent: "I know that I might not be a good teacher, but if I did make it my profession I sure would be a lot better than Mr. Smith." In defensive devaluation each of these comments serves the same purpose, even though their delivery becomes more "sophisticated': concentrate on the weaknesses of another in order to avoid my own.

Fear of rejection is one of the most powerful adolescent fears, and frequently is the cause of defensive devaluation. For many youngsters the need to protect against rejection is so powerful they exhibit the same behavior *as neurotic adults.* The following quote, for example, is intended to describe the *neurotic adult* fear of rejection; however, it also is an accurate description of many *normal adolescents'* fear of rejection:

> He rejects others because he anticipates that they will reject him. His hostility emerges in sarcasm, negativism, and withdrawal. He is quick to feel slighted. If he is not invited somewhere, he feels discriminated against. If he is kept waiting in a store, he is convinced the clerk thinks he is unimportant. Exposed to a minor criticism or even a kind sugges-

tion, he retreats from the situation. Others have to go out of their way to reassure him if they want him to feel accepted. The outcome of his feeling of rejection is that he is afraid to relate closely to a significant other. (Stein, 1972)

It is precisely because of this highly developed fear of rejection that so much adolescent behavior is defensive, protective and fearful.

Postscript

In this chapter we have overviewed the use of defense mechanisms in the adolescent population. All youth use them, sometimes to excess. Defense mechanisms are employed for several reasons. First, adolescence is a period of high anxiety, and humans at all ages use defense mechanisms when burdened with anxiety. Second, teens often lack the insight to cope with their problems in a rational way; therefore, they rely upon irrational solutions. Third, adolescents have not yet learned to recognize when their thoughts and actions are influenced by defense mechanisms; therefore, checks upon them are minimal.

All defense mechanisms share one common feature: they distort reality in order to reduce anxiety. As a rule, this distortion makes one less able to deal with reality, and in the long run, produces more anxiety than it reduces. In such instances, defense mechanisms are a handicap. Periodically, however, defense mechanisms provide necessary breathing room and help to keep the world within manageable limits, thereby becoming assets. Adolescents, unfortunately, are poor at predicting when the defense mechanisms they employ will prove to be assets or handicaps.

Closely allied, but not as psychologically complex, are what Karen Horney called the *protective structures*. Defense mechanisms and protective structures complicate the adolescent's struggle between the rational and irrational forces within his growing personality, creating a battlefield in which the adolescent sometimes becomes a casualty, but most typically, is only a combatant awaiting veteran's discharge into adulthood.

Section Two

The Three Ages of Adolescence

A Prefatory Comment

A modest controversy continues as to whether adolescence should be divided into substages; I believe that it should. Considerable insight is gained to the adolescent character when we recognize that growth unfolds in a mildly predictable manner, and as a consequence, early adolescents are considerably different in temperament and ability from late adolescents.

The categories employed in this section provide sound *generalizations* about a significant percentage of youth in our culture. The limitations which derive from partitioning adolescence into early, middle, and late are not as severe as those which come from the attempt to characterize youth under one expansive term "adolescence." This opinion is voiced by DuLit (1979) when he asserts: "For an adolescent psychiatrist on the subject of adolescent development, the three things are: *early* adolescence, *middle* adolescence, and *late* adolescence. No adolescent psychiatrist worth his salt fails to make those distinctions or some equivalent." He then adds: ". . . given the rapid rate of change from 12 through 20, the term adolescent is just too broad, too global, too overinclusive" (p. 17).

The idea of dividing adolescence into three ages is not new. It was used in early writings of Harry Stack Sullivan, and employed by many of the psychoanalysts including Peter Blos. Sullivan conceived of adolescence as being divided into three segments: *pre*-adolescence, *early* adolescence and *late* adolescence. *Pre-adolescence*, according to Sullivan, is characterized by the need for a close personal relationship with another person, usually of the same sex and similar age. These relationships nurture the foundational skills for interpersonal intimacy. During pre-adolescence the youngster begins to experience loneliness because the need for companionship is so forceful that its loss creates a fearful feeling of emptiness. *Early adolescence* witnesses a shift of interest from same-sex to opposite-sex companions. Learning to transact interpersonal relationships is a major preoccupation of this age. Sullivan believed that puberty created a sense of "lust" or genital sexuality, which monopolizes the desires and thoughts of young people.

Although Sullivan overrated the urgency of early-adolescent "lust," he rightfully pointed out the numerous complications which arise when genital sexuality is blended with the need for interpersonal intimacy. Finally, *late adolescence* is the last stage before adulthood, and for most individuals it marks the time when they integrate sexual impulses with interpersonal needs. This also is a period of significant intellectual growth, and equally important, it is a time when one's sense of self-respect must be actualized. (For a more comprehensive analysis of the significant events leading up to what we generally call "adulthood," see M. M. Marini, 1984).

Peter Blos believed that adolescence is best understood as three distinguishable periods — which he labeled *early adolescence, adolescence proper,* and *late adolescence.* During *early adolescence* youth make the transition from same-sex friendships to heterosexual friendships. *Adolescence proper,* according to Blos, is characterized by a reduction of emotional investment in people and objects which acquired their significance during previous stages. This distancing from previous "investments" prompts a reassessment of fears, conflicts and ambitions which came into being during earlier adolescent periods. As emotional attachment to these bonds weakens (or disappears) the adolescent reinvests this energy in new relationships with the real *and* ideal world. Thus, adolescence proper is a period of new attachments, new emotional investments, and new vulnerabilities.

Blos suggests that the adolescent vulnerability to depression and nostalgia is an emotional reaction to bidding farewell to earlier attachments and love objects.

Late adolescence unfolds a more consolidated outlook. The ego strengthens. Sexual identity becomes more finalized; egocentrism diminishes, and is replaced by a more "other-oriented" perspective. The late adolescent image becomes more constant because it tends to be more stable in all areas of the personality.

These mini-overviews of Sullivan and Blos represent a limited sample of writings which support adolescence as a three-part time zone. The reader should find this an effective way to understand the skills, virtues, and limitations of the adolescent population. Breaking adolescence into three separate periods will add to our knowledge of adolescence and reduce the validity of Kagan's assertion that: "It is a paradox that adolescence should be a period of greatest concern to parents and youth and the era least well comprehended by psychologists" (1972, p.vii).

6
The Early-
Adolescent Period:
A General Overview

Adolescence covers too many years and too much growth to be properly understood as only one developmental period. The differences between the early and later years of adolescence are profound. The most consistent error that adults make is to treat early adolescents as if they were more mature and self-directing than they are, and to treat late adolescents as if they were more juvenile than they are. We prematurely impose "adolescence" on youngsters who are child-like in the substance of their personality — especially the 11-, 12- and 13-year-olds; and then during late adolescence when they are ready to grow into adult maturity we tend to perceive them as full-fledged adolescents rather than as the young adults they are.

When adolescence begins youth have been out of childhood less than a year. Their lives have been lived as children and childhood is what they know best. Nevertheless, the body grows steadily toward puberty, and the world over, the attainment of puberty is the sign that childhood has seen its day. Early adolescents straddle the world of child and adolescent, sometimes thinking as one then as the other, sometimes feeling like one then like the other, sometimes looking like one then like the other. To think of them as children is wrong. To think of them as fully developed adolescents is also wrong.

Osterrith (1966) reminds us that ". . . it may not be a bad thing to recall at the outset that adolescence is above all . . . the normal and unavoidable continuation of childhood." With regard to understanding psychological makeup, he claims, it is important to note: "There is little doubt that the psychic structure of the adolescent has its roots in childhood and that many of the characteristics that are generally considered as typical of adolescence appear and are already present during late childhood" (p. 11).

These are years of learning new roles and rules, and of accepting a body which changes significantly every six months or so. The pull comes from adolescence; the push, however, comes from childhood and it flavors all experience and tastes. Just as late adolescents take into the adult world the remnants of their adolescent perceptions and attitudes, early adolescents bring powerful segments of their childhood into adolescence. For all of these reasons the earliest years of adolescence can, in a loose sense, be thought of as "child-adolescence." The term suggests a mixture of the two worlds, and makes clear the fundamental differences between this age and the final period of adolescence known as *adult*-adolescence. The period sandwiched between these two vital times of life is *middle* adolescence and it is here that youth most honestly resemble the images our culture holds of "adolescence."

The Body

Two separate growth periods are experienced during early adolescence. Developmental psychologists call them *latency* and *puberty* and the differences between them are remarkable. The latency period is a time of stable, consistent growth; by adolescent standards it is comparatively trouble-free and uneventful. The puberty period, and the time immediately before it, is a zesty, fast-paced era with body parts undergoing remarkable growth.

Sexual maturity begins at puberty. In girls, it is signalled by the first menstrual flow. For boys, the signs are less definite, with the most reliable indicator being the presence of spermatozoa in the urine. (The reliability of this signal is offset by the fact that it requires a microscope, a scientist who knows what to look for, and a urine specimen.) To state that the puberty for male *or* female is announced by *one* particular event is unfair because puberty is a process that affects all body subsystems and includes much more than *only* sexual maturity.

(It is worthy of mention that few psychologists observe in young women the traits which psychoanalysts believe are associated with menarche. Psychoanalysts claim that the first appearance of blood may induce ideas of genital injury or reactivate sexual conflicts, fears and anxieties within the girl. Although some girls experience anguish during their menstrual periods, the psychoanalytic belief that girls associate menarche with excretory soiling, with loss of sphinctor control, or with masturbatory guilt is rarely reported by young girls to anyone.) (Whisnant, 1975).

The hormones responsible for masculine traits (androgens) and those responsible for feminine traits (estrogens) are both produced in *every* person. However, with puberty there occurs a sharp increase in the production of estrogens in girls, and in boys a corresponding increase in the production of androgens. These hormones catalyze the growth of all primary and secondary sexual characteristics. *Primary* sexual characteristics concern those parts of the anatomy directly involved in reproduction, particularly the genitalia. *Secondary* sexual characteristics are traits common to males or females, but not directly involved in reproduction. For males these include deepening of voice, growth of body hair, expansion of chest cavity; for females, rounding of the pelvis, growth of breasts, increase of fatty tissue.

The first menstrual flow begins for about 75 percent of all girls during the twelfth, 13th, or 14th year. The *average* age is about 12 years, ten months; however, the "normal" range can be extended two years in each direction. The menstrual cycle tends to be inconsistent and somewhat unpredictable the first year or so after it begins, and the fact that a girl menstrates does not confirm that she is able to conceive or bear a child. The ovaries may not be able to produce eggs capable of being fertilized, and the uterus may not be sufficiently mature to house a fetus.

Puberty occurs later for boys than for girls in accord with the fact that girls are, as a rule, developmentally more advanced during the first fifteen years of life. Most girls complete the puberty growth spurt between their 13th and 14th birthdays, while boys continue until the 15th birthday and beyond. This age difference in attaining maturity carries considerable social implications.

For boys and girls alike, a number of similar events take place during puberty. The skin becomes coarser and more porous; the sebaceous glands become more active and produce an oily secretion which contributes to the adolescent's vulnerability to complexion problems. The composition of sweat changes, becoming much stronger in odor. All these combine to make youngsters more self-conscious and to tax their self-image and their self-confidence.

The head and face demonstrate noticeable growth during the early-adolescent years for both sexes. The nose tends to become longer and more conspicuous; the jaw, especially in boys, assumes a more angular and impressive prominence. Sometimes the upper part of the face grows more rapidly than the lower, providing an incongruous, but developmentally natural, appearance. The extremities of the body are the first to reach full adult size; consequently, they are out of proportion to the rest of the body.

Even the naive or disinterested observer will notice the dramatic changes in height and weight which typify the early adolescent. Boys commonly begin the ninth grade a full three inches taller and 20 or more pounds heavier than they were at the end of the eighth grade. Neither is it uncommon for a 12- or 13-year-old girl to sprout upward three inches, develop a noticeable bustline, gain 10 to 15 pounds, round out in the pelvis, and lose facial baby fat within a four-or five-month period. As youth stretch upward, basal oxygen consumption increases; they are obliged to eat more because they need more to sustain normal body operations. As the skeleton lengthens, the need for calcium and phosphorus increases; muscles must expand to handle the burgeoning body and, consequently, the need for protein and exercise increases. Not uncommonly, rapid growth in height results in awkwardness. Muscles are not efficient in controlling the body and the youngster must adjust to the fact that the body does not fit into the same space it once did.

Considerable difference in muscle tissue exists between the sexes. From the earliest years boys possess greater muscle volume whereas girls have more fatty tissue. By adulthood the male leg contains only about eight percent fat, while a woman's contains about 18 percent. Even with difference in fatty tissue, boys and girls have the same relative strength to body weight *before* puberty; after the onset of puberty, however, boys show an increase in relative strength which, when linked with other sex differences such as the larger heart and lung of the male and the greater stamina of his muscles, usually results in the male being more suited for activities requiring strength and endurance. To impress this point remember that when 11-year-olds arm wrestle, a girl is as likely to win as a boy; when 15-year-olds arm wrestle, a girl rarely is able to defeat a boy.

The Effects of Physical Growth on the Early Adolescent

Puberty takes a personal toll. It is difficult to imagine otherwise. The most notable consequence is a general preoccupation with the body, with the way it looks and how it feels.

Few youngsters of this age take their bodies for granted. They worry about how it looks to others, even though they possess some idea as to whether it is attractive by general standards. They are far more likely to believe a negative comment about their appearance than a positive one; therefore, they experience considerable anguish from ridiculing peers or critical adults. The diaries of adolescents often indicate dislike of their bodies, as typified by this entry from a nervous boy:

> I feel self-conscious. I don't want to be handsome, but I hate my present appearance. Weak, pale, small ears, big nose, 'peach fuzz,' weak chin. Now my mouth is out of shape and I cannot smile, for Dr. Singer put my brace back yesterday. (Kiell, 1964, p. 54)

All youth harbor feelings of inferiority about their bodies and in few areas are they more easily wounded. To alleviate tension they make fun of one another. On a given day this playfulness may or may not be taken seriously, so the game holds some peril despite its therapeutic utility.

The extent to which youngsters view themselves in relation to their bodies is given considerable weight by some psychologists. For example, Stein (1972) claims: "The body-image remains the core of the self-concept throughout life." Although this assessment seems steep, it lends credence to the importance of the relationship between body-perception and self-perception.

Because most adolescents lack confidence in themselves, they look to others for cues about their appearance, their attractiveness, and especially their femininity or masculinity. They need good news from outsiders and when they don't get it, are likely to think poorly of themselves. On the other hand, their understanding of outsiders is wobbly, and praise may bring a mere shrug of the shoulders or a what-do-you-know snarl. Adults, as a rule, resent this and when it continues too long they stop providing the ego-bolstering essential to the self-doubting youth.

The unpredictable temper associated with adolescence begins to manifest itself near puberty. Emotions, though they are not as rich as they will be in a few years, add their weight to body anxiety, daily living more burdensome than it was during pre-adolescence. Psychologists have long noted this as the age when moodiness begins to assume its distinctly adolescent tinge.

Blos (1970) clarifies the emotional significance of puberty with this statement: "Puberty constitutes a period of intensified stress, and, as a consequence, it readily *exposes certain inadequacies of psychic structure that were previously*, for all practical purposes, *either nonexistent or seemingly irrelevant*" (p. 9). The question of whether the implosions of puberty are the result of rising "instinctual tensions," as psychoanalysts claim, merits more analysis that this chapter permits.

Pain, of course, is not only of the *psychological* variety although psychologists are fond of thinking so. Growing muscles ache and irritate; girls often experience discomfort in the developing breasts and in the abdomen area during menstruation. Skeletal joints, especially in the feet and shoulders, sometimes smart. The growing body creates its own discomfort and when it is aggravated by psychological pressures, by inferiority feelings and self-doubt, or by peer ridicule or adult avoidance, the growth process is more difficult.

In essence, the growing and unfolding body profoundly affects the early adolescent personality. Every important theorist acknowledges its significance in molding the subjectivity of adolescence. Some writers, such as Anna Freud, believe that puberty is the most significant event in the second decade of life; others, such as Karen Horney, downplay physical puberty, and instead focus on family and culture in the formation of the adolescent personality. Whatever the theoretical orientation, during early adolescence the body assumes a significance unequalled in other developmental periods.

The Social and Private World During Early Adolescence

The social requirements of early adolescence centre upon living with peers, the pressures of competing within a limited circle of comrades, and mastering the rules of social survival. The mastery of these requirements demands time plus an exceptional amount of trial and error. Coping with bullies, rule freaks, and friends who own desired playthings or who possess money are unavoidable facts of social life. Most importantly, one must learn to do well whatever is prized, or to compensate in ways that make oneself the prize. The peer group acquires such power during early adolescence that frequently it avoids parental demands as well as personal beliefs. Many an early adolescent has sold out personal convictions because of peer pressure.

The peer group holds power because peers determine *social acceptance* and they also determine *social rejection*. To go against the crowd one risks ostracism or ridicule — two of the gravest fears among comrade-conscious youth. Most youth of this age possess neither a well-developed sense of selfhood nor a crystallized morality; as a result the restraints which hold back a more mature personality do not press as heartily on the early adolescent. When identity becomes more established, and moral outlook more principled, standing up to peers increases. Until then, peers and self live an uncomfortable alliance, each incomplete without the other, but often miserable when together. This "uncomfortable alliance" is virtually universal among early adolescents in our culture although in less complex societies it does not appear to be as prevalent. (Interesting research on these ideas has been compiled by A. Yarcheski, 1984).

Sex role learning is important for knowing what is *un*feminine or *un*masculine because youngsters at this age by no means have a clear outlook as to what is appropriate. They are impressed, however, with what is *in*appropriate, because it is easily spotted and easily ridiculed. The *fear of ridicule* is a basic fact of early-adolescent life, which contributes both to their conformity and their desire for friends who will not take advantage of them.

Personal attachments lack durability, and interpersonal bonds are more easily severed than will be the case in a few years. Emotion is a life force but not a dominant one. When contrasted with the *child*, the early adolescent experiences a far greater breadth *and* depth of emotion. When compared with late adolescents, however, he aligns more closely with childhood. One of the most exciting features of the next age of adolescence (middle adolescence) is the crossover in this alignment, that is, the transition from childlike to adultlike emotional fabric.

This is not to say that emotions are even. Anger can border on the savage. Sorrow induced by rejection can rip the seams of an otherwise domestic personality. Jealousy, envy, and spite reach remarkable depths. The major differences between the emotions now and during the older years are measured in time and expense. Early adolescents (who forget more quickly than they will in a few years) remember painful emotions dimly; they make amends with greater promptness than they will in the future. In all, emotions are not as soul-shattering as they will be, and considering the limited range of early adolescent adaptability, this is just as well.

Because of their limited emotional range, few youngsters of this age experience sexual passion as adults know it. Intimacy is not a major life experience because the self is insufficiently developed to permit genuine symbiosis; religion lacks emotional fervor but for many youngsters it holds a matter-of-fact seriousness. Each of these developmental consistencies yields to time and growth, but for now they take the form we associate with the early adolescent rather than with the late adolescent.

The foregoing observations are in accord with Erikson's psychosocial theory of development, and create the opportunity to remind the reader of two important assumptions Erikson holds with regard to adolescent development. First, individuals at every growth stage possess the ability to contribute in important ways to their own growth; therefore, growth is not completely dictated by the external environment, by maturational timetables, or by the actions of the growing person; rather, adolescent growth is a continuous, on-going interaction among all three. Second, the peer group actively shapes the direction in which growth can take place, and thereby tempers the power of the self to determine all aspects of personal behavior.

In essence, Erikson reminds us of a painfully obvious fact: youth are not merely a product of their social environment; they are a mixture of "brewed" and "brewsmaster," and unfortunately for the youth-watcher, it is virtually impossible to know when they are more one than the other.

Social Outlooks During Early Adolescence

The view of society held by most youngsters is not overly encouraging because the egocentrism of their personal thinking expands into an ethnocentrism of their social thinking. This age tends toward a kind of "high nationalism" which reflexively concludes that a country should always do whatever is in its own best interest. Early adolescents do not understand well the social forces of history nor do they have much comprehension of international power struggles. Their understanding of society is based more upon platitudes and pledges than on genuine insight. They frown upon anyone who opposes their country and usually believe that those who do so are perverted, malicious, or just plain stupid.

Few youngsters view their society with detachment, and even fewer are able to isolate its inferior institutions from the superior. Although they know that defects exist, they accept them as legitimate blemishes on an otherwise attractive face. Their sense of social identity is based upon authority rather than upon a concept of justice. (In this regard, they are similar to many adults, though an important difference exists. For adults, the *capacity* to make such distinctions goes unused; for the early adolescent, the capacity is not as yet formed).

Junior high school teachers and principals have learned it is not wise to have youngsters judge their peers who have broken a school rule. First, their punishment is often vindictive and far more punitive than the violation warrants; second, they often allow a guilty offender to escape punishment if he or she is liked by the judges. Of the three ages of adolescence this is the most corruptible because it is least bound to concepts of justice and because it is least able to resist peer pressure.

At this age youth are inclined to view the world as a place to be run and organized. Why they are inclined this way when they are simultaneously egocentric and self-centred is not clear. Adelson, in an extremely thought-provoking essay on the political imagination of youth, offers this not-so-flattering assessment of youthful authoritarianism:

> What accounts for the authoritarian animus among the young? They are, to begin with, preoccupied by human wickedness. They see man as tending naturally toward the impulsive and the anarchic. They are Hobbesian — it is the war of all against all. They do not seem to have much faith in — or perhaps they do not cognize adequately — the human capacity for self-control, or the demands of conscience. (1972, p. 117)

It is a good time for "isms." Nationalism, Catholicism, Nazism or any other "ism" finds a good audience here. "Isms" learned in the home are acquired with least questioning. The great age of doubting is not far away, however, and many "isms" acquired in early adolescence are abandoned during the intellectual revival of middle adolescence.

Neither history nor the future holds the importance they will acquire adolescent ages. Again Adelson makes a relevant observation.

> In the *early years of adolescence the child's mind is locked into the present.* In pondering political and social issues he shows little sense of history or a precise and differentiated sense of the future. The past is not seen to weigh upon the present, via precedent and tradition, nor can the child perceive the manifold and varying potentialities within the present. The young adolescent will rarely look back to the antecedent sources of

the present, and when he thinks of the future, or is forced to by the question we ask him, he can imagine only the immediate and direct outcome of a current event.

During the middle years, we begin to see a distinct, though modest, extension of temporal range. A sense of the past begins to appear. (1972, p. 110)

Gangs and cliques are common. They represent an ideal way to escape the world of adults, to establish a diverse identity which includes things forbidden at home, and to achieve greater competence within the peer world.

Early adolescent gangs are capable of savage and brutal acts. Group behavior attains the "lowest common denominator" with alarming swiftness. Egocentric rigidness, when combined with fear of peer rejection and the craving for peer praise, produces behavior which easily becomes pathological. The worst within human nature is easily kindled by the early adolescent "pack" mentality, and the student of adolescent psychology who overlooks this fact blinds himself to a significant reality of this time of life.

Almost everything in the social world is interpreted through an underdeveloped sense of morality. In school, for example, rules are thought good if they favor "me," and bad if they do not. At home rules are obeyed more from habit (or fear) than from conviction of their intrinsic merit.

Early adolescents confront the unpleasant fact that rational thought does not always produce acceptable solutions. They find that the self does not always obey the dictates of the rational mind, and they sometimes wish their easygoing lives hadn't been interrupted by the advancement of reason. Feeling and reason, as healthy adults know, do not always concur. Compromises which require suffering and anguish must be made.

The social world also changes. Friendships are taken more seriously and, though group acceptance is important, its limits are starting to recede. This age requires a friend who can be trusted, who can listen, who is worthy of sharing important events. Praise is not as readily or as categorically accepted as during the past three years. Thirteen-year-olds receive parental or teacherly praise with a casual, almost detached air because the self is in such disarray that it is easy to be unimpressed by praise from another disorganized person. Paradoxically some adults wield extraordinary influence merely by a brief compliment. Teachers possessed of this skill may become the most influential adults in the life of the early adolescent.

The peer group is difficult to assess. For some, its grip becomes tighter than ever; others display a remarkable immunity to it. As a rule, however: "Peer group conformity tends to be at its strongest during early adolescence, especially the years from 12 to 14. Peers are especially likely to encourage or support one another in behavior that would be devalued by the adult community during these years" (Newman & Newman, p. 259).

Popularity is an important consideration but rarely is it pursued at any price. Some early adolescents make up their own minds regardless of group demands. Peer groups lose their randomness as individuals search out friends who blend without excess hassle. For many youngsters this is the age when evening activities are scheduled because insufficient time exists during the day. Clubs, athletics, and study groups all vie for limited time and energy. Adults should not deceive themselves in this matter: habits acquired at age 13 are capable of diverting normal adolescent development. Good habits do not assure positive growth nearly as consistently as bad habits contribute to negative growth. Most textbooks are overly polite, as though embarrassed, when it comes to the adolescent's capacity for pathology. Every city in North America has early-adolescent prostitutes, junkies, pimps, habitual vandals, and thieves. Heroin addiction among early adolescents is a national disgrace in the United States and Canada.

Home and Family During Early Adolescence

It comes as a surprise to many students of adolescent psychology that the home remains the psychic and physical frame of reference during early adolescence. Conflicts with parents are frequent but not fundamental. The surge for freedom is so hampered by financial dictates that youth of this age rarely think about leaving home for good, and even more rarely actually do so. *Serious* runaways almost always are fleeing a painful or abusive homelife.

Practical reasons contribute to the fairly stable home-family relationship of this age. Early adolescents have almost no way to support themselves outside the family. Neither do they have a place to live. They can be detained by the authorities when they do not attend school. These shackles, however, are not as restrictive as they appear once the nature of the early adolescent is taken into close measure. For example, few youth of this age strongly desire economic independence, and few as yet despise school enough to choose from the few available alternatives. Most youth retain strong emotional ties with their parents and find them more comforting and humane than virtually any other adults in their social world. These ties are not strained excessively by conflicts of interest. Parents don't worry too much about the sexual habits of their children. Automobiles are not yet an important part of their social life, nor are liquor or drugs. Exceptions abound, to be sure, but in only mild degree when compared with the upcoming years. Daniel Offer, who has conducted what is possibly the best research to date on *normal* adolescents, notes that the "generation gap" is not as bad as is commonly thought, and that for the most part adults and their teenage children get along fairly well. His research indicated "that for the majority of teenagers we have studied there is no major gap of understanding and communication between the generations." (1969, p. 204)

Moral Outlook During Early Adolescence

Moral outlook and religious belief tend toward the conventional. Most youth adhere to the religious denomination of their parents (if they have one), and accept matter-of-factly the moral precepts upon which it is based. Differences of opinion exist, but they are founded more frequently upon dissatisfaction with rules than upon a basic difference in metaphysics or axiology. Puzzles (such as the purpose of life) do not register deeply on the early adolescent because the mental capacities required for such contemplation are not fully developed, and because the intellect has all it can handle with day-to-day matters.

Religious experiences do not carry much emotional significance. What clergymen call "genuine" religious conversions rarely take place at this age. Religion is viewed somewhat like the government: it is there, it is adhered to, and it should be respected. Youth of this age are incredulous of adults (or peers) who claim to be atheists because this makes them at odds with established authority, and also because a God-less universe is incomprehensible to most of them.

Youth at this age talk a great deal about hypocrisy, but show only an impoverished understanding of it. They rarely recognize it in themselves, and for the most part, it is a scapegoat term used to show dislike for others. This is a difficult age for understanding the subtle nuances of adult interpersonal exchange. They continuously find themselves in situations where they don't like what they see or resent what they are expected to do but are unable to put a finger on the precise reasons. This is frustrating and they soothe their anxieties by thinking adults hypocritical, or by not thinking about it at all. Both options have numerous takers.

Early adolescents (as is also true for late adolescents) have particular trouble with double standards. "Double standard" has several meanings; one usage refers to behavior accepted in one situation but outlawed in another. For example, cheating on income tax may be considered "part of the game" by a businessman, but when one of his own employees cheats on the job, he is fired. What is "right" in one situation is "wrong" in another. A second example of double standard occurs when behavior is acceptable for one sex, but not for the other. (For instance, married men have "mistresses," whereas married women commit adultery.) A third form of double standard refers to behavior which is later denied; in other words, participating in an activity but refusing to admit to it, or lying about it. This last form is quite common during the teen years because adolescents engage in a good deal of behavior they simply deny. As one would expect, this most commonly occurs in regard to behavior thought to be morally wrong by adults. Adolescents tell lies because they continually find themselves in situations where honest reporting causes considerably more strife than does false reporting.

Dishonesty irritates parents and contributes to their feelings of suspicion suspiciousness. This, in turn, offends the adolescent's growing sense of independence and increases resentment of parental constraint. Few adolescents escape the dilemma; for the most part, however, they prefer to accentuate the double standard of others and overlook their own.

Sexual Curiosity During Early Adolescence

A significant amount of wholesome curiosity surrounds sexuality during the adolescent years. *Practical* questions about the mechanics of sexuality (What position do you get into to have sex?) are foremost in the minds of many youths. *Personal* questions about the psychology of sexual behavior are also of concern. "How do you know if a girl wants to have intercourse with you?" Questions which relate to the *social* dimension of sexuality are likewise pondered. "How do you act the next day when you see a boy at school that you had sex with the night before?"

We must keep in mind that sexual behavior is a novel experience for most youths between the ages of ten and 16 and even for the "experienced," a great number of questions remain unresolved. Here we shall present some of the questions which early adolescents frequently ask about sexuality. Some questions are of a general nature whereas others are highly specific and, as we shall see, they relate to physiological fact as well as cultural myth.

Typical questions from early adolescent boys concerning sexuality

Boys are particularly concerned about their sexual anatomy and worry whether they are normal. Most 13-year-old boys, for example, do not know why they sometimes get erections when they are not thinking about girls. Most boys (especially between 12 and 14) are concerned with the length of their penis and the density of their pubic hair; boys of this age commonly are convinced that they do not "measure up" to other boys and thus become uncertain of their sexual development. Boys also worry about their testicles and wonder if something is wrong if one is lower than the other. They do not fully understand as yet that sexual development is a highly individualized matter; consequently, anxiety occurs when they observe that their own biological unfolding is not exactly the same as that of their peers. (Girls commonly consider their breasts unattractive if they do not evidence the full, rounded contours of "playmate" models.)

Questions regarding masturbation are especially important to the early adolescent boy. He wants to know if masturbation will cause him to be unable to function properly with girls, if it will cause emotional strain, if it will reduce athletic prowess and if adults or girls are able to tell when he has recently masturbated. Most boys also are curious about the incidence of masturbation: How often should you do it? Among early adolescent boys curiosity exists as to whether masturbating with another boy makes you "queer." Sexual behavior is a mystery to most boys in their early teens and the fertile imaginations of older friends cater to this burning curiosity with an abundance of fact *and* fantasy. For many boys (especially those of the middle economic class) this is the first age when much thought is given to the sexual activities of their own parents. (Mitchell, 1971)

Young boys are curious about nocturnal emissions. They want to know if wet dreams signal something wrong, or conversely, if they are a sign of maturity. They want to know if girls have them and, if not, why not. Boys sometimes ask if it is possible to have emissions during the daytime or if they ever happen in public as is sometimes the case with erections.

Quite obviously, boys are concerned with female anatomy. With regards to menstruation they want to know how much blood is lost during the menstrual flow. Boys also wonder if menstruation takes the girl by surprise or if girls know in advance when they are about to menstruate. (It is instructive to note that both boys and girls are extremely concerned with the *predictability* of sexual events. They want to know if sexuality is going to take them by surprise.) Boys are curious about female breasts: How soon does milk get into a girl's breast? Are breasts just globs of fat? Why do girls become aroused when you play with their breasts?

For many early adolescent boys the mechanics of reproduction are unclear. For example, the relationship between sexual intercourse and pregnancy is not clearly understood. Some boys believe that pregnancy will always occur if the male reaches orgasm while inside the female, thus indicating that they do not understand the ovulation cycle. Others believe (though the incidence of this belief is not as great) that pregnancy is assured once penile penetration has taken place. Among 10-, 11- and 12-year-olds it often is not understood that the penis must be erect before sexual intercourse can take place. Many youths, even those in later adolescence, do not understand the concept of artificial insemination and cannot provide any kind of explanation as to how an animal (or human) could become pregnant without first having sexual intercourse. (Mitchell, 1974)

Because our society is preoccupied with sexual behavior early adolescents become aware of most topics of sexual interest. They want to know what is wrong with pornographic movies and books; they want to know why men are so impressed with female nudity while women *seem* considerably less impressed with male nudity. Early adolescents frequently do not understand the contractual arrangement between prostitute and client, nor do they seem aware that adult sexual behavior is partially motivated by non-sexual factors such as acceptance or submissiveness. For the most part, the early adolescent is naive about not only the mechanics of sexuality but also its motives.

The early adolescent frequently is rather puritanical in his outlook toward sexual behavior; chained to the moral dogmatism of childhood, he readily condemns that which he considers wrong. Also, because the biological impulse toward sexual experimentation is still several years from its peak level, the 10- to 13-year-old may have a "take it or leave it" attitude. (Mitchell, 1972)

Typical questions from early adolescent girls concerning sexuality

In many respects the early adolescent female approaches heterosexual behavior in a more sophisticated and personal way than her male counterpart: several developmental factors contribute to this difference. First, girls mature earlier than boys; therefore, they become preoccupied sooner with the transition from childhood to adolescent sexuality. Second, girls in North American society have sexual responsibilities avoided by boys. For example, an early adolescent girl (especially between the ages of 13 and 15) may discover that her social acceptance can be seriously damaged by gossip related to her sexual behavior. Though our society is showing signs of equalizing moral codes, it remains commonplace for a sexually adventurous girl to be thought of as a harlot while an equally active male is thought of as virile and manly. For girls, even during early adolescence, social stigma surrounds sexual behavior. Boys, for the most part, are exempt from such pressure, and thus often have a different outlook on sexual conduct.

Girls, like boys, have *specific* as well as general sexual curiosity. Male anatomy, especially the genitals, concerns adolescent girls. They are curious about erections. Do erections always occur when a girl sits on a boy's lap? Can boys get them whenever they want? Is an erection highly pleasurable? What makes an erection go away? When a boy gets an erection when he is with a girl does this mean he has to have sex with her? Does a boy have to lose his sperm before his penis will become small again? How big is an erect penis? Does it hurt when a penis enters you?

Girls of this age are also curious about wet dreams. Interestingly, female questions regarding nocturnal emissions are quite similar to those which boys themselves ask. Do wet dreams occur during the day? Can they happen without warning? Are they harmful to sexual growth? Girls are curious about sexual intercourse. From the physiological point of view they want to know if intercourse is painful, if it causes bleeding and how the penis actually gets into the vagina. From a personal point of view, they want to know if sexual intercourse can become "habit-forming," if boys like you less or more after intercourse and how one knows if one has reached orgasm. Occasionally, a girl will inquire if intercourse will stretch her vagina out of shape, if boys know how many times a girl has had intercourse by the size of her vagina, and if boys automatically dislike a girl who has had sexual intercourse with another boy.

Girls are much more interested in the specifics of *reproduction* than are boys during the early adolescent years. Among the more common questions concerning reproduction are: Is birth painful? Why does the mother sometimes die in childbirth? How does the baby get out? What does the doctor do during the birth of a baby?

Girls also want to know about embryology and fetal development: How do babies get deformed? Can you decide whether you will have a boy or a girl? What does "planning a baby" mean? Where do twins and triplets come from? Can you have a baby without a man's help?

In talking with early adolescents about sexual behavior one is struck by the greater female interest in contraceptives. Girls sometimes ask if boys ever have "periods" when they cannot impregnate. Girls invariably bring up the topic of birth control before boys. They ask about hysterectomy and even vasectomy more frequently than boys, and appear to have more personal involvement in the biological consequences of human sexuality. Most early adolescent girls ask about "the pill'; some demand to know why they cannot use it at ages 14 and 15, while other girls consider the use of the pill morally wrong and claim they would never use it. Most girls are interested in learning about those days in the menstrual cycle when the greatest possibility of becoming pregnant exists.

Girls are curious about petting, but indicate some concerns not shared by boys. For example, girls frequently ask how to "stop" a boy when she doesn't want him to go any further. Boys rarely ask the parallel question. Girls also want to know why boys are so interested in petting and why they try to do so even when the girl says "no." Girls also are curious about social distinctions made by boys concerning girls who go "all the way" and those who don't.

For the most part, the first years of early adolescence (10 to 12) witness considerably less interest in sexual matters than do the last years (13 to 14). Sexual curiosity, like other forms of mental adventure, is influenced by the environment in which the person lives; thus, it is difficult to distinguish "natural" from "acquired" sexual curiosity. A certain amount of sexual curiosity is an inevitable part of early adolescent growth and, even though varying from individual to individual, it shows some consistency and uniformity, thus again permitting the psychologist to observe the continuity of early adolescent life.

Postscript

What then are the dominant traits of the period of life we here call "early adolescence'? First and foremost, this is a period of significant growth. Puberty is the reality around which it revolves; it influences how youth think about themselves, and, of course, it influences their interest in the opposite sex.

Social growth is likewise important. As the peer group increases in power one of the most important life requirements is to cope effectively with it. Youth of this age go to school and their social life is inseparable from it. "Fundamentally, for most American 12-year-olds, school is where it's at. School occupies the time and concerns of all the people you know — your friends, your parents, people you meet" (Martin, 1972, p. 189).

The home is equally important and it has not as yet become the source of major conflict typical of later adolescence. The bulk of one's social energy is spent learning to become competent with peers. The larger society is not an overly important concern; of far greater importance are the mini-societies to which one belongs.

Intelligence is blossoming but it is not as sophisticated as most youngsters believe it to be. The ability to make sound judgments, to hypothesize cogently, and to detach from selfish interests are poorly developed.

To highlight the fluctuating intellect, and as well, the vascillating abilities of the early adolescent, Adelson notes: "The 13-year-olds seem to be the most labile of our subjects . . . In a sense they are on the threshold of mature modes of reasoning, just holding on, and capable of slipping back easily. Their answers are the most difficult to code, since they often involve an uneasy mixture of the concrete and the formal" (p. 192).

The body remains healthy despite its prodigious growth, and even more significantly, the early adolescent abuses it considerably less than do older adolescents. Suicide is rare, as is homicide. Pregnancy is infrequent. Social pathology and mental breakdown are not major problems; they await further aging. By middle- or late-adolescent standards it is a remarkably trouble-free time of life.

The self-centredness of the early adolescent is a mixed blessing, yielding dividends as well as penalties. Not infrequently it promotes an imperviousness to the larger environment, fostering an exaggerated sense of the role one plays in day-to-day realities. Gifted adolescents, for example, typically infer that their excellence in sports or schoolwork is exclusively a function of their own efforts and abilities, overlooking completely the significance of their coaches and teachers. Such self-centredness irritates the adult but seems perfectly natural to the egocentric early adolescent.

This inclination toward elevated grandiosity should not be confused with conceit because it derives primarily from a failure to comprehend all the ingredients to the interpersonal puzzle rather than from a genuine sense of superiority.

Adolescents who overrate their own significance are extremely critical of the shortcomings of others. To them the idea that *everyone is what they are because of their personal efforts* is attractive because it simplifies complex realities, and even more importantly, because it harmonizes with their egocentric nature.

If one were to divide human life into three broad categories: childhood, adolescence, and adulthood, the early adolescent years, more than any other, would be a mixture of the first two. These years are difficult to document because childhood imperceptibly blends and overlaps with adolescence. Boundaries are not clear, definitions are not crisp, body impulses are not precise, and social patterns are not constant. The single word which encapsulates its spirit is *transition.* The stability of childhood vanishes, replaced by the uncertainty of teen existence. In the early adolescent years, one bids farewell to childhood and begins the arduous trek to adulthood. One writer put it his way:

> In the space of three years the change is drastic. At 12 (usually seventh grade) they are clearly on one side of limbo, at 14 on the other. I always saw my high school students as people becoming adults. They had the size and shape of adults, the physical and mental abilities of adults; they were clearly becoming someone. Early adolescents are a different story. They are also in the process of becoming, *but they move erratically back and forth between the world of childhood and the world of adolescence.* (Martin, 1972, p. 187)

During early adolescence popularity achieves lofty prominence. Peer rejection results in so much trauma that for many 13-year-olds a sense of *accomplishment* is felt when an evening with peers brings no ridicule or rejection. Few experiences are more important than peer acceptance, and few more painful than peer rejection.

The occasional adolescent concern with death usually does not reflect a morbid preoccupation; rather, it more closely resembles curiosity. (I stress this because some psychologists, especially those closer to the end than the beginning of life, project a gloom onto these adolescent inquiries which simply does not belong.) Thomas Cottle makes this point with fine literary clarity:

> When young people inquire about death, their words almost convey a charm, not a gaiety, of course, but hardly the lugubrious grays and blues of the words directed to death whispered and written by those who

recognize that their life lines have begun to trail out behind them. (1971, p. 339)

All in all, early adolescents are more social than philosophical, more impulsive than reflective, more experimental than cautious. Their sense of self is not well-defined because they are in the process of discovering what they like and dislike, what they are good at and bad at. Their morality is based more upon what they have absorbed from their culture than from thoughtful evaluation. Their conscience is more pragmatic than ideal, and certainly more egocentric than altruistic. Their important life achievements are skills which allow them to survive with a decent amount of recognition and esteem; their concerns are immediate rather than distant. They are not brutal in the Hobbesian sense, but closer to it than most modern psychologists are willing to admit. (William Golding's portrayal of early adolescent youngsters in *Lord of the Flies* is reasonable.) They are not naturally cooperative as some of the "man-is-good" anthropologists such as Ashley Montagu would have us believe, but they *are* capable of genuine sharing — under the right conditions.

They are *easy* to teach because they believe in the power of authority, because their thought is geared to assimilate rather than to analyze, and because they have limited ability to disagree with ideas or facts beyond their experience. They are *difficult* to teach because they think they know more than they do, because they question better than they understand, and because their powers of induction are still quite weak when compared with those of adults.

7
The Early
Adolescent Period:
Some Specific Considerations

In the previous chapter a *general overview* of the early adolescent years was our focus. In this section we will address the specific issues dealt with in the first part of the book; i.e., storm and stress, identity problems, sexuality, and defense mechanisms; and in addition, egocentrism and narcissism.

The intent of this chapter is to indicate how the basic issues of adolescent psychology are influenced by age, how their effects modify with the passage of time, and how the general circumstances of culture act upon youth.

Storm and Stress During Early Adolescence

In assessing the relative stressfulness of different time periods it is vital to distinguish between *profound* and *non-profound* stress. Profound stress sustained over a period of time results in self-destructive symptoms, in exaggerated use of defense mechanisms, in neurosis, or even psychosis. Non-profound stress, on the other hand, is not debilitating even when sustained over a long period of time. It causes anguish; it creates irritation and inconvenience; it disrupts friendships. However, it rarely leads to neuroses. The distinction between profound and non-profound stress is critical when evaluating early adolescence because it is a period of abundant, but, as a rule, non-profound stress. Psychologists who claim early adolescence is a period of extreme stress, such as Anna Freud, tend not to emphasize the differences between these two types of stress.

Extreme emotional dislocation is rare in the early adolescent community because it is a period of *relative* ease. However, it is inaccurate to think of this period as being stress-free — it most assuredly is not.

Areas of High Stress: Many youngsters suffer considerably from trying to accommodate to the endless demands made by "friends." Hypocrisy and self-centredness flourish at this age, and they contribute immeasurably to stressfulness.

Self-concept and self-identity also cause the early adolescent a good deal of anguish. The self, in its often tortured dialogue, experiences anxiety on a fairly protracted basis. Self-doubt increases fearfulness. All in all, the internal world is stressful for many youngsters during their early teens.

Parental conflict is, in many households, at a lifetime high. Fighting and bickering reaches such extremes that many parents would abandon their teenager if they could get away with it. When early adolescents run away from home, it is usually because of household fighting.

In fairness to parents, it should be pointed out that early adolescents are frequently argumentative, persistently egocentric, and self-indulgent. Their inflated sense of maturity causes them to resent their household and their lack of status within it.

In fairness to the early adolescent, it should be pointed out that many parents are completely out of touch with their adolescent children. Some parents are abusive or indifferent, while others are punitive and jealous. These conditions make life miserable for the early adolescent.

Household strain carries over to school and some youngsters too frightened to act out at home do so at school, thereby increasing stressfulness at a location second only to the home in emotional significance.

Much adolescent overconfidence and conceit cannot be accepted at face value. All too frequently this is merely a cover-up for personal insecurity and social uncertainty. Even though adults are often intimidated by this assertive style it is worth bearing in mind that "the swaggering bravado so typical of the adolescent age is a thin disguise for self-doubt, inadequacy, or fear. Those who are afraid and cannot admit it must have recourse to some pretense, designed as much to convince themselves as others" (Blos, 1941, p. 284).

Areas of Low Stress: The interpersonal battles which produce profound stress are less prevalent during early adolescence than during middle or late adolescence. Frustrated sexuality is avoided precisely because of immaturity. The anxiety of lover's quarrels, or the pain of romantic rejection, each of which torments the middle or late adolescent, are rarely experienced in the early adolescent community.

In a similar vein, excesses of alcohol and drug abuse are less frequent than in the circles of older brothers and sisters.

Meaninglessness and purposelessness, which are perhaps the most powerful precursors to adolescent suicide, are not abundant during early adolescence. The cognitive centres vital to a philosophical inquiry have not attained prominence among the youngest adolescents — thus they are not likely to be philosophically disillusioned. Likewise, the great metaphysical issues of religion do not excessively burden — meaninglessness is, in general, a late-adolescent phenomenon.

The early adolescent rarely holds ideological conflicts with society. Societal alienation, social disenfranchisement, or anomie are rarely found among early adolescents. Finally, the pressures of responsibility are comparatively absent because youth of this age do not have much responsibility. This liberation from responsibility is part of the *moratorium* which embraces virtually all of early and middle adolescence, and for many youth, late adolescence as well.

In summary, early adolescence *is* a period of abundant stress, but essentially of the non-profound variety. Daily routine is riddled with skirmishes and bickering, but the majority of young people accommodate rather well to the storm and stress of the age. Unfortunately, the same cannot be said for middle and late adolescents, as we shall see in forthcoming chapters.

Identity During Early Adolescence

The fundamental requirement of early adolescence, as far as identity is concerned, is to replace the childhood with an adolescent identity. This is not an easy task, but, for the most part, one the youngster is eager to achieve. The farewell to childhood is sorrowful for few teens; they view childhood as beneath their station. It is not until pressures and anxieties begin to burden the personality that the memories of tranquil childhood hold much allure.

Early adolescence is the most sheltered of the adolescent ages. There is very little involvement with the dominant society. For the most part, this suits the early adolescent just fine because the building blocks of their evolving identity are based upon school, peers and home. Learning the rules and regulations of the adolescent community is a full-time undertaking. Middle and late adolescence witnesses a gradual expansion into the outside world, but for now the frame of reference is narrow, and the identity which springs from it, limited.

Every adolescent strives to be good at something, and when it appears to them that they are not good at anything (a common inference) they mask their disappointment with attitudes of indifference or resentment. Interestingly, when young people are convinced of their own incompetence, these attitudes become part of their identity, and contribute to the sense of low self-worth so commonly observed in the adolescent community.

Foreclosure at this age is extremely rare. Most youth find the possibilities facing them too vast to conceptualize, much less render a decision upon. Equally important, most early adolescents are too consumed with *learning to be an adolescent* to foreclose upon their identity. They resemble the university freshman recently arrived from a small town, overpowered by bigness and complexity, who spends all of his energy "just learning my way around."

Fidelity, the desire to show allegiance and dedication, is a genuine force during early adolescence but, for the most part, lacks clarity and direction. It is impeded by egocentrism, which prevents the early adolescent from getting too far outside himself. Fidelity, however, does make its presence felt. Friendships during this age are powerful and, in *many* instances, durable and long-lasting. Early adolescents almost universally believe in faithfulness and dependability. Interestingly, they often hold others, especially adults, to higher standards of fidelity than they themselves manifest.

Identity *crises* are rare. Identity *bewilderment*, however, is frequent and painful. The individual is changing so rapidly, often in unexpected and feared directions, that confusion about identity is typical. However, the failure, rejection, and fearfulness which nurture genuine identity crises *usually* do not occur until middle or late adolescence. In this matter, as with so many others, the early adolescent simply has not accumulated sufficient negative experiences to undergo major emotional dislocation.

In summary, early adolescent identity is largely confined to a moratorium-protected environment, and transpires within a comparatively limited social setting. The disorders of identity occur with greater frequency during the final, rather than the first, trimester of adolescence. Once the initial requirements of peer survival have been mastered, the adolescent is better suited for the outward sojourn into a more ruthless universe, and it is there that the brutal battles of adolescence are fought, won and lost.

Sexual Interests During Early Adolescence

The opposite sex is not well-regarded. Males have little interest in females although they recognize that to get along with them is necessary. Girls, because they are closer to puberty, and because the menstrual flow personalizes their awareness of reproduction, have slightly more advanced sexual interest. However, the attraction which exists between the sexes is based more upon preparing for future demands than upon present impulses and, most assuredly, it lacks what adults call "sexual chemistry."

In day-to-day behavior one observes very few indicators of the libidinal rush which Freud viewed as the dominant reality of this time zone. Flashes of it are observable, but rarely does the youngster convey the impression that he or she is on the verge of losing some kind of cosmic struggle with sexual urges and impulses.

In a rather matter-of-fact essay on the behavior of early adolescents in the schools, Martin (1972) includes the following observation:

> Twelve-year-olds hang around in groups by sex. It is a rare exception when a member of one sex risks associating with members of the opposite sex. The students make this issue an important one, for example, when they work in groups and strongly prefer one-sex grouping. The attitude displayed toward the opposite sex is often humorous — "Ugh, she's a girl" — when you realize what he will be saying in three years.

Sexual desires do exist and they do lead to sexual activity, though sexual intercourse is comparatively rare at this age. Almost all researchers of adolescent sexuality conclude that fewer than ten percent of boys and girls have experienced sexual intercourse before age 14. The sexual impulse is not keenly genital, and does not possess its own independent force. Sexual interests are greatly influenced by novelty, by curiosity, and without doubt they are less intense than during late adolescence. Sexuality is less passionate and less erotic. Sexual abstinence rarely produces the feelings of emptiness or the sense of frustration which is associated with late adolescent and early post-adolescent abstinence.

The nature of sexual *feelings* during adolescence is not agreed upon by theoreticians. Freudian-oriented psychologists believe that puberty brings powerful sexual passion which the adolescent learns to sublimate or repress. Developmental psychologists, as a rule, do not agree; they claim that sexual passion is weak, and of minimal influence for the early adolescent.

> It is also likely that the sheer intensity of passion that is so urgent in the older adolescent is attenuated at this earlier age. The tension that is so overpowering in the 17-year-old is more like a tickle at 11 and, hence, more easily put aside. However, the 11-year-old knows that his time is coming and he must prepare for it. (Kagan, 1972, p. 95)

It should not surprise us that psychologists differ in their assessments of sexual feelings. Some psychologists conclude that youngsters should be encouraged to sample a variety of sexual activities, including intercourse. Others do not. Laufer, for example, maintains that *important differences exist between early and late adolescents in this area.* He states:

> Sexual intercourse *early* in adolescence should be viewed with caution; we should not assume that it represents the adolescent's ability to accept his physically mature body. It may also hide a fear that something is wrong with himself, either mentally or physically; the behavior is then an effort to establish (unsuccessfully) in his mind the belief that he is normal.

Such behavior will have different meaning for the older adolescent who is nearer to emotional maturity. (1974, p. 36)

For the most part, this observation by Laufer, especially the final sentence, represents not only the mainstream of psychological thought on the matter, but also finds general agreement among parents, educators and teenagers themselves.

Defense Mechanisms During Early Adolescence

Early adolescence witnesses a great variety of defense mechanisms, although the *consequences* of their use, and the *reasons* for their use are not as profound as in later years.

The need to constantly defend against criticism or ridicule inclines the young person to engage in extensive *rationalization*, in which he provides plausible (but unlikely) reasons for his behavior. In addition to the criticism of peers, early adolescents also must respond to their rejection of their own nature. This provides a perfect scenario for *projection*, whereby the young person excuses his limitations with "everyone does it." Disowning projection (projecting to others desires or fears repressed within oneself) however, is less frequent. *Suppression* is widespread primarily because it is not as powerful as repression, and merely displaces temporarily an unpleasant thought or fantasy. This displacement serves an important function because the adolescent cannot handle all the anxiety-producing thoughts which populate his consciousness — some have to be dismissed.

Identification is a widely-used defense mechanism. The early adolescent is susceptible to a remarkable range of identifications and, without doubt, the media sensationalizing of rock stars and sports heroes makes it easier for youngsters of this age to "identify" with an assortment of images unavailable to by-gone generations.

Early adolescents are not long out of childhood and many of its features remain with them. Temper tantrums, pouting, refusal to eat, and other *regressive outbursts* are not unusual. The normal adolescent encounters so much peer ridicule for regressive outbursts that they eventually lose their effectiveness. However, many youngsters employ them at home if parents tolerate them, are frightened by them, or, as is sometimes the case, encourage them in order to prove to themselves that their adolescent is still a child.

The *protective structures* are likewise abundant. *Blind spots*, which cause the individual to overlook what everyone else sees, are typical. *Compartmentalization* is widely used because the interpersonal world is complex and because the "concrete" thinking habits of the early adolescent encourage a compartmentalized understanding of the world.

At this juncture we do well to remember that early adolescence is only the beginning of the teen years and that virtually every domain of growth is a considerable distance from completion. As Newman & Newman pointed out in their excellent overview, when describing the early adolescent as an "unfinished product":

> The point is that in thinking about early adolescence, we must remember that we are thinking about an unfinished product. This is not the end but only the beginning of the formation of a life pattern of social interactions. During these years, we are looking at peer group interaction in its formative phase. We are looking at heterosexual intimacy as it just begins to be expressed. We are focusing on the earliest, most tentative steps toward autonomy from parents, many years before a true camaraderie can even hope to be formed (1979, p. 216).

Before proceeding to the next adolescent period we shall briefly investigate two aspects of adolescent development which exert considerable impact on behavior, emotion and thought: *egocentrism* and *narcissism*. These are not unique to early adolescence; however, they are introduced in this chapter because much of their middle and late adolescent character can be traced to the early adolescent years.

Egocentrism

In its literal meaning egocentrism refers to regarding the self as the centre of all things, or as having little or no regard for interests other than one's own. In psychological usage, egocentrism refers to the inability to understand (or perceive) points of view other than one's own. In this section we shall consider egocentrism as the inability to see the world independently of one's vested interests. For the most part, egocentrism is a limitation not only intellectual but also emotional.

Egocentrism molds information so that *its relationship to the person* is more important than the information itself. Everything is filtered through "me"; and it is the relationship to "me" which establishes the *value* and the *truth* of information.

Egocentrism blurs the distinction between what is of concern to others, and what is of concern to "me." The egocentric person assumes that what interests him *is* of interest to others. Because adolescents are concerned with themselves, their experience, and their appearance, they egocentrically conclude that everyone is aware of them, and of their every action. Their self-consciousness and their exaggerated sense of self-importance derive in great measure from their egocentricity.

Information which agrees with egocentric desires is assimilated *with for greater ease and establishes a much stronger foothold,* than information which does not. As a rule, egocentrism weakens during the course of adolescence, while objectivity strengthens. When the opposite is true, that is, when egocentrism increases and objective thought decreases, it is not unusual for the adolescent to experience personality deterioration, neuroses, or some other aberration of the growth process.

William James thought that egocentrism could be understood as *an ongoing subjective syllogism.* He observes that: "It appears as if all our manifestations of selfishnes might be the conclusions of as many syllogisms . . . thus: Whatever is me is precious; this is me, therefore this is precious; whatever is mine must not fail; this is mine; therefore this must not fail, etc." (p. 205). The "Egocentric Syllogism" is nearly universal among adolescents, and without doubt contributes immeasureably to their self-centredness, their preoccupation with their social microcosm, and their unawareness of realities which adults take for granted.

The imaginary audience: A fascinating example of adolescent egocentrism is the tendency to anticipate in the mind's eye how other people will react in a real or imagined meeting. Elkind termed this phenomenon *the imaginary audience* (1967).

Imagining oneself as a cheerleader before thousands of fans, or as an athlete performing an unbelievable feat, or as a sexual adventurer applauded by one's peers, are common fantasies. Most imaginary audiences are awestruck by the splendor of the adolescent. Some audiences, however, are condemning and may require the young person to deliver a scathing indictment of their stupidity, or moral backwardness — a task they perform with zeal, and often rehearse in their private moments.

The thoughts surrounding an imaginary audience range from the totally unreal (being begged to speak before the United Nations) to the likely (anticipating a meeting with the school principal). Unfortunately for the adolescent, the imaginary audience usually behaves differently than the *real* audience. For example, new clothing which brings incredible reactions from one's imagined audience goes unnoticed in the real world; a new hairstyle envisioned to bring rave reviews from the opposite sex does no such thing; acquiring an automobile, which supposedly brings friends, does not. *It is the constant conflict between what happens in the real world and how it differs from the imaginary world which, in time, erodes the imaginary audience and gradually makes the young person less egocentric.*

A second example of adolescent egocentrism has been labeled by Elkind as "the personal fable." *Personalfable:* A story about oneself which is greatly distorted, sometimes completely false, which the adolescent nevertheless accepts as true, is known as a Personal Fable. The central theme to all fables is the uniqueness of "me." It is a fable of one's brilliance; a monologue of grandeur in which the adolescent is convinced that he experiences things no one else can comprehend, with an intensity no one else can equal. As Elkind says: "only he can suffer with such agonized intensity, or experience such exquisite rapture" (1967, p. 1030).

The following dream, related by a 14-year-old boy, with its emphasis on his special uniqueness and his being the centre of attention, encapsulates the basic ingredients of both the imaginary audience *and* the personal fable.

> I dreamt that one afternoon I walked out on our porch headed for the swimming pool when I observed . . . bleachers with some 2000 spectators sitting and waiting for me to swim. I was so taken aback by this event that I decided to favor them by walking on the water. My repeated success in performing such a feat brought the audience to its feet, then its knees in admiration and homage. (Thornburg 1982, p. 106)

The elements within this dream are classic examples of adolescent egocentrism. Many youngsters truly believe that their emotions are of universal significance, and symbolic release in dreams, fantasies and fables are not unusual.

The imaginary audience and the personal fable attain considerable importance during adolescence and these egocentric phenomena do not disappear *merely from advancing age.* The imaginary audience weakens when the adolescent recognizes the ways in which it differs from the *real* audience. The fantasy of the imaginary audience simply does not equal reality.

The personal fable begins to erode as the adolescent gains more first-hand knowledge about other people and realizes that his own inner world is not radically unique, nor composed of singular experiences. This knowledge about the inner working of other people derives from intimacy relationships, and from the confidential exchange which comes with friendship and comradeship. Therefore, just as *real* interaction with other people weakens the power of the imaginary audience, *real* knowledge about other people weakens the personal fable. In essence, adolescent egocentrism is overcome by a twofold transformation: "On the cognitive plane, it is overcome by the gradual differentiation between his own preoccupations and the thoughts of others; while on the plane of affectivity, it is overcome by the gradual integration of the feelings of others with his own emotions" (Elkind, 1967, p. 1033).

The realization that personal experiences are never completely understood by others often creates within the adolescent a sense of dismay. Fantasizing about oneself as being a significant person while at the same time observing that most people are not concerned about "me" at all is a devastating perplexity to many young people. And for many of them this sense of dismay lingers for several years.

To sum up, as much as the intricacy of the subject permits, the imaginary audience and the personal fable begin to lose their influence when the adolescent:

1. accepts matter-of-factly that others don't understand completely what it is like "to be me";
2. works systematically at getting others to understand why he does things the way he does;
3. explains inner experiences without an overpowering sense of urgency;
4. calculates the reactions of others realistically;
5. realizes when he is the object of conversation and when he is not;
6. can arrive at a social gathering without excessive self-consciousness. (It can be stated with considerable certainty that very few early or middle adolescents possess these six traits. It is not unusual, however, to observe them among *late* adolescents.)

Young people never *completely outgrow* egocentrism. However, the extent to which it overrules the thinking process definitely diminishes as age increases.

Egocentrism is a significant limitation within the adolescent character because of its pervasive impact on thought and emotion. It colors reality with personal hues which falsify and distort. It realigns ideas to reflect the needs of the thinker. In essence, it strives to make reality fit the desires of the person.

In the young person's struggle to attain an honest and objective understanding of the world, few factors interfere more than egocentrism.

Narcissism

Narcissism is the force within the personality which impels one to become the focus of everyone's attention. It is the global fascination with oneself *and with the thrill of experiencing oneself.* Egoism and egotism are parallel concepts in that they emphasize an excessive pride in oneself, an excessive reference to oneself and one's importance. Narcissism discourages interest in others, except as they pertain to oneself.

Narcissism, while "natural" to adolescence, begets a fascination with oneself at an age when learning about, and creating empathy with, others are necessary life skills.

Narcissism is not merely an infantile carryover from childhood, without redeeming features. It keeps youth "in touch with themselves," and nourishes self-assertion in a world that consumes it. Adolescence without narcissism is, emotionally speaking, a vacant reality. Vitality, flamboyance and creativity are manifestations of it; there is no sense of heroic individuality without it.

Egocentrism and narcissism both benefit when the self is elevated or praised. When they "take over" the personality, however, a pathological condition known as the Narcissistic Personality Disorder occurs.

The Narcissistic Personality Disorder

This condition is characterized by a grandiose sense of self-importance and by a consuming need for constant attention and admiration. It is usually accompanied by disturbances in interpersonal relationships, especially tendencies toward exploitation, feelings of entitlement, and a lack of empathy. It is a disorder, not a condition of normal development. However, flashes of it characterize virtually all adolescents, and for this reason we gain insight into normal adolescence by investigating an exaggerated condition.

Extreme self-absorption causes one's abilities and achievements to be radically overestimated. However, it is not unusual for feelings of greatness to alternate with feelings of unworthiness and incompetence. For example, a student who ordinarily receives 90s, may feel himself to be a total failure when receiving an 80 or 85.

The Narcissistic Disorder is characterized by unrealistic goals of unlimited wealth, power, or prestige; ironically, when these goals are pursued (whether attained or not) it is often with a "driven, pleasureless quality, and an ambition that cannot be satisfied."

Even though individuals with this disorder are constantly seeking admiration they usually possess low self-esteem and a fragile sense of well-being. In response to criticism "there is either a cool indifference or marked feelings of rage, inferiority, shame, humiliation, or emptiness." These reactions to criticism are far more devastating than the disappointment which accompanies frustrated narcissism among normal adolescents.

Another prominent feature of the Narcissistic Personality Disorder is the expectation that one should receive special favors without assuming special responsibilities. When challenged by others the narcissist claims it is *their* selfishness which makes the relationship unbalanced. Because the submissive person is least able to defend himself, the narcissist often surrounds himself with submissive, non-assertive individuals. (The narcissist's ability to exploit weak individuals is a significant variable in adolescent sexuality *and* adolescent pregnancy.)

Relationships with others are based upon aggrandizement of one's self, and as a result, relationships lack reciprocity. However, the narcissist usually denies the superficiality of his relationships. Instead, he projects the superficiality *onto the partner,* and thereby feels even further justified in abusing the partner.

At the subjective level, depressed mood is extremely common. Frequently there is painful self-consciousness, a preoccupation with grooming and chronic envy of others. Personal weaknesses are justified by rationalization, or by lying.

The Narcissistic Personality Disorder results in impairments in interpersonal relationships, in occupational functioning, or in schooling. It is a genuine psychiatric disorder, and should not be equated with normal adolescent narcissism. Nor, however, should it be thought of as being *totally* different. In essence, the difference between the two are of degree. For this reason, "normal" narcissism must be given serious consideration when analyzing the adolescent character.

The Impact of "Normal" Narcissism on Adolescent Behavior

One consequence of narcissism is the tendency to respond positively to people who make oneself the object of attention. As a result, most adolescents are silently, yet forcefully, attracted to anything which satisfies their elemental selfishness.

Conversely, the narcissistic element within adolescents causes them to be repelled by people, or events, which detract from their feelings of prominence. The net effect is that youth are impelled toward self-aggrandizement in their friendships and are repelled by individuals who do not acknowledge their uniqueness. It is this latter fact which permits youth to hold intense dislike for someone they do not even know as long as this person fails to take note of their "specialness" (this tendency is especially exasperating to teachers, coaches, and others who discover that a youngster "hates" them even though they have never interacted personally with each other).

We can easily observe how narcissism encourages the formation of defense mechanisms. *Emotional insulation* helps the narcissist minimize emotional investment in others and it keeps others distanced so that their criticisms cannot register. Typically, the narcissist prefers the convenience of fragmented social relationships, therefore *compartmentalization* is widely used. Most common however, are *rationalization* and *denial*, the bulwark defenses for individuals constantly required to justify their selfish nature. Because narcissists do not like to be "pinned down," or to make commitments, *elusiveness* is a common tactic.

Even normal amounts of narcissism help produce a suspiciousness towards people who, for whatever reason, do not think the young person is "anybody special." This suspiciousness contributes to a unique brand of "mini-paranoia" easily observed among highly narcissistic youth. Shapiro described suspiciousness this way, and its relevance to adolescent narcissism should not be underestimated.

> Suspicious people, in general, do not ignore a piece of data; on the contrary, they examine it quite carefully. But they examine it with an extraordinary prejudice, dismissing what is not relevant to their suppositions and seizing on anything that confirms them. The fact is, furthermore, that their dismissal and disregard of anything that does not confirm their prior supposition is an active and intentional process. (1965, p. 75)

Suspiciousness is not universal to the adolescent community but it is a hallmark of it. And, as Shapiro comments, additional aspects of the suspicious personality can be seen in adolescent habits. ". . . they operate from the outset on the assumption that anything that does not confirm their expectation is mere appearance. Thus, they would say that they are interested in penetrating the sham, the pretense, and the superficial . . . But this need not prevent us from noticing *that the underlying truth invariably turns out to be precisely what they expected it to be in the first place*" (1965, p. 58).

With the foregoing in mind, we may infer that much of the suspicion and resentfulness of youth is anchored in, and caused by, their narcissism.

Incorporating normal narcissism into its opposite — selfless love — without obliterating it, is a necessary step in achieving personal identity. During adolescence incorporation of the narcissistic into the altruistic is encouraged by intimacy and friendship at the interpersonal level, and by the weakening of egocentrism at the psychological level. For many youngsters it is the most difficult adjustment of the teen years.

A feature typical of highly narcissistic youth is that they cause more misery and hardship for others than they themselves experience. They are unaware when they trample on the feelings of others, and when they are aware it rarely causes much anguish, and most assuredly, does not change their behavior. This imperviousness yields mixed dividends: in some instances it allows the person to be socially assertive and, as a result, get his own way more frequently than could a more timid or "other-oriented" individual.

In summary, elements of narcissism exist within every adolescent. The most exaggerated example of narcissism is a condition known as the Narcissistic Personality Disorder — a phenomenon which is rare in the adolescent community. However, narcissism exists within all adolescents in lesser degrees and, as a result, it usually is a significant factor in adolescent behavior. The greater one's narcissism, the more self-centred and manipulative one behaves. And even though narcissism contributes to a self-centredness of which society disapproves, it is not, unto itself, a psychiatric disorder. Nor is it brought into existence by a malfunction within the socialization process. Narcissism, like egocentrism, is basic to human nature, and its adolescent form is merely one of many forms it assumes in the course of one's lifetime.

Postscript

The beginning years of adolescence are easy to define in terms of biological growth and mental advancements, but they are difficult to define in terms of psychological growth because of the overlap between childhood and adolescence during this time of life.

Storm and stress is mixed. In many regards, household conflicts are at a lifetime high, causing parents to wonder what kind of a monster their easygoing child has turned into. Household conflicts, though numerous, *tend* to be of the minor variety. However, the peer group often creates major turmoil, and learning to deal with it is one of the primary growth requirements of this age.

Identity does not reach mature heights during early adolescence, but it definitely towers over the childhood identity of a few years prior. The world of peers, once again, exerts its influence. The young person's sense of "Who am I?," "Where am I going?," and "What is life all about?," remains juvenile in its scope, especially when compared with the more complex identity searching of the late adolescent. Identity problems tend to be more social than metaphysical; therefore, to the early adolescent the *quest* for popularity is more consuming than is the *meaning* of popularity. The distinctions between the two preoccupies the middle or late adolescent, but rarely his younger brothers and sisters.

Interest in the opposite sex is genuine, but ignites very little action. Social gatherings become progressively more mixed, with boys sometimes approaching civility in their conduct. But even though interest in the opposite sex is percolating, day-to-day activities tend to involve same-sex groups. In virtually all cultures of the technological world we observe a distinct absence of "love" or romance during the early adolescent period. Sexual passion, so abundant during late adolescence, exists in modest degree only. For the most part, this is an age of social internship during which the complex skills of interpersonal relationships are refined. Until this refinement takes place, sexual intimacy is avoided. This generalization is not unfailingly correct, but the vast majority of young people adhere to it.

Defense mechanisms are everywhere observable in the early adolescent community. Very few people of this age can cope with the confusion and bewilderment of the peer group (and homelife) without using defense mechanisms. The most common are *rationalization* (especially giving acceptable reasons for unacceptable behavior), *projection* (especially attributing to others the worst of one's own nature), and *regression* (especially pouting and temper tantrums).

Egocentrism is at its most powerful during the early adolescent years. It influences thought, perception and emotion to a remarkable degree. For most individuals it tends to gradually weaken as they grow through the adolescent years. Egocentrism, of course, never completely disappears, but by late adolescence it is far more under control than during early adolescence.

8
The Middle-Adolescent Period:
A General Overview

Middle adolescence, more than any other time, resembles our cultural image of the adolescent. It is a time when the childlike features of early adolescence are outgrown, when the body begins to look adultlike, but it also is a time when the personality features of early adulthood are not finalized. During middle adolescence, one is neither child nor adult; one is in between. The term "adolescent" suits perfectly. Mid-adolescents are close to adulthood in the areas that count — body maturity and intellectual ability. In fact, if those indicators measure "adultness," most adolescents would be considered adults. However, there is more to adulthood than a body which is able to reproduce and a mind which is able to calculate swiftly or to reason systematically.

The Body During Middle Adolescence

During the middle adolescent period the body continues to grow, although the *rate* of growth is lower for both boys and girls. By the 14th year girls have achieved about 98 percent of their adult height, whereas boys only about 90 percent. Both sexes continue to add weight for the next several years; however, a great proportion of this weight gain is represented by muscle volume for males and by fatty tissue for females. The *accelerated growth spurts* characteristic of early adolescence are not typical (especially for girls) but growth does continue.

The most impressive body changes include the following: (1) Expansion of skeletal growth which results in the body proportions characteristic of early adulthood. (2) Altered body composition with a greater abundance of muscle for males and increased fatty tissue for females. During this period, males become measurably larger and stronger than girls for the first time in the life cycle. (3) Increased maturity of the circulatory and respiratory systems leads to increased strength and endurance; as a result there is considerable increase in athletic capacity. (4) The continued development of the reproductive organs and the secondary sexual characteristics.

For both sexes these changes are noticeable and unmistakable. The vast majority of youth becomes capable of reproduction, and many exercise this capacity. Finally, all of these body advances contribute to the general physical appearance of adulthood.

The *early* adolescent is easy to spot because his features are tinged with childish traits; the middle adolescent much more closely resembles the adult, though not as precisely as during late adolescence. The face is more adult-like because the bones of the face grow faster than those of the cranial vault; thus the prominent nose and the angular jaw (especially in boys) assert themselves. Sex differences become more visible. The male forearm, which is larger relative to body height than the forearm of the female, is more conspicuous. Boys are distinguishable by their larger shoulders, their relatively narrower hips, and their larger legs relative to trunk length. Girls are more adultlike in appearance because breast development is almost complete and because skeletal growth has almost stopped, thus leaving the middle adolescent girl with her adult body proportions (if weight does not increase too much). In primitive cultures where age is not counted in years, girls are expected to begin childbearing at this age.

The image of the middle adolescent as a non-stop eater has some basis in biological fact. Of the first twenty years, the greatest caloric requirement for sustaining growth is witnessed during this time. At about age 14, girls are at the peak of their daily requirements, about 2,800 calories. Boys at age 14 require about the same amount; however, by age 17 they require almost 3,400 calories per day in order to sustain their *normal growth*. Sound nutrition remains a crucial growth necessity as much as during the tremendous growth years of childhood and early adolescence (Barnett, 1972). Abuse of nutrition is common, often resulting in obesity. Many adolescents consume more calories than they need for growth, adding considerable weight. Obesity is inversely related to socioeconomic status, being "six times as common among women of low economic status as among those of high status" (Katchadourian, p. 153).

The Intellect During Middle Adolescence

The mental advances of adolescence begin during *early* adolescence. They are described in this chapter because it is not until middle adolescence that they achieve consistency in day-to-day living. During middle adolescence, the *consequences* of mental advancement are unmistakably present, whereas during the previous age they are spotty and less substantive.

Six general trends dominate the intellect during middle adolescence, exerting influence on two crucial aspects of adolescent life: *moral decision-making,* (the way one makes moral decisions) and *introspection* (the way one thinks about one's own personality).

The first feature of middle adolescent intellectualism is that thought becomes more abstract. The facility for dealing with hypothetical and theoretical ideas expands considerably. Abstract thought fosters greater interest in the *ideal*, the *probable*, and the *nonphysical*; therefore, thought becomes less bound to the narrow conclusions of the earlier adolescent years. Mental preoccupation with nonphysical concepts such as soul, eternity, and death is common. Matteson (1975) observes: "In middle adolescence, young people begin to understand the future realities available to them and they invest themselves emotionally in planning for the future."

The second feature: *Thought becomes more comprehensive.* When solving problems children do not recognize that an unexplored possibility may be as correct as the more obvious and blatant possibility. Adolescents are more thorough — they look at more sides of an issue, and are less likely to be duped. Their thought is more comprehensive, and less susceptible to errors of omission; as a result they are superior thinkers not only in a general sense, but in specific, practical ways as well.

The third feature: *Thought becomes the object of its own action.* The adolescent discovers that mental conclusions do not come into existence on their own, but that they result from preceding mental processes. Thought is increasing in *comprehensiveness* as well as in powers of *hypothesizing* and adolescents apply these skills to their own thought process. They review the product of their thought to see how it stacks up, to see if it is consistent, and if it does justice to the problem.

Thinking about one's own thoughts is often an emotional experience which gives rise to confusion and bewilderment, and in this regard, intellectual advancement causes emotional difficulties. The adolescent world is filled with inconsistencies and incongruities. Adolescents note with surprise that opposite emotions (such as love and hate) exist side by side within them; they notice that one day they behave one way, another day another way. They also recognize inconsistencies in others. Middle adolescents are, as Arnold Gessell says, "amateur psychologists who hold an intuitive grasp of their own psychological being." They see traits in their parents which before went unnoticed, and, if they hold parents in unrealistically high esteem, the pedestal upon which they stand is likely to collapse.

The ability to think introspectively allows greater precision of thought and increases the detection of mental errors. On the other hand, it encourages self-doubt by examining ideas from outside the egocentrism of early adolescence. It deprives adolescents of the mental dogmatism to which they became accustomed during childhood and forces upon them the burden of intellectual freedom. The mental process which permits scientific thought is the same process which introduces the anguish of self-analysis, and which interrogates weakened or hidden parts of the personality.

A fourth feature: *Thought becomes more propositional.* A proposition is any statement capable of being believed, doubted, or denied. Propositional thinking allows one to investigate ideas beyond reality as *it is now* understood. It allows manipulation of facts, and freshness of viewpoint. Adolescent political thought, for example, undergoes important changes because of the increased ability to create and examine propositions.

> Ordinarily the youngster begins adolescence incapable of complex political discourse . . . By the time this period is at an end, a dramatic change is evident; the youngster's grasp of the political world is now recognizably adult. His mind moves with some agility within the terrain of political concepts; he has achieved abstractness, complexity, and even some delicacy in his sense of political textures; he is on the threshold of ideology, struggling to formulate a morally coherent view of how society is and might and should be arranged. (Adelson, 1972, p. 106)

In significant measure, the sophistication of political thought which evolves during these years derives from an increased capacity for propositional thought.

A fifth feature: *Thought becomes less egocentric.* Adolescents become increasingly capable of thinking from points of view other than their own, even though they are likely to think egocentrically when the object of thought is close to their emotional centre. However, in areas of *minimal* ego-involvement, egocentrism decreases. When applied to mathematics, for example, the adolescent mind is amazingly free of egocentrism. As has been stressed throughout this book, however, adolescents rarely completely shake the influence of egocentrism when thinking about themselves.

A sixth feature: *Thought becomes more future-oriented.* Inevitably the future works its way into the thought patterns of adolescents because, as they approach adulthood, they face decisions which influence the rest of their lives. Their ability to hypothesize allows them to consider numerous possibilities, and the ability to think propositionally allows them to assess the plausibility of all these options.

Because of these six mental advances, middle adolescent thought undergoes several changes:
1. It goes beyond the real to deal with the ideal;
2. It goes beyond the physical to deal with the hypothetical;
3. It goes beyond fragments to deal with wholes;
4. It goes beyond what *is* to deal with propositions which ask "what if"?;
5. It goes beyond the present to examine the future.

All mental activity becomes more complex during middle adolescence and yields thoughts unavailable to a mind governed by simpler processes. New realms of insight open, and the world becomes more complex as the mind grasps a greater number of relationships, infers a greater number of possibilities, and conceptualizes richer combinations of ideas.

The intellectual metamorphosis of middle adolescence nourishes identity formation and, ironically, also encourages identity crises. In fact, *the entire process of identity* cannot be separated from the mental growth of adolescence: "It must be clear that without the skills of hypothesis-raising, conceptualization of the future, logical problem solving, and the ability to anticipate consequences of an action, *work on identity formation could not really begin.*" Likewise:

> Without the capacities of formal thought, identity would be tied to the observable, the readily measurable or manipulatable dimensions of experience. But with the door of abstract reasoning opened, identity becomes a vision of what might be possible as well as of what has already been experienced. Because of formal thought there is a chance to conceive of an identity that is a unique integration, a new combination of past, present, and future that takes a person along a new course. (Newman & Newman, p. 366)

The connective links binding personality to the thought process are everywhere observable during the adolescent experience. The capacity to think in new and advanced patterns poses problems that the ego struggles with — frequently in vain. Haviland and Scarborough (1981) in their description of the adolescent thought process make these important comments:

> In reading, conversations, and daydreaming, the teenager develops theories about the differences between how the world is and how the world could be. Morality, political views, religious commitments, parental ideals, and other assumptions are critically inspected and often found lacking. Elaborate fantasies for utopian societies, pious adherence to religious sects, and enthusiastic involvement in the political sphere are not at all unusual among adolescents carried away by idealistic beliefs about what could be accomplished, or despair about society's current ills. Interestingly, the despair itself is a relatively new attitude toward reality, *one that seems to emerge from the ability to think about non-reality.* (p. 57)

Thus, normal cognitive growth, in addition to opening up a new world of science and philosophy, also adds to the burden of a personality troubled with self-analysis and interpersonal conflict.

The Effects of Mental Growth on the Middle-Adolescent Personality

Five general reactions are commonly associated with increased mental growth during middle adolescence.

1. *Expanded external awareness.* The narrow, confined world of childhood explodes; increased intellectual powers bring into focus aspects of the social and physical world which heretofore were ignored. Political, economic, social, and moral systems are seen from a perspective possible only with the onset of formal thought. Adolescents are rarely content merely to observe new discoveries; they apply propositional and hypothetical thought and, as a result, gain insight as to "why" and "how." The wonder of discovery is periodically blunted because some discoveries are difficult to assimilate, and as a result, confusion and disillusionment establish a foothold.

The net effect of expanded external awareness is twofold: (1) the adolescent becomes involved in discovering the systems upon which the social and physical world operate and, at the same time, becomes less involved in himself, and (2) the adolescent discovers imperfections which before went unnoticed. Some youth accept matter-of-factly that things are not ideal; others are emotionally shaken when they discover the world is not as they thought it was.

2. *Enriched internal awareness.* The basic skills of the intellect are applied inwardly as well as outwardly. Thus, adolescents become obsessed with *introspection.* They want to know about their strengths and weaknesses — how they stack up. They thrive upon "instant replay" of daily events, and before falling asleep they may in their mind's eye run through an event of social importance a dozen times.

The self does not wait to be discovered; it projects its own feelings, desires, resentments and insecurities. The rational mind attempts to understand these realities and organize them into cohesive and manageable units, but in no way is it responsible for their existence.

Sociologists and psychologists have long debated whether each person has *several* selves. William James entered this debate and concluded what must seem reasonable to most scholars of adolescent psychology: ". . . we may practically say that he has as many different social selves as there are distinct *groups* of persons about whose opinions he cares. Many a youth who is demure enough before his parents and teachers, swears and swaggers like a pirate among his 'tough' young friends." To lend generational balance, he adds: "We do not show ourselves to our children as to our club-companions, to our customers as to the laborers we employ . . ." (p. 190). This notion of "several selves" has considerable merit; however, on the whole, it creates an image of a fragmented person which does injustice to the self we experience phenomenologically. Therefore, in this book little mention has been made of the "several selves" concept.

Thus, increased mental capacity makes possible the complicated form of exploration which leads to different kinds of adolescent identity crises. Mental power does not cause these crises; it is merely the tool by which the ego attempts to understand its own inner workings.

3. *Coping strategies become more systematic.* An important result of formal thought is that it results in a greater ability to understand the principles upon which other people (or objects) operate. Adolescents apply this knowledge to their advantage. They learn from experience that the school principal can best be dealt with when addressed as "mister," when respect is shown, and so on. They *anticipate* that what worked for principal A probably will also work for principal B, as well as for, say, policeman C. Coping strategies result in more diversified social behavior, greater resiliency, and greater premeditation.

Adolescents know that they must deal with 6-year-olds differently than two-year-olds and, as a result, they develop better strategies for supervising younger children. They recognize that employer-employee relationships are not the same as other adult-adolescent relationships; they recognize that their own behavior influences how others respond to them. In a phrase, adolescent behavior becomes more premeditated and more strategic.

4. *Idealism is tested.* Some adolescent idealism is little more than childlike naivete, as when parents are thought to be perfect or authority figures exempt from human failings. Other forms of adolescent idealism are dignified and philosophical and worthy of serious consideration. Adolescents may demand to know *why* food cannot be more equitably divided among society's citizens. They are not impressed with economic explanations, with tradition, or with political policy. If these do not jibe with what is right, they reason, so much the worse for them; if they do not accord with what is ideal, they must be changed. (This outlook stands in marked contrast with the rigid, authoritarian outlook of the early adolescent, and contributes significantly to a reduced ethnocentrism during middle adolescence).

The loss of idealism is not accepted gracefully. Bitterness, cynicism, resentment, apathy, and rebelliousness are common symptoms of squelched idealism. Interestingly, adolescents are able to accept *intellectually* the limitations of idealism before they are able to do so emotionally. (One must have a philosophy of adolescence to decide whether this is a strength or a limitation of the adolescent character.)

Despite negative experiences, many positive effects accrue from testing idealism. Adolescents are forced to sort the naive from the philosophical; they must realign their conception of how the world operates and recheck their own biases and prejudices, each of which contributes to intellectual expansion and to a more mature and complex personality.

5. *Self-doubt increases.* One of the major characteristics of formal thought is the ability to countercheck the thought process. The ability to doubt the product of one's own thought represents a fundamental difference between the adolescent and the child and even though it benefits thought, it taxes self-concept. It is an especially heavy tax because most youth already are burdened with uncertainty about social acceptance and inferiority about body image.

Self-doubt is soothed by certainty; therefore, dogmatism holds a special allure. Expanding intellectual powers, however, quickly advise of the limitations of dogma, and as a result, adolescents strive for intensity of *emotion*, which is more difficult to deny or refute. We thus witness an interesting paradox of adolescence: increased intelligence encourages the search for intense emotionalism.

It is obvious that advancements in mental growth create numerous psychological dislocations, and in some instances, considerable anxiety, and it is equally obvious that the ability of the adolescent to cope effectively with them greatly determines the extent to which daily life is filled with storm and stress.

Free Will During Adolescence

The nature of free will during adolescence is a puzzlement to psychologists and to adolescents alike. There can be no doubt that adolescents are capable of assessing, evaluating and questioning; they demonstrate autonomy by resisting environmental pressures, and by making choices which agree with moral viewpoints. Each of these tendencies helps paint a picture of self-direction and free will. The painting, however, is no masterpiece! Flaws fill the canvas, and gaps dot an otherwise rich landscape. For example, the adolescent is not free from social urges which give direction to thought. The adolescent usually does as he wills, but the will itself is guided by developmental needs for recognition, assertion, and acknowledgement.

The adolescent is less egocentric than the child, but nevertheless demonstrates considerable self-centredness in daily mental habits. Though capable of impartial reasoning with topics such as algebra and astronomy, the adolescent rarely displays impartiality of thought when dealing with topics such as the rights of parents, or the tendency of a sweetheart to flirt with competitors. The closer an issue moves toward one's emotional centre the more biased thought becomes.

Adults lose sight of the fact that an adolescent who demonstrates objective thought in one area evidences only dim objectivity in others. The growth of the intellect does *not* guarantee the ability to think objectively about oneself. Adults (for the most part) are considerably more able than adolescents to overcome egocentricity. We do not here wish to engage in a metaphysical discussion of the nature of free will; rather, our intent is merely to indicate that the adolescent is not a completely free agent when formulating viewpoints. Reasoning about matters distant from the self is considerably more advanced than reasoning about issues close to one's emotional centre. The adolescent is, in a very realistic sense, semi-free. To assume that he is totally free is fiction. To assume that he is incapable of free thought is likewise fiction. His range lies somewhere in the middle ground between childhood and adulthood, on some terrain resembling the child, and on others the adult.

Social Living During Middle Adolescence

Middle adolescents are more disciplined when it comes to *choosing* friends; they are less likely to mix with peers only because they are from the same neighborhood or classroom than is true for early adolescents. They also are better at avoiding self-defeating "friendships" filled with continuous bickering; they are better able to deal in a civilized way with the opposite sex whether or not a romantic interest exists. Dating is more common and *may* result in genuine romance and intimacy, a trend which rarely occurs during early adolescence.

The peer group, of course, plays an important role in the life of the adolescent. For example, many youth, when given the opportunity to speak in a frank manner, appraise their peers in ways similar to adult appraisals of these peers. Adolescents ably recognize faults in their friends, admitting, for example, that one girl may be deceitful, while another is honest. Most adolescents are fairly adept at analyzing their own personality strengths and weaknesses, though for the most part they tend to overplay their weaknesses. When *adults* point out the weaknesses in a friend, most adolescents feel compelled to rally to the defense, pointing out the positive traits which counterbalance the deficiencies. The next day, however, when interacting with another peer, the boy who the night before vigorously defended his friend may gossip about his deficiencies, excluding from the conversation the positive traits he so gallantly paraded before his parents.

The desire to assume important roles is a source of strife in many households, especially those which afford little opportunity for the youngster to do "worthwhile" work. Conflict also exists when the adolescent competes with one parent for the affection of the other. Peter Blos describes what he calls a reawakened "family romance" when the daughter secretly wishes that her father will find her more attractive, or more desirable, than her mother. Or when the son secretly wishes his mother will find him more attractive than his father. Blos suggests that even though this "family romance" is waged in a subtle manner, it nevertheless creates tension within the family unit. It is interesting to note, however, that parents, social workers, or psychologists rarely report observing this phenomenon in action; like many other psychoanalytic concepts, it lacks verification.

This is a critical age for adjustment to school. Youth for whom school is *not* socially rewarding, or for whom the learning does not improve job prospects, are more likely then ever drop out. Youngsters to whom school offers social rewards *and* provides the credentials for future "success" rarely drop out. For them school is the most important fact of their social lives, and eventually, of their professional lives.

Companionship in the adolescent community is not always as it appears. The untrained observer concludes because teenagers cluster that they necessarily share a common bond of friendship or derive a sense of genuine companionship from their physical togetherness. This, however, is not always the case. In many regards, adolescent gatherings resemble middle-class cocktail parties where people are tossed together in close proximity, chatting with one another, smiling, as though things could not be better. Despite the appearance of cordiality which first strikes the observer, the actual interpersonal dealings may or may not be sincere, and may or may not be based on friendship. Companionship by no means automatically exists simply because a group of people are thrown together (whether by protocol or necessity) and are required to interact with one another.

By participating in a group the adolescent acquires greater competence in negotiating his interpersonal world. He must be in a group to learn the group. Thus, the *need* for belonging is a gravitational factor in teen groupings but it does not follow that a *feeling* of belonging emerges. Friedenberg, in a significant statement on North American youth, puts it this way:

> Groups of juveniles are not friendly; and strongly-felt friendships do not commonly form among them, though there is often constant association between members of juvenile cliques. They are not there to be friendly; they are there to work out a crude social system and to learn the ropes from one another. To some extent they behave like the gang in an office, jockeying for position within a superficially amiable social group. (1964, p. 44)

Adolescents come together *from the fear of isolation* as much from the desire for friendship. Not uncommonly, a group will hang around for an hour or more with virtually no attempt at conversation and with little concern for their peers *as persons*. Often as not, exchange centres upon ridicule or abuse; talk may take the form of bragging or complaining, but no serious attempt is made to speak with conviction or honesty. In short, the gathering exists because the participants partially fulfill mutual needs for togetherness or affiliation and also prevent aloneness and isolation.

Mixed emotions permeate adolescent companionship. On one occasion, the adolescent may feel warmth for his comrades; at another time, hostility. Mixed feelings are natural because every individual is continuously subject to judgment by peers, with verdicts sometimes favorable but at other times punitive. Because he is dependent upon comrades, he dare not alienate those who determine his significance. Ironically, the evaluators themselves are evaluated in a "perpetual certification by peers," each as insecure as the others and none more powerful than the totality.

Adolescent disputes are easier to understand once one recognizes that adolescent groupings, by their very design, contribute to alternating feelings of self-importance and self-debasement. The uncertainty of their social network adds pressure to an already difficult time of life, resulting in periodic outbursts of self-assertion. Such gestures, so typical of the middle adolescent years, represent the beginning of the group-person divorce proceedings which last throughout the rest of adolescence.

The adolescent attraction for stability, continuity, and durable strength is considerable. For some youngsters these needs are expressed through religion; for others, through the timelessness of chemical nirvana; for still others, through an established political party. The quest for security is hampered by relationships which are fragile and easily disrupted. Experience, plus the increasing awareness of the selfish nature of every person, engenders the realization that relationships not only are rare, but highly improbable. Therefore, even though adolescents value durable companionship, they are aware of the life forces which go against it.

Pathology During Middle Adolescence

Virtually all areas of self-destructive behavior show an upswing during middle adolescence. The suicide rate continues to escalate as does the incidence of homicide and physical assault. Death from accidents increases, with automobiles leading the fatality list. Drug-related deaths, especially overdoses, and suicides while under the influence of drugs or the depression induced by them, also increase. The more severe psychiatric ailments such as depression, schizophrenia and paranoia also demonstrate a significant increase over the early adolescent years. Common to all of these difficulties is the fact that they increase during the coming years, and the suffering they cause likewise continues. Virtually all forms of personal and social pathology show a gradual increase throughout the adolescent period, with early adolescents exhibiting the least, late adolescents the most, and with middle adolescents somewhere in between.

Weiner and Del Gaudio (1976) analyzed psychopathology in relation to age and concluded that suicide and schizophrenia are extremely rare during the earliest years of adolescence, but increase steadily into the late adolescent years. The generalization which most accurately describes the relationship between age and psychopathology during adolescence is this: as age increases so also does the incidence of serious emotional disturbance (Mitchell, 1980).

Postscript

Differences between the early and the middle adolescent are considerable The early adolescent has been out of childhood for only a short while; child traits permeate personality, tastes and inclinations. Middle adolescents come to grips with a new body and, as a result, perceive themselves more as adults than as children. The early adolescent displays weak skills in dealing with the opposite sex, while the middle adolescent is considerably better not only with the opposite sex, but with adults as well.

Mental growth shows great improvement even though *initial* breakthroughs take place during early adolescence. Each mental advance represents an improvement over its early adolescent character and produces more scientific and philosophical thought, the end result being a more idealistic, more theoretical, and more sophisticated thought process.

Mental growth embraces the outside world, and fosters awareness of political and social systems previously unnoticed. It creates a keener awareness of the inner workings of the personality; it encourages introspection, and indirectly, self-doubt and self-criticism. It permits coping strategies to become more systematic, thus activities are negotiated with greater premeditation and with more emphasis on outcomes.

The social world undergoes significant change, primarily in the direction of greater autonomy, increased interest in the opposite sex and more complicated relationships within the family. Same-sex groupings are less popular than during early adolescence, but remain the dominant medium for interaction with peers. Mixed-sex gatherings provide the experimental arena for deeper relationships, and an opportunity to practice social skills.

Romantic involvements during middle adolescence traverse a remarkable spectrum, ranging from superficial, naive "puppy love" to fully blossomed mature love. In the middle of this continuum exists a compromise: "having a girlfriend" or, "having a boyfriend," which tend to be attachments characterized by familiarity, fidelity, and shared intimacies. It is not a mini-version of mature love but neither is it only an improved version of early adolescent affiliation. Unquestionably, it is more substantive than popular caricatures portray, and, also unquestionably, it is less spectacular than the youth it embraces claim it to be.

Konopka (1976), reporting the results of hundreds of interviews with adolescent girls, claims that the most highly valued qualities in boyfriends (and girlfriends) are loyalty, understanding, and consideration as well as being a person whom one can confide in and share with. This supports the notion that adolescent relationships are governed by the same principles which regulate adults relationships.

Incidentally, for those of you sensitive to the occasional reference in this chapter to what seems like "stereotyped" adolescent behavior, it probably is. One of the ironic twists to the study of adolescent psychology is that it addresses both true and false stereotypes about the adolescent community. However, the array of stereotypes we associate with adolescence is not unique to humans; several of our evolutional cousins such as the chimpanzee and the gibbon also manifest age-related mannerisms usually associated with human adolescence. Jane Goodall, studying chimpanzees in East Africa, noted that adolescent chimps were especially prone toward confusion and turmoil when it came to learning their new adult roles, and generally made a nuisance of themselves among the older adults before settling into their young adult period. Ellefson (1968) noted that adolescent gibbons are more "helter-skelter" than their sedate elders, that they over-react far more frequently, and that they chatter excessively, sometimes aimlessly. Experienced animal watchers claim that distinguishing adolescent from adult primates can usually be achieved simply by looking for *stereotypic human adolescent mannerisms*, particularily confusion about adult roles and responsibilities, playful jousting, preoccupation with the opposite sex, and hyperactivity.

Therefore, with full awareness of the foregoing, we may conclude that in our study of adolescence we uncover the typical as well as the atypical, and the humanly unique as well as a few evolutional realities which we share with other species.

9
Middle Adolescence:
Some Specific Considerations

Thus far we have described, in general terms, some of the significant variables which influence growth during the middle adolescent period. In this section we shall deal with the specific topics discussed in Chapters 1-4 in order to clarify how these issues pertain not only to adolescence in general, but to middle adolescence in particular.

Storm and Stress During Middle Adolescence

Areas of increased storm and stress:

In general, young people improve their capacity for realistic self-evaluation during the middle adolescent period. Increased cognitive abilities combine with increased interpersonal experience to produce an assessment of self which becomes increasingly realistic. This increased accuracy of self-assessment, ironically, is a primary cause of anguish because honest news is not necessarily comforting news. Youngsters of this age who are weak in general abilities, or low in social attractiveness can no longer hide from these deficits. Consequently, *many* youngsters openly face the realization that they have a limited future in school-related professions; that they are physically unattractive; that their true aptitude makes unlikely the brilliant future envisioned at a younger age.

Coming to grips with personal limitations frequently deteriorates into self-pity. Most youth accept their limitations, but a significant number cannot accept any contradiction to the narcissistic premise of their lives, and spend their adolescent years hating the society, and the people within it, which undervalues them.

Most emotions increase in power during middle adolescence. That is, jealousy, the emotions of anger, especially hatred, flood the personality with stressful anxiety. For many youngsters the emotional richness of mid-adolescence is a scourge rather than a blessing.

The insecurities of romantic involvements begin to appear in middle adolescence. Most youngsters avoid them simply by avoiding romance, but for those to whom romance comes, so also does turbulence. Late adolescence, more so than middle adolescence however, is the theatre where the beauty and the beast of romance take centre stage.

Thus far we have confined our attention to aspects of adolescence which, although essentially "normal," increase grief. And, in a book which has as its focus "normal adolescence" this is understandable. However, our understanding of storm and stress remains unbalanced if we fail to take note of the irrational side to adolescence. Therefore, youngsters who in the course of their childhood have acquired an irrational hatred of themselves, or an irrational fear of others, or overpowering feelings of inferiority, rarely find that adolescence brings any relief. Defects of personality acquired during childhood as a rule become more profound during adolescence and they contribute greatly to storm and stress. For many youngsters these defects convert painful normalcy into neurotic pathology.

Therefore, we may conclude that during middle adolescence many factors contribute to increased storm and stress, most notably: (1) an increased awareness of personal limitations causes a certain amount of anguish and despair; (2) an increase in the power of emotions creates a roller-coaster effect which magnifies the impact of all emotional experiences — the positive as well as the negative; (3) anxiety associated with romance and sexuality increases, and; (4) some of the immaturities of childhood which remain within the personality cause increased anxiety and tension because they interfere with effective interpersonal relationships.

Areas of decreased storm and stress

Middle adolescence brings some relief from the troubled moments of early adolescence, the most important being a refined capacity to survive within the community of peers, and an uplifted ability to survive within the household. These encouraging advances on two vital fronts add tremendously to middle-adolescent confidence and well-being.

By the middle teens most youngsters have learned to satisfy their needs for belonging and esteem without subjecting themselves to the humiliations and juvenile rituals which flourish during the early teens. They learn to choose friends with an eye to their decency, and they learn to avoid peers who are self-destructive. They also hold a greater appreciation for the weaknesses within their own personality, and they are more insightful about how to retain reasonable equilibrium. In sum, they benefit considerably from what they learned during early adolescence.

Household relationships improve with increased ability to "read" parents. Receding egocentrism liberates youth from expecting the world to accommodate them, and a more honest awareness of limitations deflates some of their narcissism. (See N. J. Bell, 1985, for an interesting analysis of the relationship between family structure and the compatability of parents and teenagers. She presents some thoughtful ideas).

Middle adolescents are beginning to reap the benefits of solid friends, genuine intimacy, and peer acceptance. They assume a consolidated posture which enhances their overall sense of well-being. This promotion in self-identity, unto itself, increases their ability to cope with stress, and, therefore, reduces it.

In summary, the middle-adolescent period is a dialectic between stress well-being, with each holding the upper hand on occasion. Although generalizations about middle adolescents are difficult to make, it seems that for most people of this age the momentum is swinging towards greater mastery of life problems. Likewise, for most young people the ability to cope with stress is increasing at the same rate, if not faster, than the amount of stress to be coped with. It is because of these observations that most contemporary psychologists do not view adolescence as a period of *overpowering* storm and stress.

Identity Formation and Identity Confusion During Middle Adolescence

Many factors which contribute to a stabilized identity score triumphs during middle adolescence. The three most significant components of adolescent identity — competence, self-esteem, and integrity — show improvement over their early adolescent status. The reasons for this are simple: the increased skills afforded by advancing age make it easier to demonstrate competence, to receive esteem, and to build one's integrity. The internship of early adolescence teaches the individual how to handle group settings, how to get along more effectively with the opposite sex, and how to earn the goodwill of adults, all of which are vital to one's sense of identity and worthwhileness.

Stevens-Long summarized the distinctions between early and middle adolescent identity with clarity and brevity:

> . . . it is premature to speak of identity in early adolescence . . . most of the work of identity formation is done in middle adolescence, and only as separation from the parent becomes clearer and more confident can we assume there is a stable sense of self. Perhaps what emerges in early adolescence is just the idea that one has a self, not how that self operates (1983, p. 305).

Role experimentation is beginning to yield dividends partly because haphazard experimentation is outgrown, and partly because failures are avoided while successes are repeated. All in all, by this age the child personality is virtually eradicated, while the adolescent personality becoming firmly entrenched.

The child feels important when loved, or when *told* he is important. The adolescent must produce, and this causes panic. For some youngsters performance is a blessing — especially those who possess valued skills. For them the fact that they are esteemed in the classroom, in the sports arena, on the street corner, or at their job takes on tremendous significance. "Legitimate" importance instills confidence and solidifies identity.

Middle adolescents experience problems with *continuity of experience* because their in-between status casts them into a variety of social contexts. The household also lacks consistency because the youngster is sometimes treated like a child and at other times like an adult. The inner world of emotion most assuredly is not continuous. Such inconsistency does not paralyze, but it does impede, an enduring identity. Some adolescents infer that a solid identity is unachievable. As a rule, this inference is short-lived and eventually most youngsters comprehend that discontinuity is a reflection of circumstance rather than a defect within oneself.

Interestingly, many youngsters do not want to move toward an adult identity, preferring instead to focus on the adolescent world, and identifying themselves *in terms of it*. They are, "total adolescents," and they fit nicely many stereotypes our culture holds about them. This does not impede later identities; it is even helpful when adult responsibilities are not available to them because it allows them to avoid the painful juxtaposition of a "mature" personality surviving within a juvenile environment — a dominant youth predicament of our time (Mitchell, 1975).

Of more serious concern, (and one to which "storm and stress" advocates pay considerable attention), is the fact that many middle adolescents experience profound identity confusion. Compared with early adolescents (as a group) virtually *all* symptoms of identity confusion increase; therefore, aimlessness, free-floating anger, depression and other symptoms of identity confusion are observed more frequently during middle adolescence.

One expression of identity confusion is the tendency for negativism to escalate into *negative identity*, whereupon the youngster not only thinks negatively, but acts out negations in hostile and disruptive ways. The pressurized lifestyle which previously produced only *feelings* of hostility now explodes into destructive behavior. In this regard the vandalism of middle adolescence is often rooted in a more profound emotional disturbance than vandalism of early adolescence because the latter is often caused by peer pressure or egocentric narrowness rather than emotional disturbance.

Identity diffusion is more common and more serious than during early adolescence because anxiety takes a progressively higher toll with each advancing year. The pathological manifestation of identity diffusion — the *identity disorder* — also increases in frequency.

In summary, for the majority of youth, middle adolescence is a period of identity growth. For some, however, it is an identity moratorium, *par excellence*. And for a lesser percentage, it is a time of identity confusion and identity pathology.

Sexuality During Middle Adolescence

Middle adolescence is the transition period from the comparative non-sexuality of early adolescence to the sexual maturity of late adolescence. In terms of incidence, *all forms* of sexual involvement increase. It is a period of experimentation, investigation, and experiencing. Masturbation increases for both sexes, as does heterosexual involvement. Intercourse remains a minority experience; however, the escalating power of sexual passion, the increased *desire* for sexual involvement (an element noticeably missing in the early adolescent), and an overall increase in general inclination, make the probability of sexual intercourse considerably higher than during early adolescence.

In a more practical vein, the *opportunity* for sexual involvement increases. Dating is more frequent, the availability of partners increases for both sexes (virtually all boys are now sexually mature), the automobile is more available, as are apartments and parentless homes. Dating, for many youngsters, takes on a more serious tone. Romance, as generally understood by adults, blossoms, and this universally increases the likelihood of sexual involvement.

Throughout North America middle adolescents are extremely ineffi-cient users of contraceptives. They uniformly believe that their sexual activity will not result in pregnancy, even when they fully comprehend the ovulation cycle and other mechanics of pregnancy. Consequently, the preg-nancy rate among the sexually active is much higher than during late adolescence or early adulthood when both partners (especially the female) are more effective contraceptive users, or more sophisticated in employing the rhythm method.

Of the numerous instances when egocentrism, rationalization, and den-ial contaminate the adolescent thought process, none is more blatant than "I will not get pregnant." It is this intellectual error, more than the fre-quency of intercourse, which results in the high pregnancy-to-intercourse ratio of middle adolescence.

Many factors influence adolescent sexuality — especially the need for belonging, the propensity for submissiveness, and the craving for sexual passion. Youngsters who receive no affection at home now comprehend that sexual intimacy offsets this. Interpersonal pressure mounts because both sexes realize that sexual involvement is essentially a matter of *choice*. The partner who chooses "NO" is, by definition, in conflict with the partner who chooses "YES." This conflict of interest complicates sexuality and introduces youth to some of its adult intricacies.

The conditions upon which marriage in our culture is predicated — love, fidelity and reciprocity — reach considerable prominence during middle adolescence. They continue to grow in the forthcoming years, but their emergence as viable forces within the evolving personality signals that the metamorphosis from child to adult is nearing completion. (See J. W. Lindsay, 1985, for a thorough analysis of adolescent perceptions of marriage).

Depersonalized sexuality and "recreational" sex are rare. These await later years when the complexities of sexuality are better mastered, and when the emotional pains of sexuality are more likely to require the anesthetic of detachment. Sexual pathology is essentially an adult phenomenon, and when it does occur in adolescence, it is usually during the later years.

In almost every way, middle adolescence is the "in-between" stage of adolescent sexuality. It is the first of many sexual proving grounds, and though vital lessons are learned from it, these lessons are more abstract than carnal, and not nearly as vital as those learned in the forthcoming late-adolescent period.

Defense Mechanisms During Middle Adolescence

As life becomes more pressured, and as the self becomes more troubled, reliance upon defense mechanisms deepens. As a rule, both of these show noticeable increase during middle adolescence, therefore, we observe a corresponding upswing in defense mechanisms and other maneuvers of psychic protection.

Sex-related anxieties become more powerful, and although most youth accommodate effectively, they nevertheless exact a considerable psychic toll. *Repression* of sexual desires, and *denial* of sexual fantasies are rather common; *reaction-formation* is less frequent than either repression or denial; however, it is more prevalent then it was during early adolescence. The essential conflict of middle adolescence involves accepting one's sexual impulses without having sanctioned ways to express them. This conflict lasts throughout adolescence and into early adulthood; its difficulty to the middle adolescent is found in its novelty, its urgency, and the lack of coping devices available at this age.

On the other hand, defense mechanisms which are reduced by intellectual examination (such as *rationalization* and *projection*) tend to lessen as the intellect progressively expands.

The need to formulate a philosophy of life, and to draw conclusions about one's personal identity, imposes upon the adolescent conflicting demands for rational objectivity and self-aggrandizing conclusions. With advancing age, the conflict between these polarities becomes more apparent to the intellect and more painful to the emotions. Many youngsters simply cannot reconcile their craving for importance with the fact of their unimportance, their need for love with their sense of isolation, their desire for intimacy with their fear of aloneness. From this quandary they must formulate ideas about their role in society, and draw conclusions about the "meaning of life." It is not by chance that identity crises begin to crop up during middle adolescence, because the inability to blend narcissistic centredness with altruistic selflessness is, in essence, the nuclear ingredient to identity crises.

Identity crises encourage the use of defense mechanisms, especially rationalization, projection, and denial. *Protective structures* also show a dramatic upsurge. *Asceticism*, as a reaction to sexual impulses and fears, shows considerable increase, and *elusiveness*, as a defense against commitment, proliferates. *Cynicism* becomes more profound for some youngsters, but virtually disappears for others; *compartmentalization* lessens for youth who acquire greater mastery over their increasingly complex environment, but skyrockets for those who are losing the battle for environmental and interpersonal competence.

Before concluding this chapter it is necessary to introduce two significant variables which influence the middle adolescent years: (1) the adolescent susceptibility to despair, and (2) the adolescent tendency toward apathy. Both of these contribute to the deployment of defense mechanisms, and, equally important, they contribute to some of the most significant disruptions of adolescence.

The Adolescent Susceptibility to Despair

Adolescence contains developmental, phenomenological, and personality variables *which heighten the probability that despair, and despair-related ideologies, will consume the individual.* In this section an attempt will be made to specify the factors which accelerate despair during the adolescent years.

First, however, a word of caution. All youth are not prone toward the despair. In fact, many youth do not experience anything which resembles it. As Offer (1969), Bandura (1980), and other contemporary psychologists have noted, some people grow through their teen years with little turmoil, anxiety or despair. This cautionary note does not blind us to those adolescents for whom despair is a major struggle. The following comments refer to a limited, but nevertheless significant segment of youth.

In our attempt to understand outlooks which diminish the significance of life, it is prudent to bear in mind that many youth not only feel insignificant, they *are* insignificant; many youth not only experience purposelessness, they *are* purposeless. Therefore, despair realistically portrays their existence.

Nor can we surmise that despair is unique to disturbed personalities. The autobiographies of many adults disclose a turbulent adolescence filled not only with self-doubt, inferiority feelings, and peer anxiety, but with despair, depression and periodic inclinations toward suicide. Kiell, whose analysis of autobiographies focused on the adolescent time zone, provides several intriguing examples of famous people whose youths were riddled with despair. Napoleon Bonaparte, one of the ablest military minds of his century, a capable and powerful political leader, and a dynamic adult personality, experienced numerous episodes of despair and sorrow. In adolescence he wrote: "Always alone in the midst of people, I return home in order to give myself up with unspeakable melancholy to my dreams." In equal measure, the French novelist Romain Rolland claimed that his adolescent years were "tragic years, unimportant only to those who would have seen nothing but . . . the familiar schoolboy existence of a restless youth. But they concealed the voracious monsters of a deadly despair. Those were the days when I plumbed the very depths of total emptiness." The despair of Napoleon and Rolland reached even greater depths for Havelock Ellis whose adolescent attitude toward life "was embodied in an 'Ode to Death' in which I implored Death to bear me away from the world on gentle wings, although at the same time I had no thought of taking any steps to aid Death in this task." And finally, to further reinforce the fact that despair finds its way into youth of low as well as high ego-strength, comes the confession of Goethe's troubled youth. "This uncertainty of taste and judgement disturbed me more every day, so at last I fell into despair . . . I found myself in the completely wretched condition in which one is placed when a complete change of mind is required — a renunciation of all that I hitherto loved and found good. After some time . . . I felt so great a contempt for my works begun and ended that one day on the kitchen hearth I burnt up poetry and prose, plans, sketches, and designs altogether, and by the smoke which filled the whole house threw our good landlady into no small fright and anxiety."

As virtually every scholar of adolescent psychology attests, the formation of personal identity is one of the paramount tasks of the adolescent. It is precisely during adolescence that our culture expects experimentation, sampling, and role playing. When these years are filled with despair, a task vital to an effective *adult* personality goes unfulfilled. The end product is a young adult who lacks self-definition, self-direction, and usually, self-pride.

Love and elation are not the most intense emotions of youth. Despair and sorrow are often equally profound; and youngsters who deeply experience them are often unable to escape their grasp. In fact, they often prefer not to escape because the allure of an emotion is not whether it generates positive or negative feelings, but rather, whether it *engenders an immersion in, and a global preoccupation with, oneself.*

If despair occurred only among the emotionally disturbed or among those who lacked genuine love relationships, it could be understood as a neurotic condition. However, this is not the case. Feelings of despair characterize many youngsters who mature into normal, even healthy, adults.

However, this does not blind us to an equally significant fact: the weakened personality *is far more vulnerable to despair and depression* than is the sturdy personality. Therefore, even though despair occurs among many youth, it is not equally distributed among them. It is far more common among the non-affiliated, among those with low self-esteem, among those who lack achievement and accomplishment, and among those with strong guilt feelings. Among those youth despair is cause for concern in a psychiatric sense. Their prognosis for an emotionally healthy adulthood is reduced, primarily because they are more susceptible to depression and its allied pathologies, and this, unto itself, makes them a less healthy population.

Despair is especially attractive to youth who perceive themselves as inferior and worthless because it cancels the achievements of others. (If the entire world is meaningless, so also are the achievements of individuals.) Ironically, this diminished perception haunts their owners *by devaluing their own achievements and accomplishments* (usually actualized during early adulthood), leaving them with a sense of insignificance toward achievements which would otherwise have engendered feelings of competence and worth within them.

Non-Rational Beliefs & Irrational Perceptions

Irrational beliefs are unrealistic ideas about how one should behave in order to be loved, to be popular, or to be successful. Adolescents are particularly susceptible to irrational beliefs dealing with "How I should behave," and "Why people don't like me."

One particularly powerful irrational belief is that it is necessary to be approved of by everyone including parents, teachers and neighbors. Ironically, for an age-group supposedly at odds with adult society, this irrational belief is rather common. Even more prevalent is the belief that all of their peers should approve of and like them. These youngsters become consumed by acceptance and popularity. If they are socially gifted they may obtain a great measure of it; however, the desire for universal popularity usually results in disillusionment.

Another irrational belief is that one should be thoroughly competent adequate, and achieving. This is rarely observed among children, but it shows dramatic increase during adolescence and an even sharper upswing during early adulthood. Interestingly, it most frequently occurs among high-competence people, and some psychotherapists think of it as an "executive ailment," or as a "perfectionist syndrome" because it is so frequently observed among high achievers.

Another irrational belief which exerts strong influence during adolescence is the belief that certain people are bad or wicked, simply because they are different, and *that they should be punished* for their differences. This belief is commonly observed among youth who desire to punish other people in order to counter unmanageable impulses swelling within themselves. This belief encourages prejudice and discrimination, especially towards groups discriminated against by society at large.

A further belief is that it is awful or catastrophic when things are not exactly the way one wants them to be. This belief, as is true for the others, may exist in either a normal or a disturbed personality. It usually emerges when the real world does not coincide with personal desires, thereby creating an incongruity which the adolescent perceives as calamatous.

At the risk of making the adolescent seem trivial, it is worth making a special note of their susceptibility to this particular belief. Early and middle adolescents are especially prone to believe that the slightest social error will invite the greatest catastrophe. Counselors and teachers know from experience how important it is to inform them that the world does not come to a halt after one has made a fool of oneself, or when one has been rejected by a peer, or when an examination comes back with a failing grade on it. With the accumulation of experience, youngsters learn to manage the struggle between their personal desires and the indifference of the outside world. The neurotic adolescent, however, develops such elaborate defenses in response to this frustration that irrational beliefs increase rather than decrease.

Two other irrational beliefs are widespread in the adolescent community: (1) the belief that one should become upset over other people's problems and disturbances; and, (2) the belief that happiness is *externally caused* and that people have little or no ability to control the things which bring them joy or cause them sorrow.

Woolfolk and Richardson (1979) have described a series of *irrational perceptions* which are common among young people.

The first irrational perception they describe is the conviction that *worry is a helpful trait*; that it "prevents mistakes and misfortune, helps anticipate the future, or gives you added control over the course of events." Worry, like sorrow, perpetuates itself when the adolescent believes it is inevitable, or that *it is a symbol of mature concern.* Adult worriers are abundant; therefore, the adolescent saddled with this misconception has little trouble locating a role model. Worry creates an urgency which the adolescent misperceives as *necessary importance,* and thereby experiences a sense of elevated significance when engaged in frenzied worry.

The second irrational perception is the belief that your emotional security and your prospects for meaningful relationships are *completely dependent upon being accepted by a limited group of specific people.* As a result, fights and arguments among peers take on enormous significance. Early and middle adolescents are especially inclined to believe that if rejected they will undergo irreversible damage.

Another irrational perception states "I am permanently inferior to my peers," and that any attempt to equal their achievements is out of the question. This overestimation of others at the expense of oneself is observed with such frequency that it can be considered, in a statistical sense, a normal adolescent phenomenon. Its "normalcy," however, does not cancel its destructive potential. This irrational perception is tailor-made for youngsters with low self-esteem, with a history of low achievement, and with parents who do not buttress their sagging self-confidence.

Competitive cultures such as our own nurture a further irrational perception which exerts profound effect: evaluating *everything in life in a win-lose perspective.* Friendships and relationships are, in essence, contests to be won or lost. Young people whose sense of worth comes from competitive achievements, or who believe that without victory they have no acceptability, are extremely vulnerable to this perception. As is true for most irrational perceptions, its presence is so abundant in the adult world that the young person has no trouble attaching himself to an adult who holds similar beliefs.

A further irrational perception inclines the adolescent to feel that people who behave differently *are immoral.* Differences between individuals are viewed as *moral inferiorities* rather than merely differences in behavior. Many adolescents so hunger for superiority that even when it is achieved only by proclaiming that someone else is inferior, it briefly satisfies their need for it.

The final irrational perception typifies narcissistic and pampered youth, and is increasingly reported by therapists and counselors: this is the perception that one has the *right* to be free from discomfort, and to glide through life with only minimal frustration. This perception is a source of considerable grief not only to adolescents who hold it, but to the parents and educators who daily interact with them. If this naive expectation lasts into late adolescence the stage is set for an antisocial or a narcissistic personality type.

Unto themselves, these irrational perceptions are not debilitating; however, when bonded with defense mechanisms, or free-floating anger, or with excessive egocentrism, they avalanche through the youthful landscape, creating chaos and magnifying the significance of pre-existing personality defects.

Apathy

The experience of apathy includes dullness of emotion, indifference to social events, insensitivity to normal passion, and general impassivity and lethargy. Apathy results from prolonged frustration — it is not a normal reaction to normal stress; it is a disturbed reaction to profound stress.

The apathetic adolescent views life as artificial and meaningless; he does not plan for the future and he is not impressed with society:

> The adult world into which they are headed is seen as a cold, mechanical, abstract, specialized, and emotionally meaningless place in which one simply goes through the motions, but without conviction that the motions are worthy, dignified, relevant, or exciting. Thus, for many young people, it is essential to stay "cool"; and "coolness" involves detachment, lack of commitment, never being enthusiastic or going overboard about anything. This is a bleak picture, and it must be partially qualified. For few young people are deliberately cynical or calculating; rather, many feel forced into detachment and premature cynicism because society seems to offer them so little that is relevant, stable, and meaningful. They wish there were values, goals, or institutions to which they could be genuinely committed . . . (Keniston, 1969, p. 243)

The apathetic adolescent usually believes that the important aspects of life are beyond control; he sees himself as a pawn, with Fate the grand master. For the most part, he is estranged from society, and commonly his identity is based on opposing societal norms, a condition Erikson calls "negative identity."

Affluence and Apathy

An irony of the modern era is that increased material wealth has produced a series of totally unexpected disorders in the psychological realm. Affluence does not create interpersonal crises, but for many youth, it compounds them. With regard to the matter at hand, there is no doubt that economic conditions encourage psychological apathy, especially among middle-class youth.

Two general economic conditions which deepen apathy are of special significance. The first is the plight of the lower class, and it is this: No matter how hard one tries, things will not get much *better.* The second condition is characteristic of the upper class, and goes like this: no matter how little one works, things will not get much worse. Both conditions minimize the person and maximize social forces beyond personal control. However, it has only been since the mid-sixties that either of these two conditions has exerted a dominant influence on *middle-class youth.*

We are witnessing a historical novelty in North America, because for the first time middle-class youth are tranquilized into apathy by their relative immobility in the economic sphere, and because of their satiation with material goods.

In times past *neither* condition one nor condition two (as described above) applied to the middle class because it has never before been as affluent as it is now, and the motivational strivings of the middle class have historically impelled it toward greater achievements and more extravagant goods. Equally significant, the parents of today's teenagers were the children of poor parents. They think in terms of "surplus" and "security," therefore, they not only have specific goals to strive towards — they also value highly a tangible "stash" in case of bad times. They grew up in an economic world where if they failed to work diligently, they could easily slip backwards beyond the rescue of their financial reserves. Their world was the perfect arena for Social Darwinism.

In the seventies a historical anomaly began to occur. Because of the relative affluence of the middle class, the youth who lived in this economic grouping found themselves in a situation where condition one *as well as* condition two held true. That is, no matter how hard they would strive, they were not likely to improve significantly upon the standard of living to which they had grown accustomed. Stated succinctly: middle-class youth in today's world enjoy a lifestyle almost as advanced as they will experience as adults. Therefore the second economic condition (no matter how little one works things will not get much worse) which historically has held true only for upper-income youth, now also applies to middle-class youth *who have learned to lower their expectations* and live a Thoreauvian simplicity.

This has been the message of various cultures which typically originate in suburbia, or the university, and relocate within the inner city. The message has been so well received that we now witness among middle-class youth an indifference toward future employment which in the past could be seen among the extremely low- or extremely high-income youth, but almost *never* among middle-income groupings.

For many middle-class youth the "real" economic problems relate only to the degree to which they wish to acquire goods on a par with those possessed by their neighbors. As far as *basic life necessities* go, no genuine problems exist. This contrasts markedly with the economic picture at the turn of the century where young people faced genuine deprivation of basic necessities if they did not work diligently at one or perhaps even two jobs.

For youth jaded and bored with the opulence of our era, apathy is a relentless companion. However, it is not a lack of interest in "things" which fosters apathy in these youth: they are apathetic because they have nothing to attach themselves to, to define themselves in terms of, or to lend dignity to their existence.

Parents who believed that their children would be motivated by the same forces which motivated them are now learning that youngsters who rebel against the pursuit of capital, but who have no other motivation, drift aimlessly and apathetically, and even worse, they hate themselves and their parents because they are forced to live in the barren limbo they together have created.

Postscript

It would be unfair to overlook the elementary and personal fact that young people require a special person, usually an adult, who has faith in them and who believes they will handle the adversities of life. This is not the same as an adult who only offers advice. Youth require an older person who has faith in them, and who will continue to believe in them even when things are not going well. This faith in "me-as-person" is vital and its absence creates adolescent disbelief toward adults.

Rollo May cogently summarizes this idea:

> When I was in college I found the experience of having some adult believing in me crucially important; and at times thereafter in my life when I was faced with fateful decisions, I found myself casting about to fasten upon one of these persons. It was not that he or she would, in my memory, tell me what to do. It was rather that at such a time it was important for my own psychological security to find somebody who believed in me. This "belief" included his or her liking me, although it was not chiefly that; it included his confidence in my abilities and other qualities which the reader can experience through his own treasuring of such persons in memory better than through my attempt at enumeration. (1972, p. 139)

As May points out, having someone who believes in you engenders strength when it is most needed. What he does not mention is that when growing through adolescence each person not only needs the additional strength which comes from having someone who believes in you, but also that when this belief is absent youth feel abandoned and become hostile towards those adults who think so little of them. (See J. J. Galbo's research on adolescents' perceptions of significant adults, 1984, for further elaboration of these ideas).

10
The Late
Adolescent Period

During the final years of adolescence youth acquire the features we associate with "adultness" and outgrow many which we associate with adolescence. In terms of mental and physical growth late adolescents *are* adults; in terms of psychological growth they are rapidly becoming adults; in terms of assuming active social roles, however, they remain essentially adolescents.

Some experts are reluctant to refer to late adolescence as a developmental stage because so little physical or mental growth occurs. Kimmel writes, "Perhaps the most striking characteristic of young adulthood in America today is that somewhat artificial way in which it was created as a stage in human development." (p. 79) It is without question, however, a *unique* age because important strides are made beyond the composition of the adolescent personality and a much tighter link with the adult personality is established.

In terms of calendar years, late adolescence embraces a larger range than early or middle adolescence. For females, late adolescence begins sooner because they complete their biological growth earlier than boys. Therefore, ages 16 - 21 can be thought of as late adolescence for early-maturing girls. For the majority of girls, however, and for most boys, late adolescence includes ages 17-21.

From Adolescence Into Adulthood

One trait of this age is the *absence* of physical growth. It is the first period in the human life cycle where the body does not grow measurably in height, width or depth, or where the skeleton does not enlarge. A similar "absence" exists with regard to mental growth, with the exception of a few mental skills which improve with experience such as word fluency. Thornburg represents the consensus in developmental psychology when he asserts that "between ages of 15 and 17 the adolescent reaches his full intellectual

157

growth potential and has a capacity similar to that of the adult" (p. 70, 1975).

If the body has ceased its growth, no such comment can be made about the ego, which is rapidly expanding its boundaries, bolstering its weaknesses, and becoming considerably more consolidated and forceful. Most late adolescents become more self-reliant because they are more sure about "who" they are, and consequently are less susceptible to peer manipulation. During *early* adolescence identity was largely dependent upon how one was assessed by peers; now the reverse is true — peers are assessed in terms of one's personal identity.

It is prudent to remember that self-esteem, no matter what the age, does not fluctuate *exclusively* in accordance with how others praise and compliment us. Our self-esteem also vacillates because of internal and sometimes non-definable factors. William James made this observation and it strikes a thoughtful chord with regard to adolescence.

> And in fact we ourselves know how the barometer of our self-esteem and confidence rises and falls from one day to another through causes that seem to be visceral and organic rather than rational, and which certainly answer to no corresponding variations in the esteem in which we are held by our friends. (p. 198)

We are thus cautioned against relentlessly searching outside the personality for changes in self-esteem; although in fairness, this is frequently where they are found.

During late adolescence most youth become better at perceiving their own personal uniqueness, and at coming to grips with "the way I am." Traits such as physical unattractiveness are assimilated in a more matter-of-fact way (though not in a way which makes the person feel *good* about being unattractive). Traits such as reliability or industry assume greater prominence because the person realizes that in the next few years competence skills and character traits are more important for adult acceptance than the standards of popularity typical of mid-adolescence.

Some interesting changes within the need structure also take place at this age. For example, late adolescents are less likely to think well of themselves merely because they are highly regarded by family or peers; they develop their own private and personal standards by which they assess their struggle toward self-importance. And it is these standards more than the opinions of others which really count. Self-importance becomes more strongly linked with *competence*; therefore, one feels important when one can *do* something important.

Robert W. White claims that at this age greater *stabilization of ego identity* occurs, whereby one's sense of identity becomes clearer and more consistent and free from transient influences; as a result, it is more inclined toward commitment. Youth achieve greater consistency in their self-perceptions and become more accepting of the positive as well as the negative aspects of their nature.

Youth of this age also become more adept at *perceiving the unique personhood of other individuals,* forcing them less than they did as adolescents into predesigned patterns. They see more clearly the individuality of parents and relatives, and for this reason adults find them easier to get along with than middle adolescents who lack sophisticated insight into the adult personality. Keniston claims that *relationships with elders* undergo moderately predictable changes especially in the direction of comprehending the individuality, the eccentricity, and the private history of older persons. He claims that during the period of *youth,* a time covering late adolescence *and* early adulthood . . . "new kinds of relationships with elders become possible . . . Without attempting to describe each of these substages in detail, the overall transition can be described as one in which the older person becomes progressively more real and three-dimensional to the younger one . . ." (1975A, p. 17).

A *deepening of interests* is another trait of late adolescents The trend is away from short-term interests or fleeting involvements toward durable and continuous investments. This is partly in response to increased cultural demands for long-term decisions, such as job and marriage, and partly in response to a personal identity which is more secure with itself and more certain about what is meaningful in the long run. This deepening of interests inclines the late adolescent to take greater interest in basic religious issues, to give more earnest consideration to marriage, and to map out long-range goals. White claims that "a general *humanizing of values*" also takes place at this age, and Kimmel says "they are creating their value system out of their growing understanding and synthesis of their own feelings . . ." and as a result they respond "with more empathy to the needs of others while at the same time they are creating their own unifying philosophy of life." (p. 93) A final characteristic of late adolescents is an *expansion of caring,* a growing empathy with others, and greater concern for their feelings.

During late adolescence the person becomes more stable in ego identity, freer in relationships, and more highly skilled at recognizing others as unique individuals who are not forced to live up to "my" personal expectations. More so than middle adolescents, late adolescents *identify themselves in terms of their involvements.* Values are more personalized and the personality attains a sensitivity unattainable during earlier years.

Late adolescents are less intrigued by immediacy (unless the future is bleak) and their thoughts live more in the future than the past, a liberation which transports them out of themselves. It should not escape our attention that preoccupation with the future and the enigmas wrapped within it become integral to the personality only after hypothetical reasoning and a probabilistic view of future time are acquired — skills which exist among late adolescents far more consistently than among early adolescents.

This also is an age when the person brings into sharper focus the differences between himself (or herself) and society. Paul Goodman describes it as the period when youth recognize the inherent struggle between themselves and the dominant society. Therefore it is an age of ideology, because without ideology there can be no resolution to the self-vs.-society struggle.

All of these advances contribute to a comprehensive maturity which places the late adolescent at the pinnacle of pre-adult development. However, despite this remarkable growth, much remains in store during the upcoming years of early adulthood, as is clearly pointed out in the following passage:

> The late adolescent has yet to confront the complex realities of the marriage relationship, parenting, or intense involvement with occupational settings. What is more, the late adolescent has not yet had to negotiate the tensions and contradictions among roles that demand creative social problem solving. In the years to come, there will be a growing appreciation for the merging of the ideals and aspirations of later adolescence and the realities of adult commitment. There will be new demands for a psychological orientation toward others and a new ability to tolerate the contradictions of adult life. Nevertheless, in later adolescence there is a convergence of new skills that makes the young person especially well suited to take on the challenges that lay ahead. (Newman & Newman, p. 395)

The Body During Late Adolescence

Late adolescence is the first period in the life cycle when significant body growth is *not* evidenced. Were it not for significant transformations in social and psychological makeup, it would be pointless to refer to it as an "age" of adolescence. This age is unique because the demands of physical growth are weak; therefore the personality concentrates on personal and social realities. The body no longer is an unfolding mystery. It simply "is." For better or worse: it is. The subjective issue changes from curiosity about what the body will be, to accepting how it has turned out, and the finality of it all induces a brand of self-acceptance which typifies the late-adolescent period.

The Intellect During Late Adolescence

Most psychologists agree that intelligence does not show significant gains after the adolescent period. Although adults benefit from increased experience they probably employ no superior mental processes in doing so. Late adolescents utilize the abilities of formal thought acquired during middle adolescence in a more sophisticated way than formerly, but this more efficient usage of talents is largely due to practice.

To brief the intellectual as well as the philosophical bent of the late adolescent Adelson says: "He knows more; he speaks from a more extended apperceptive mass; he is more facile; he can elaborate his ideas more fluently. Above all, he is more philosophical, more ideological in his perspective on the political order. At the same time he is consciously, deliberately an ideologue" (p. 192). Without question, the late adolescent is not in the same league as the middle adolescent as far as versatility of the intellect is concerned.

Psychological Makeup of the Late Adolescent

The inner workings of the late adolescent are similar, in some respects, to those of the early and the middle adolescent. The need for approval, acceptance and belonging remain strong and motivate a great deal of day-to-day behavior. The desire for reassurance, contact comfort and achievement persist as they did during earlier years.

Psychological needs such as achievement, independence, belonging, and role experimentation exist during *all* adolescent ages. With late adolescence, however, many individuals become more intent on achieving certain goals and establishing new kinds of security. The need for peer acceptance ebbs considerably, because choices about the "who" and "what" of daily living are made in a more straightforward manner and are left less to chance and circumstance.

Stereotypes

Any book which purports to cast light on the adolescent reality must address itself to popular stereotypes. One such stereotype is that youth, as a group, are hyperactive, and that their flightiness places them at a disadvantage in situations where calm and composure are required. As with most stereotypes born of time and observation there is a measure of truth to these generalizations. During the short history of adolescent psychology, the pros and cons of hyperactivity have been described. In all probability, random hyperactivity is as plentiful in childhood and adulthood as during adolescence. However, virtually all documents written by adults who supervise adolescents note greater fidgetiness and lack of body restraint among *early* adolescents than among *late* adolescents.

Erik Erikson points out that one expression of youth "is the craving for locomotion, whether expressed in a general "being on the go," "tearing after something," or, "running around"; or in locomotion proper, as in vigorous work, in absorbing sports, in rapt dancing . . . and in the employment . . . of speedy . . . machines." Erikson, however, does not subscribe to aimless nervous mobility, noting that "being on the go" finds expression when it appeals to "moving something along towards an open future." He here lends significance to the directionality of energy, pointing out that "societies offer any number of ritual combinations . . . to harness youth in the service of their historical aims . . ."; however, and of importance to youth watchers, especially those dismayed by the "randomness" of youthful behavior: ". . . that where societies fail to do so, *these patterns seek their own combinations*, in some groups occupied with serious games, good-natured foolishness, cruel prankishness, and delinquent warfare." Because societies differ in their aims for youth, and their opportunity for meaningful goals, youthful searching ranges from "helter-skelter" to the supremely refined. Therefore, to employ the insight of Erikson one final time, "In no other stage of the life cycle, then, are the promise of finding oneself and the threat of losing oneself so closely allied." If Erikson is correct, restless mobility characterizes many youth; however, the degree to which this energy is harnessed is, in large measure, determined by the dominant society and the offerings it makes available.

Many stereotypes are not true for *late* adolescents but are fairly accurate for the early or middle adolescent. Consider the following statement by Anna Freud, which is thought by *some* psychologists to be an honest description of the entire adolescent experience:

> Adolescents are excessively egoistic, regarding themselves as the centre of the universe and the sole object of interest, and yet at no time in later life are they capable of so much self-sacrifice and devotion. They form the most passionate love-relations, only to break them off as abruptly as they began them. On the one hand they throw themselves enthusiastically into the life of the community and, on the other, they have an overpowering longing for solitude. They oscillate between blind submission to some self-chosen leader and defiant rebellion against any and

every authority. They are selfish and materially-minded and at the same time full of lofty idealism. They are ascetic but will suddenly plunge into instinctual indulgence of the most primitive character. At times their behavior to other people is rough and inconsiderate, yet they themselves are extremely touchy. Their moods veer between light-hearted optimism and blackest pessimism. Sometimes they will work with indefatigable enthusiasm, and at other times they are sluggish and apathetic. (1937, p. 149-150)

Although Anna Freud believed that these comments accurately describe adolescents in general, other psychologists are not impressed with this assessment as far as the *late* adolescent is concerned. Very few late adolescents, even those receiving psychotherapy, behave in a way which would incline an observer to assume that they think of themselves "as the centre of the universe and the sole object of interest." The dominant trend at this age is, in fact, the diametric opposite, namely a concern with "outside" realities, the nature of society, and the pull of the future. Few adolescents, before the age of 16, "form the most passionate love relationships"; the norm at this age is limited sexual interchange and weakened passion. As Offer, in his study of *normal* adolescents confirms, most youth are not raging rebels; they do not alternate between "blind submission to some self-chosen leader and defiant rebellion against any and every authority." They are neither blindly submissive nor defiantly rebellious; they are more bent upon "moderation." Whether adolescents in our society "throw themselves enthusiastically into the life of the community" is not known because virtually no opportunity exists for them to do so. Therefore, Anna Freud's description of adolescence is completely out of sync with the late adolescent experience. If any age of adolescence comes close to fitting this description it is middle adolescence; for both late adolescence and early adolescence, however, it is totally inappropriate.

In some respects Anna Freud's misrepresentation of adolescence is typical of all psychoanalytic thinkers; however, it is not *unique* to them. Typically, for example, school administrators think of adolescents as bound to the deficiencies Freud attributes to them. Likewise, government officials often believe youth are considerably more juvenile and childlike than they truly are. As a result, most government programs offer trivial involvements for adolescents when, in fact, they are capable of sophisticated and advanced workmanship, especially after ages 16 or 17.

Intimacy During Late Adolescence

As has already been noted, during late adolescence the individual acquires a strange sense of personhood, becomes more stable in ego identity, and is less monopolized by egocentrism. The desire to share with, and care for, another person encourages not only romantic and sexual bonding but also close friendship and sharing.

Intimacy may or may not lead to sexual relationships. In our culture it tends to do so when the partners are of the opposite sex, when they love each other, or when either partner genuinely desires sexual relations. When partners are of the same sex, *close friendship* is the most common expression of intimacy. Intimacy occurs only when both partners are fairly secure in their own identities, or know themselves well enough to represent themselves authentically to the partner. As Erikson points out, "It is only when identity formation is well on its way that true intimacy — which is really a counterpointing as well as fusing of identities — is possible." This is a primary reason why intimacy, in the sense presently used, is not much evident in earlier periods of adolescence. Erikson goes on to indicate that "The youth who is not sure of his identity shies away from interpersonal intimacy or throws himself into acts of intimacy which are promiscuous without true fusion or real self-abandon." (1968, p. 135) "True fusion" and "real self-abandon" are vital to understanding intimacy because they convey the genuineness of the merging of two personalities.

Intimacy is not an easy topic for the psychologist to research, but unquestionably it is more forceful during late adolescence than during earlier years. For example, Douvan and Adelson interviewed adolescent girls to discover their feelings towards friends. One of their findings was that *pre*adolescent and *early* adolescent girls were not overly interested in the personal qualities of their friends; rather, they were more concerned with sharing activities with them. When asked to describe "what a friend ought to be like" the *early* adolescent girls mentioned considerably fewer personal qualities than older girls. In summarizing research findings such as this, Galatin notes:

> Both in middle and late adolescence, girls defined their friendships in terms of virtues like loyalty, the ability to keep confidences, emotional support, and common interests. The researchers concluded that *these older subjects were much more capable of establishing a relationship with another person, of truly sharing experiences and being responsive to their friends.* (1975, p. 127)

The opposite of intimacy is what Erikson calls "distantiation," which is "the readiness to repudiate, isolate, and, if necessary, destroy those forces and people whose essence seems dangerous to one's own." Within most adolescents the need for distantiation increases when intimacy fails, when the self is too long unacknowledged, or prevented from asserting itself. The result of distantiation is "the readiness to fortify one's territory of intimacy and solidarity and to view all outsiders with fanatic overevaluation of small differences between the familiar and the foreign." (1968, p. 136)

Intimacy is significant not only because it nurtures belonging and affiliation, and encourages love relationships: it also is *vital to the formation of effective ego strength.* Every individual's sense of identity depends upon verification from another self; and, every person, to become strong and effective, must inhabit some form of intimacy with another person. Glasser comments:

> To develop an effective ego, a person must have a meaningful, two-way relationship with someone in which the ego of the giving person is available for use by the receiving person in a consistent atmosphere of some love and a minimum of hostility or anger. (1970, p. 50)

The fear of intimacy: All forces within the personality do not push toward intimacy because in it is much to be feared.

Intimacy requires closeness, trust, and reciprocity, and is actualized only when both partners possess the strength and maturity to cope with these requirements. When genuine intimacy is nurtured into existence it brings with it pre-existing weaknesses within one, or both, of the partners, which went unnoticed during previous conditions of isolation or pseudo-intimacy. These pre-existing weaknesses strain the relationship, and sometimes even destroy it. Therefore, the young person not only encounters the strain of adjusting to another person, but must come to grips with deficiencies within his own personality which have been silently filed away, or defensively avoided. In this sense, even though it is among the most profound youth experiences, intimacy also exposes the weakest and least desired aspects of the growing personality.

Intimacy panics youth whose personal boundaries are so poorly defined that it makes them fear they will be lost or obliterated by it. We time and again observe youngsters, especially early and middle adolescents, who simply have not established an appropriate self-identity for shared intimacy. They are better geared to *receive* intimacy *than to give it;* they are better prepared to deal with their own anxiety than with the anxiety of the partner; and, they are more inclined toward individualism than reciprocity. In sum, they are not mature enough for intimacy or the demands it makes upon the ego.

Intimacy contains another demand which many youth are not ready to experience. It requires a loosening of selfish preoccupation, and a lessening of basic egocentrism. Therefore, before the adolescent will endorse an intimacy relationship it must contain elements of gratification which offset the loss of self-primacy. Stated succinctly, intimacy must offer considerable rewards, and little pain, for it to be "worthwhile" to egocentric youngsters.

Erikson claimed that intimacy is the true test of one's sense of identity. "True engagement with others is the result and the test of firm self-delineation" (1959, p. 110). There is little doubt that passing this "true test" is beyond the maturational grasp of many youth.

Finally, intimacy contains within it a genuine possibility of rejection which many youngsters fear because the *pain of rejection carries more profound significance than does the pleasure of intimacy.* Therefore, the pleasure of genuine intimacy, as well as the anguish of shattered intimacy, usually does not occur until the early adult years.

The Fundamental Needs of Adolescence

Throughout this book there is only slight reference to the "needs of adolescence." This is partly because many of the needs traditionally attributed to youth overemphasize the infantile nature of adolescence (popularity, status, acceptance) and therefore, are descriptors of early adolescence rather than of adolescence in general. It is also, in part, due to the ill-defined nature of needs and the corresponding vagueness which accompanies their articulation. However, few questions in adolescent psychology are more significant than: "What are the basic needs of youth?"

To answer this question meaningfully one must do justice to adolescence as a distinct period of life and at the same time do justice to the adolescent-as-person. Hadley Cantril (1964) has done this effectively. Based upon his ideas and insights, the following are presented as the fundamental requirements of youth in our culture.

1. *The adolescent wants security, in both its physical and its psychological meaning, to protect gains already made and to assure a beachhead from which further advances may be staged.* The adolescent's psychological makeup requires that he be able to perceive the world as predictable and orderly, allowing meaningful preparation for the future.

2. *The adolescent craves sufficient order and certainty in his life to enable him to judge with fair accuracy what will or will not occur if he does or not act in certain ways.* According to Cantril, people want to be certain "satisfactions already enjoyed will be repeatable and will provide a secure springboard for take-offs in new directions." Not only do youth crave sufficient order but they actively embark on activities which will promote and guarantee it. The need for order and certainty is strong enough within some individuals to override other needs. Thus, for some adolescents the need for

order is stronger than the need for novelty or perhaps, even for independence.

3. *Adolescents continuously seek to enlarge the range and enrich the quality of their satisfactions.* Adolescents do not remain content with past achievements; they move on after continuous gratification of any need. Cantril asserts the search for increasing satisfaction takes place at two general levels: (1) learning new methods of satisfying consistently recurring needs, and (2) developing new needs which require completely new forms of satisfaction. From this perspective, adolescent behavior which is classified as "troublesome" may be little more than awkward attempts to discover novel, stimulating ways to gratify needs for which conventional gratification has become boring. The adolescent need to enlarge the range and quality of satisfaction is the forerunner of the adult need for self-actualization, and is a postscript to the childhood need for exploration.

4. *Adolescents are creatures of hope and are not genetically designed to resign themselves.* Youth resist fatalistic resignation (and as noted elsewhere in this book, they become susceptible to psychiatric symptoms when they do become "early-resigned"); this resistance encourages their propensity for idealism and for future directedness.

5. *Adolescents have the capacity to make choices and they desire to exercise this capacity.* To ask an adolescent to live a lifestyle in which he cannot make meaningful choices is contrary to his basic makeup. Not only does he prefer to make choices, he derives considerable satisfaction from doing so. This need, like all others, is susceptible to distortion by various defense mechanisms but, nevertheless, is a reality. The need for choice begins to make itself known in early childhood, with the blind gestures of self-assertion characteristic of the "terrible twos" an early manifestation, which gradually becomes incorporated in a more mature form by the preschool years.

6. *Adolescents require freedom to exercise the choices they are capable of making.* (An important interjection here is worth the reader's time: too many contemporary psychologists confuse this need with the need to make decisions, in general. Therefore, they blur the distinction between important decisions and insignificant decisions.) Adolescents want to "exercise the choices they are *capable* of making." When their environment does not accommodate this need typical for most youth today, they suffer from infantilization and other ailments which exist in abundance in our culture but which, for the most part, are improperly diagnosed as "normal" to the adolescent period.

7. *Adolescents want to experience their own identity and integrity.* Many psychologists overlook this need and many more are reluctant to consider it as a primary need. Although each individual learns various ways to achieve both identity and integrity, the desire to experience integrity pre-exists as

an attribute which adolescents bring to all social interaction. When the environment affords little opportunity for meaningful participation and involvement, the need is frustrated, creating a sense of bewilderment.

8. *Adolescents want to experience a sense of their own worth.* Although each person receives satisfaction from achievements and triumphs, he also has the desire to be accepted in and of himself, with no ulterior reasons or motives. This need for primary-approval is basic to all intimacy relationships, and resembles what Buber calls the "I-Thou" relationship.

9. *Adolescents seek some value or system of beliefs to which they can commit themselves.* This need is sometimes described as part of "man's religious nature." However, whether viewed from a religious or psychological perspective, this propensity urges youth to conceptualize beliefs about a reality greater than oneself.

Maslow stresses the pathological consequences of not having a system of values:

> The state of being without a system of values is psychopathogenic, we are learning. The human being needs a framework of values, a philosophy of life, a religion or religion surrogate to live by and understand by, in about the same sense that he needs sunlight, calcium or love. (Maslow, 1962, p. 206)

This need draws to our attention the integrated nature of values and psychological needs. The interrelationship can be seen at two levels: the first, as Maslow claims in the above quote, indicates that people suffer in a psychiatric sense when they are devoid of a value system; the second, (as Cantril has suggested) throughout this assemblage of needs, adolescents possess a number of psychological needs which both directly and indirectly *encourage them to create a system of values.*

10. *Adolescents want a sense of surety and confidence that the society of which they are a part holds a fair degree of hope that their aspirations will be fulfilled.* This postulate is a synthesis of several previous needs, including hope, order, identity, worthwhileness, and future preparation. An environment which does not allow gratification fosters frustration.

Love, Belonging and Esteem Needs During Adolescence

Abraham Maslow claims that all individuals are motivated by needs for love, belonging and esteem.

Of the love and belonging needs Maslow says:

> He [man] will hunger for affectionate relations with people in general, namely, for a place in his group, and he will strive with great intensity

to achieve this goal. He will want to attain such a place more than anything else in the world and may even forget that once, when he was hungry, he sneered at love . . . One thing that must be stressed at this point is that love is not synonymous with sex. Sex may be studied as a purely physiological need. Ordinarily sexual behavior is multidetermined; that is to say, determined not only by sexual but also other needs, chief among which are the love and affection needs. Also not to be overlooked is the fact that the love needs involve both giving and receiving love. (1943, p. 70)

If belonging and love needs receive prolonged gratification the person eventually becomes motivated by *esteem needs.* Maslow understands esteem needs in this way:

All people in our society . . . have a need or desire for a stable, firmly (usually) high evaluation of themselves, for self-respect or self-esteem, and for the esteem of others. By firmly based self-esteem we mean that which is soundly based upon real capacity, achievement, and respect from others . . . Satisfaction of the self-esteem needs leads to feelings of self-confidence, worth, strength, capability, and adequacy of being useful and necessary in the world. But thwarting of these needs produces feelings of inferiority, of weakness, and of helplessness . . . (1943, p. 391)

Love needs, for the most part, are satisfied by parents during the childhood years; however, with the onset of adolescence parental love is not sufficient. Adolescent love needs are satisfied by a combination of deep friendships, romantic involvements, *and* familial love.

The belonging needs pose more practical and pressing problems than the love needs — especially during early and middle adolescence. This is partly because youngsters are uncertain to whom they should be affiliated. Cliques, gangs, and groups are formed with considerable premeditation because greater status is attached to some groups than others. Like their parents, adolescents prefer high-status over low-status groups. Few adolescents will pursue the high-status group at any cost, but all things being equal, they prefer what is most highly regarded in their circles.

With regard to belonging however, the adolescent measures closely the evidence. Some groups simply are not worth belonging to. They do not encourage, do not flatter, and they do not take their members seriously. Therefore, youngsters abandon groups which offer little. This capacity for social experimentation sometimes impedes a durable sense of membership or a genuine sense of belonging. Consequently, the need for belonging often goes unsatisfied even though the adolescent lives in a world of peers mistakenly perceived by adults as "companions."

On the other side of the coin, some youth experience a durable and unswerving sense of belonging. Not only do they possess a strong sense of family affiliation, but they also have attachments with peers and adults. Further, some adolescents have a sense of belonging because of their values, beliefs and ideas. As Fromm points out, even individuals without a *personal* support network may achieve a sense of belonging: "An individual may be alone in a physical sense for many years and yet be related to ideas, values, or at least social patterns that give him a feeling of communion and 'belonging'" (1946, p. 19).

Esteem needs also pose special problems because most youth are not clear about what constitutes esteem. They recognize that much of the praise they valued so highly only a few years ago now means considerably less; they also know that what one person holds in high esteem another may hold in low esteem. In essence, esteem is difficult to satisfy in a personality not yet crystallized its own identity.

Some youngsters, however, have no such problem. They know exactly *what* they admire, and they know exactly *whom* they admire, and this clarity enhances the satisfaction of their esteem needs. Ironically, these same individuals often suffer when their outlook changes, because it bewilders them that they could have been so certain about what they esteemed only to see it change and modify with age. This bewilderment may deteriorate into cynicism, or even nihilism, and thereby transform a relatively stable, clear-thinking youth into an unstable, frightened individual.

The sense of inferiority which inhabits the adolescent personality also impedes the esteem needs. It is difficult to feel good about oneself when one is haunted by self-doubt and inferiority. Many youth deny the authenticity of people who offer praise or love because their self-doubt is too forceful to accept it. During middle adolescence this conflict is one of the primary struggles. Remember, the adolescent turns to peers for validation and confirmation; and in many facets of daily living — especially in the school environment — peers *determine* whether the traits, mannerisms or skills of a person are valued or devalued.

The consequence of the foregoing is that even though the adolescent struggles to satisfy needs for love, belonging and esteem, the constraints of interpersonal environment, the limitations of the household, and weaknesses of personality make consistent gratification of these needs extremely difficult. The inability to gratify these needs is a vital fact because *unsatisfied needs produce anxiety*. Therefore, in addition to satisfying the needs for love, belonging and esteem, the adolescent must pursue them in a state of comparatively intense anxiety — the presence of which exaggerates egocentrism and makes even more difficult the satisfaction of these basic needs.

Postscript

In most regards the late adolescent makes significant strides toward adulthood, and in many important ways outgrows the juvenile traits of early and middle adolescence. The growth traits of this age are not as definable as those of earlier adolescent periods but there is no doubt that late adolescents become more self-directing and less manipulated by peers. Identity becomes defined more in terms of adult competencies than of adolescent mannerisms.

The late adolescent is better able to perceive the uniqueness of others and less inclined to view them merely as "outsiders"; interests deepen and a greater interest in metaphysical issues appears; values become more personalized and more humanized.

The body does not evidence significant growth in height, weight, depth, skeletal alignment or general appearance. This is especially true for girls, with boys being more inclined to increased growth during this age.

The intellect does not undergo any significant increase in power; however, it benefits considerably from experience and greater consolidation.

Late adolescents are more stable than some psychologists (such as Anna Freud) believe. They also are less rebellious and less anti-establishment than many commentators believe.

Intimacy is a more powerful force than it was during middle or early adolescence and is more integrated with sexuality. Intimacy requires a stabilization not found during earlier adolescent periods. The intimacy *partner* assumes a progressively more important role in the life of the late adolescent.

Sexuality increases in activity and passion. The physical desire for sexual play increases; the need for intimacy increases; and, the individual is better equipped to handle the interpersonal complexities of sexuality than during earlier adolescent years.

11
The Late Adolescent:
Further Observations

Thus far we have described in general terms some of the significant developmental and personality variables which influence growth during the late-adolescent period. In this section we shall deal with the specific topics discussed in Chapters 1-4 in order to clarify how these issues pertain not only to adolescence in general, but to late adolescence in particular.

Storm & Stress During Late Adolescence

Perhaps more than during either early or middle adolescence, late adolescence is a period when generalizations about "emotional makeup" are difficult. The primary reason for this is found in the polarization of response to stress. That is, some individuals (the majority) have effected a workable balance between daily tension and emotional stability. This is induced by a variety of factors, including increased mental skills and interpersonal abilities, an intensified unity of character, and greater competence in coping with daily routine. In terms of the storm and stress debate, these late adolescents have attained a considerable degree of stability, and navigate their emotional storms with acceptable expertise. These youngsters are described by Offer, who specializes in the "normal" growth process, as having grown through adolescence in a "continuous, and fairly uneventful" fashion. They are a low-risk group for becoming psychiatric casualties, and are extremely unlikely to commit suicide, or to find themselves in a self-defeating cycle of emotional destruction. Within this group we observe little of the classic storm and stress. Estimates of their numbers range from 25-50% of the total age group — so they cannot be thought of as exceptions to the larger tendency toward stressful adolescence.

Equally true, however, is the fact that considerable numbers of late adolescents experience an escalating pyramid of anxiety. For these young men and women storm and stress is more psychiatrically damaging than during either early or middle adolescence.

The indicators of severe psychiatric problems — suicide, homicide, neurosis, chronic drug or alcohol dependency — occur with greater frequency during late adolescence than during early or middle adolescence. In a similar vein, youngsters who show signs of emotional instability, deteriorating ego strength, or anti-social tendencies during their early adolescent years often experience an upsurge rather than a downturn of these traits, with the consequence being a lifetime high not only in storm and stress, but also in more profound disorders, some of which are resistant to change even with professional assistance.

Pressure and responsibility increase dramatically during late adolescence. The comparative immunity of the moratorium is receding, and the pressurized world of adult responsibility is rapidly closing in. In elementary terms, the egocentrically narrow and artificially restricted world of middle adolescence is being replaced with the harder and more depersonalized "real world." All youth know the distinction between their protected status and the "open season" of adulthood. For some this change of status is a long-awaited liberation from juvenile constraints; for others, however, it is a condemnation into a world they cannot cope with, and a small percentage of them are, psychiatrically speaking, destroyed by it.

The anxiety which typifies so many late adolescents does not magically disappear with early adulthood. On the contrary, it usually continues to escalate. Therefore, during the early twenties storm and stress can be summarized in the following manner: Those individuals who have attained a general mastery of their life demands, who have secured intimate lovers and friends, and who have incorporated the future into their identity, encounter life stress, but rarely collapse in the face of it. On the other hand, individuals who possess low competence and who have mastered few aspects of their environment, who lack durable love relationships, or who fear the future, are much more likely to experience profound storm and stress, and their psychological condition is better described in psychiatric terms than in the more juvenile caption "storm and stress."

Identity During Late Adolescence

Although identity is not finalized during adolescence, it comes closer to its adult posture than at any other adolescent stage. This is partly because it is the closest to adulthood in terms of calendar time — but this is only part of the reason. It is also true because the growth transformations necessary for an adult identity do not mature until late adolescence.

The *moratorium*, while drawing to a close for many, lingers into the twenties for others. Regardless, the experience gleaned from this sanctuary greatly enhances the confidence of most young people which results in adultlike behavior without completely abandoning the adolescent style. Late adolescents, with far greater effectiveness than their younger underlings, assume adult roles and responsibilities, although the *inclination to do so* varies considerably from youngster to youngster as well as from subculture to subculture. As a generalization, the lower one's socioeconomic status, the earlier one assumes adult roles and responsibilities within that group.

The late adolescent handles roles which, for the most part, are beyond the scope of early or middle adolescents, most notably: spouse, parent, university student, and full-time employee. In some respects, these "adult" roles require a developed identity; however, among some individuals we observe virtually no change in their "sense of identity," only a change in day-to-day behavior.

Some young people cannot handle the responsibilities associated with marriage, employment, and so on, while others take them in stride. It is unfair, however, to conclude that those who effectively handle adult roles *necessarily* possess a more "mature" sense of identity. The failure to accommodate to a role may occur because of weaknesses with the personality, *or, because the role itself* opposes honest individuality. Both are commonplace. (However, when late adolescents fail to handle the requirements of a job, or of marriage, or whatever, they consistently imply that *it is the unbearable demands of the role*, and not weaknesses within themselves, which caused the failure).

Pertaining to the "malfunctions" of the identity process, there is no doubt that late adolescence is the most psychiatrically profound time within the entire adolescent period.

The minor forms of identity confusion, such as the *identity crises* and *negative identity*, are difficult to summarize because they often take conflicting courses. For example, an identity crisis which troubles the middle adolescent, and may even cause his parents or teachers to suspect that he requires professional counselling, may disappear in late adolescence. In a similar vein, *negative identity* (which usually is a more troublesome matter during middle adolescence) may weaken into "free-floating pessimism," which, while unpleasant, certainly is not a psychiatric malady.

However, the evidence does not warrant such a relaxed attitude toward the more profound identity problems. *Identity diffusion* often becomes a serious ailment in late adolescence. *Identity disorders* tend to become more devastating as age increases. The impending demands of marriage, the marketplace, or moving away from the household make it virtually impossible for older adolescents to hide from the limitations of character which were less taxed in earlier years. The unfortunate consequence is that for many youth the "identity confusions" of adolescence become the neuroses and psychoses of adulthood.

A factor which significantly influences identity formation during adolescence — especially late adolescence — is one's sense of personal worth. It is especially significant in our culture as one approaches adulthood because it is at this time that the ideas about personal worth attained during middle adolescence meet head-on with the demands of "personal worth" expected of adults. A few comments will help clarify this issue.

Worth and Worthwhileness

The adolescent period is a difficult time of life for feeling worthwhile. Primarily, this is due to three general circumstances. First, little opportunity exists for youth to engage in worthwhile work or to participate in inherently meaningful activity. Second, the youth culture itself is riddled with hyprocrisy, power politics, and short-term strivings. Third, the school setting, in which youth spend most of their daylight hours, tends towards artificial rules of acceptance and over-reliance on ritual and conformity. In this section the focus will be on point number one. While points two and three are of considerable significance, they have been extensively described and analyzed elsewhere (Mitchell, 1975 & 1979).

Youth low in self-worth invariably think *poorly* (not neutrally) of themselves; they resent themselves with the same matter-of-factness that they resent other people whom they consider worthless. This is of extreme import because if we are inattentive to it, our understanding of adolescence is seriously flawed.

Reflect just for a moment on the day-to-day habits of most middle-class youth. They go to school; they eat; they hang around; they visit; they watch television; they search for diversion; they work odd jobs. There is nothing intrinsically wrong with any of these activities. However, to engage in this routine day after day, month after month, even year after year eventually brings forth the ego-deflating conclusion (first unconsciously, then consciously): "I don't do anything of importance; therefore, I myself am of no real importance." It is a conclusion difficult to deny because our culture measures the importance of a person by the importance of his actions.

Worth, of course, is not based *solely* on what each person does. Nor would we suggest that it should be. However, *as far as the adolescent is concerned*, self-worth cannot be separated from what one *actually does*. Living in a social context where it is difficult to find worthwhile activity *while at the same time emotionally requiring it* is part of the adolescent worth predicament.

As Kurt Lewin noted, adolescence is a marginal status in our society — a time zone between puberty and adulthood when the individual acquires skills to better cope with the demands of parenthood, occupation, society, and self. The entire preparation process, however, is contingent upon two key factors: (1) the parent society's willingness to involve itself in the process, and (2) the youth's desire to enter into the adult world. The smooth transformation from adolescence to adulthood is sabotaged when youth feel that the dominant society is unworthy of their allegiance and, therefore, refuse to participate in it, or when youth feel themselves incapable of performing adult roles, and therefore flee from them.

We are confused by adolescents because even though they are our children, they cannot be understood as children. We mistakenly think that if we give them affection and love, their sense of worth will flourish. This is not true for adolescents even though it is fairly correct for younger children. Love and affection given to children satisfies their sense of worth, or, at the very least, it offsets their feelings of nonworth or worthlessness. Giving love and affection to adolescents satisfies only their need for love and affection; it has little impact on their feelings of self-worth. Worth during adolescence (and, in this regard, it differs significantly from childhood) is based upon *doing*, not merely receiving. Youth must do something important, something worthwhile, to establish their sense of personal and social worth. That we fail to understand this elementary fact of adolescent psychology contributes immeasurably to worth pathos in our culture.

It is a bit disconcerting that a message as basic and straightforward could get lost in the shuffle of modern psychology's attempt to understand human behavior. However, few textbooks of adolescent psychology deal with worth, worthwhile work, and, in general, worthwhileness. A series of lesser concepts (such as self-concept, and self-esteem) have taken their place in theory and research, and for the most part, a dignified assessment of youth is less possible as a result of this shift in emphasis. As Hadley Cantril claims:

> *People want to experience a sense of their own worthwhileness.* A human being wants to know he is valued by others and that others will somehow show through their behavior that his own behavior and its consequences make some sort of difference to them in ways that give him a sense of satisfaction. When this occurs, not only is a person's sense of identity confirmed, but he also experiences a sense of personal worth and self-respect. These human cravings seem to be at the root of man's social relationships.

Cantril then adds:

> People acquire, maintain, and enrich their sense of worthwhileness only if they at least vaguely recognize the source of what personal identity they have: their family, their friends and neighbors, their associates or fellow workers, their group ties of their nation. (1964, p. 134)

Sexuality During Late Adolescence

By every important indicator, sexual activity and sexual passion increase during the late-adolescent years. For couples "going steady," sexual play is the norm. By age 19 more than half of the girls have experienced sexual intercourse, and the incidence for girls with steady boyfriends is considerably higher. Sexuality has a more intense nature than during early or middle adolescence, and the person is more likely to develop a strong romantic link with the sexual partner, and to think in terms of marriage. This, of course, does not hold true for all youth, and some engage in "recreational sex," which is essentially physical and genital in nature, and does not require genuine intimacy. It differs from the shallow sex play of the early adolescent in that genital pleasure is more intense and sexual passion more fully experienced, even though the treatment of the partner may be similarly superficial.

Three traits characterize late-adolescent sexuality which are substantially less prevalent in earlier ages. First, the physical desire for sexual activity increases because the sexual impulse is stronger than ever before in the life cycle. Second, the psychological need for intimacy becomes intertwined with sexuality more than at previous ages. Third, the individual, having weathered the social internship of early adolescence, and the courtship ritual of middle adolescence, is *more ready* for the interpersonal difficulties associated with sex. The end result is that youth of this age are more sexually active, more easily aroused by a sexual partner, experience their sexuality more intensely, and are more likely to think of marriage or coupling than during earlier adolescent years.

Rollo May describes four kinds of love in the Western tradition and it is interesting to evaluate them within the context of developmental age, especially with regard to the differences between the early adolescent and the late adolescent. The first is *sex*, "or what we call lust, libido." The second is *eros*, "the drive of love to procreate or create," what the Greeks call the urge toward "higher forms of being and relationship." The third kind of love is *phillia*, which is friendship or brotherly love. The fourth is *agape*, "the love which is devoted to the welfare of the other." Each kind is within the emotional grasp of the late adolescent. Among early adolescents, however, they fall, with only modest exception, on barren soil.

Age imposes general parameters on sexuality, but does not dictate its expression. Thus, there is no doubt that some adolescent sex is lust or "libido"; some is *eros* ; some is friendship, and some is love. But no reason exists to think that it is always the same. Adolescent sexuality is determined by adolescence, *and* sexuality.

Virtually all relationships deepen during late adolescence and early adulthood, not only because one's identity becomes more established and the capacity for intimacy enriches, but also because self-conscious inhibitions weaken to permit a deeper flow of experience. On this final point Symonds claims that one reason young adults are better at dealing with intimacy problems is that "the things feared in adolescence *are less fearsome after they have been experienced.*"

The sexual impulse is strong for late adolescents as a group, but not necessarily for all individuals. For example, Jense's statement that "Sex urges come upon them like a 10-ton truck. The urges are inescapable; something must be done with them" (p. 142), unquestionably is an overstatement. So is Anna Freud's belief that with adolescence the "relation established between the forces of the ego and the id is *destroyed*, the painfully achieved psychic balance is upset, with the result that the inner conflicts between the two institutions *blaze afresh*" (1936, p. 158). What Jense and Freud say holds true for some youth but certainly not for all of them.

The adult evaluation of adolescent sexuality is a bewildering mixture of detached objectivity and hypocritical disengagement. For example, in his overview of adolescent development Winder (1974) comments: "Young people are preoccupied more frequently than adult society would care to admit, with heterosexual daydreams and masturbatory fantasies" (p. 76). The substance of this comment hinges, quite obviously, on the adult who is doing the admitting. However, a better understanding of adolescent sexuality is achieved when we remind the reader that it is adults, not adolescents, who financially support the pornography industry, the enterprise of prostitution, swinging-singles clubs, exotic dancers, and an infinitude of sexual variations (both legal and illegal) found in virtually all cultures of the industrialized world. Therefore, whether the "heterosexual daydreams or masturbatory fantasies" of youth are merely a prelude to the highpowered realities of adult sexuality, or represent a transitory preoccupation, it can be said with certainty that adults are far more sexual in their activities and their fantasies than their novice adolescent children.

Defense Mechanisms During Late Adolescence

A certain irony characterizes the late adolescent use of defense mechanisms because even though life pressures and major conflicts increase, the use of certain kinds of defense mechanisms tends to decrease. The reason for this is that the philosophy of life which is gradually forming displaces some of the viewpoints anchored in rationalization, projection or other defense mechanisms.

On the other hand, youngsters who have established a pattern of avoiding reality or of distorting their interpersonal world by persistent use of defense mechanisms find the increased strain of late adolescence too much to bear. Rather than reassessing their naive or irrational viewpoints they entrench themselves more deeply within them.

As is true for middle adolescents, the late adolescent attains greater insight into not only the workings of his own personality, but also the motivations of others. Therefore, the defense mechanisms which plague the early adolescent, especially rationalization and projection, become less of a problem to the normal older adolescent. On the other hand, the struggle with inner impulses, especially sexuality, and the anxiety of low self-esteem may become so powerful that defense mechanisms are the only way the late adolescent can maintain equilibrium.

A further factor which magnifies defense mechanisms is the emergence of *guilt*, especially the guilt of worthlessness, of feeling unloved, or of feeling incompetent. Guilt is shielded with an abundance of defense mechanisms, especially *insulation, repression,* and *asceticism.*

Hypocrisy and Prejudice

Some adolescent-watchers emphasize that the teen years are a period of idealism, that youth are strongly opposed to deceit or deception, and that they place great emphasis on truth and fidelity. They also conclude that "to be true to oneself" is the paramount axiom of the adolescent years. In a phrase, many commentators argue that youth are not hypocritical. For the most part, this is false. Youth *are* idealistic; however, they also are pragmatic, and frequently they do whatever is required for personal advancement, for peer acceptance, or for increased status.

At least four kinds of adolescent behavior can be described as hypocritical. These include: (1) the tendency to pretend to be what one is not; (2) the tendency to pretend not to be what one is; (3) the tendency to talk negatively about peers in their absence but positively about them in their presence; and (4) the tendency to behave and speak in whatever manner is most advantageous to oneself. The adolescent is inclined toward all these forms of hypocrisy for numerous reasons, some of which are developmental in nature and will be outgrown.

Hypocrisy requires skills and talents not available during the pre-adolescent years. To be hypocritical one must recognize the distinction between public appearance and private experience. It requires the ability to remember accurately and plan systematically a complex series of actions, always distinguishing within one's own mind that such behavior is a mixture of parade, charade, and fact which must appear genuine to the observer. Hypocritical behavior, in most respects, is beyond the capacities of the child, who does not clearly understand that thought is private and cannot be read infallibly by outsiders, and that personal motives cannot be omnisciently detected by others. The adolescent, on the other hand, is aware that thought is private, that motives are ambiguous, and that deception often goes undetected. Teenagers are considerably better at hypocrisy than their younger brothers and sisters because they possess the tools for its proper execution and can better transact the complex procedures required.

Adolescents are more impressed with the hypocrisy of adults than with their own, and they can be relied upon to document the daily hypocrisies of· their elders; however, the intelligence which allows such insight is not sufficiently impartial to objectively investigate its hypocrisy. Stated succinctly, adolescents are aware of the hypocrisy of others to a much greater degree than they are of their own. Their understanding of adult hypocrisy is often sophisticated and, on occasion, exceeds that which adults themselves possess. The issue, however, is not how accurately adult hypocrisy is understood, but how inaccurately adolescents perceive their own hypocrisy.

Numerous factors contribute to hypocrisy. Adolescents, for example, are constantly confronted with situations where they *pretend to be what they are not*. They are expected to be content with school when they rarely are; they are expected to be honest with parents, but, when they are, chastisement is often the reward. Therefore, the stage is set for one type of hypocrisy: pretending to be what one is not.

Pretending *not to be what one is* contributes also to hypocrisy. Adolescents are expected *not* to be angry or resentful but, in fact, they often are; they are expected *not* to behave contrary to parental expectation when they often do; they are expected *not* to feel jealousy or possessiveness even though these feelings surge through them. In essence, adolescents are expected by peers, adults, parents, and teachers not to be, not to feel, and not to desire many of those very things which constitute a genuine share of their daily existence.

These first two types of hypocrisy, in great measure, are a consequence of living in a social world filled with contrary rules and expectations.

More serious forms of hypocrisy also come into play during these critical years including slander and self-centred expedience.

Adolescents are, in many respects, status seekers and pyramid climbers. They are strongly influenced by peer pressure, power politics, and the need to belong: thus, they become prospects for the web of social maliciousness we sometimes associate with junior executives. When the need for group acceptance becomes overwhelming, as it indeed does for many adolescents, the ability of the group to manipulate is proportionately increased; on the other hand, when the group strongly desires to admit a particular person, the greater is the ability of the individual to manipulate the group. Adolescents who find themselves on the weak side of the exchange are easily enticed into a array of behavior they otherwise would avoid. Of the extremes to which an adolescent will go in order to win group acceptance, hypocrisy is one of the more moderate.

The adolescent whose conscience is not overly burdened with moral rules is able to handle the "requirements" of cut-throat social life more easily than companions who reflect upon the moral rightness of their conduct. Inevitably, the adolescent must come to grips with the non-authenticity of hypocrisy, whether it is socially effective or not. Thus, a natural consequence of adolescent hypocrisy is a "mini-crisis" in moral viewpoint, usually occurring during the late-adolescent years after the turmoil of early adolescence has taken its toll.

The final form of adolescent hypocrisy is the hypocrisy of expediency. The adolescent who says what the school principal wants to hear, who behaves in the way the gang leader expects, who fakes sincerity to win the confidence of a sweetheart, is acting out a false role. Role playing is not itself hypocritical. However, when one portrays the role as real when it is not, this is hypocrisy. On this count, adolescents are guilty time and again. They manipulate others by appearing innocent when they are not, or by appearing expert when they are novices. Hypocrisy of this type can be likened to that of the imposter, the conman, or the charlatan, and even though such prototypes are stylish nowadays deceit is its foundation.

Neither are lying, cheating or stealing foreign to the adolescent character. Kiell (1964) in an intriguing overview, concludes that these activities hold considerable prominence in the lives of normal adolescents. After analyzing several hundred autobiographies, Kiell reports that memories of adolescence often included incidents of lying, cheating and stealing. One autobiographer claimed that at age 13 "I became such an adept in the infernal art of lying, that I was seldom guilty of a fault for which I could not invent an apology capable of deceiving the wisest." Another biographer reflecting on his youth claimed: "We liked to steal, but we didn't like to think about it, *not as stealing.*" Another stated: "I did not exactly want to steal the money, I wanted to steal the employment of it." A classic example of rationalization blended with candor. As Kiell points out, however, "The experimental stealing the adolescent engages in is not serious and usually is outgrown as the superego develops greater stability." The point should not be lost, however, that *until stability is attained*, many adolescents are prone to dramatic episodes of lying, cheating and stealing.

Many adolescents remain underdeveloped (sometimes impoverished) in the capacity to apply moral beliefs to their daily lives, and they are likely to "understand" their personal conflicts with stereotyped slogans, or naive platitudes, rather than with genuine insight. It is interesting to note that research on cheating among university students supports the thesis that it is tolerated by most students, and viewed as a practical necessity by others. As Kiell points out, this is neither a historical nor a geographical novelty:

"The social sanction of cheating by students is not a phenomenon peculiar to life in the United States. It is to be found also in China, Russia, India, France, England, Brazil, and Scotland . . ."

Most experts specializing in adolescent psychopathology concur that lying, cheating, and stealing, unto themselves, are not indicators of a disturbed personality. For many youth, this behavior can cautiously be called "normal." As with hypocrisy, developmental conditions contribute to these character limitations. Kiell summarized it this way: "The adolescent who *persistently* lies, cheats or steals is expressing a symptom of acute personality disorder. The adolescent who manifests such behavior *occasionally* has not yet established fully effective controls to prevent the outbreaks" (p. 830). This assessment of the "progressive improvement" of moral decision-making is appropriate for the entire adolescent period, but it is especially valid for the early and middle adolescent.

Adolescents tend to outgrow their brands of hypocrisy, replacing them in time with adult variations. Adolescents are comparatively exempt from the universal adult hypocrisy which decrees that others should 'do as I say, not do as I do'. Adolescents tend not to be overly prescriptive about what others (especially peers) should do.

Adolescent hypocrisy tells us a good deal about pressurized life and how the personality juggles to preserve itself in a social network which often does not take it seriously.

Adolescent Prejudice

Prejudice is more complex than hypocrisy. Its origins are more vague, and its purposes less detectable. Nevertheless, it *is* widespread in the adolescent community, at times existing even when the specific prejudice is not found in the adult community. Adolescent prejudice is directed against the different and the weak, and it is especially prevalent when the different *are* weak.

In a comprehensive investigation of adolescent prejudice, Glock & Wuthnow draw this conclusion about anti-Semitism among the young: "Our initial descriptive examination of teenage anti-Semitism produced a fair share of surprises . . . the most disturbing was the sheer amount of hostility toward Jews expressed by teenagers." The researchers were also surprised to discover "that so many negative stereotypes received majority or near majority support . . ." (1975). Although Glock & Wuthnow admitted surprise that racial and ethnic prejudice is widespread among adolescents, it is doubtful whether school teachers, social workers or probation officers would be surprised.

It is not known what causes prejudice. Glock & Wuthnow claim that prejudice "is nurtured especially among youths who have not developed cognitive skills and sophistication to combat it" (p. 164). However, the varieties of elitism found among the highly educated seemingly contradicts this. The authors themselves caution: ". . . if group differences are real, which . . . they sometimes are, the cognitively sophisticated may be more prone to a hostile response because the reality of the differences will be more visible to them" (p. 166).

Prejudice places someone, or some group, on a lower level than oneself. At first glance this seems insufficient to account for its existence; however when one takes into account the precarious status of many youth, and how easily they are rejected, the value of "knowing" others are inferior is not only comforting; for some it is necessary.

Prejudice allows one to direct hostility to a particular group and to feel *morally superior* while doing so. Prejudice is seductive to the adolescent because scapegoating hostility and establishing a sense of moral superiority are ways by which the struggling person maintains some sense of adequacy.

Prejudice provides clarity and many youngsters would rather be prejudiced against a group than be unclear about what to think of it. Prejudice, to them, is less a problem than uncertainty.

Finally, some adolescents are prejudiced simply because they have learned it. Their friends, their parents, their teachers, are prejudiced and they acquire it just as they acquire any other dogma.

After investigating over 1,500 boys and girls aged 11-16, Frenkel-Brunswik and her research associates isolated traits which characterize individuals high in prejudice and ethnocentrism. Foremost among their findings was the rejection of "out-group" individuals and a naive and selfish acceptance of "in-group" individuals.

Prejudiced adolescents are highly critical of "weakness" and they mistrust minority groups which lack "official" status. They sharply dichotomize sex roles, and not infrequently, prejudice-oriented boys display a profound dislike of women and girls. They not only perceive the opposite sex in stereotyped fashion; they also believe in the truth of these stereotypes. They hold exaggerated concepts of masculinity and femininity, and disapprove of those who differ from them, especially males who have "feminine" traits, or females who have "masculine" traits.

Prejudiced adolescents hold wealth in exceptionally high regard. The contempt they hold for the weak is reversed in their admiration of the powerful. Money is viewed as a source of friends, and their interpersonal world is often structured in such a manner that it becomes so. Interestingly, the *parents* of prejudiced adolescents have an exaggerated concern for social status; they are highly concerned with upward mobility, with "right" versus "wrong" people, and they show resentment and dislike for low-status people.

Prejudiced adolescents need right and wrong answers to moral questions; they perceive issues from an "either-or" framework, and consistently see issues as "black" or "white," but rarely as "grey." Prejudiced young people also tend to hold a catastrophic conception of the world, presumably because *their personal insecurities are projected outwards*, resulting in a readiness to perceive catastrophies in the outside world. They are more impressed with superstition than their unprejudiced peers, and are far more likely to believe that events are caused by chance than by underlying social forces.

In summary, prejudice is part of a world outlook which derives partly from beliefs acquired from parents and other social agents, and partly from personality limitations which are appeased by prejudice and hatred. The traits most typically associated with adolescent prejudice include:
1. glorification of the in-group and vilification of the out-group
2. strong conformity, with underlying feelings of rage and resentment
3. either/or perceptions of social events and interpersonal relationships
4. general submissiveness toward authority while, at the same time, resentment and dislike of specific authority figures
5. status and conformity consciousness derived from parents

The ingredients which encourage hypocrisy and prejudice during adolescence include (1) the inability to objectively assess the beliefs of others, (2) the tendency to think in "either/or" categories, and (3) the inclination toward ethnocentrism. The defense mechanisms which allow hypocrisy and prejudice to thrive (especially projection, denial, and emotional insulation) are widespread during adolescence, and they contribute in great measure to the young person's failure to understand his own hypocrisy and prejudice.

Postscript

The late adolescent years bring adolescence to a conclusion, but they do not resolve the fundamental problems associated with youth, nor do they render finality to the storm and stress which sometimes characterize it.

The late adolescent, in North American culture, is something of a lost entity because he, in many respects, has outgrown stereotypic adolescent mannerisms, but has not found a comfortable zone in the world of young adults in which to stake a claim.

We frequently hear that the *early* adolescent lives in a transitional world, alternating between childhood and adolescence. A similar transitional status defines the late adolescent also; however, an important distinction exists between these groups which makes the comparison less real than it appears. Mainly, the late adolescent is better prepared to deal with the adult world than the early adolescent is to deal with the adolescent world. The late adolescent possesses many adult traits, and generally speaking, his personality is "ready" for additional responsibilities and an expansion of identity. Similar observations may be made about the early adolescent; however, we must not forget that the early adolescent possesses less intellectual power and less emotional depth, and therefore is less capable than older adolescents.

Our culture is making genuine efforts to "infantilize" youth for longer and longer periods. The late adolescent is something of a victim in this process — but not categorically. The most severe implication arises when youth choose deviant, or self-destructive, means to "prove" that they are no longer children, thereby simultaneously confirming and refuting that they are.

A Final Postscript

While writing about youth, charting their customs, and analyzing their psychological makeup, we must caution against being overly sober and straightforward. All the business of youth is not serious. Carefree rambunctiousness and spontaneous zaniness are as vital to young people as are their needs for work and involvement or esteem and belonging. Indeed, youth without frivolity is a contradiction. What better time of life to mock, ridicule, and spoof than during this time of relative immunity from responsibility and accountability? Adults make rules; hence, they are made the brunt of jokes when the rules fall through or prove absurd, much as adults ridicule politicians and their blunders.

Adolescents are proud of their blossoming wit (brought into existence by refinements in intellectual maturity) and flash it frequently. They make startling comparisons or sensitive allusions; they dearly enjoy a play on words and their vocabulary is filled with words holding double or triple meanings. Saying only half of what they mean, leaving the rest to the imagination, always brings self-knowing laughter, as does pretending to take oneself seriously when peers know that one is only mocking the earnestness of the conversational partner.

Humor is a universal safety valve which youth utilize well to render a stupid situation tolerable or a frustrating situation whimsical. Without it, tense situations become desperate, desperate situations become unbearable, and unbearable situations become neurotic.

Laughter holds remarkable survival value. Without it, mundaneness converts to apathy and, except for blind hostility, apathy is the most destructive adolescent experience. Youth laugh at themselves, for themselves, and among themselves in order to preserve themselves with enjoyable dignity.

Laughter is the means by which they show their robustness by not taking someone or something else seriously, while simultaneously proving that they take themselves at least seriously enough to stand in judgment of someone else.

Humor is also a counteroffensive against boredom and having nothing to do. Voltaire helps bring this message home by reminding us that boredom is not unique to our youth or even our century:

> "Which is worse — to be ravished a hundred times by Negro pirates, to have one's rump gashed, . . . to be cut to pieces, to row in the galleys, . . . or to sit still and do nothing?"
> Candide answered thoughtfully, "That is a great question."

Humor and laughter are vital to youth, just as in a healthy society youth is vital to humor and laughter.

References

Adelson, J. "The Political Imagination of the Young Adolescent." In *12 to 16: Early Adolescence.* Ed. Jerome Kagan and R. Coles. New York: Norton Publishing Company, 1972.

Adelson, J. and R.P. O'Neil. "Growth of Political Ideas in Adolescence." In *Adolescent Behavior and Society.* Ed. R. Muuss. New York: Random House, 1971, p. 192.

Adler, A. "Individual Psychology, its Assumptions and its Results." In *Varieties of Personality Theory.* Ed. H. Ruitenbeek. New York: Dutton Company, 1964.

Agee, Vicki L. *Treatment of the Violent Incorrigible Adolescent.* Massachusetts: Lexington Books, 1979.

Allport, G.W. "Crises in Normal Personality Development." In *Teachers' College Record,* 1964-66, pp. 235-242.

_____ *Pattern and Growth in Personality.* New York: Holt, Rinehart and Winston, 1937.

American Psychiatric Association. *Diagnostic and Statistical Manual of Mental Disorders.* Third Edition, Washington, D.C., 1980.

Anthony, L. "The Reactions of Adults to Adolescents and Their Behavior." In *Adolescence: Psychosocial Perspectives.* Ed. G. Caplan and S. Lebovici. New York: Basic Books, Inc., 1966.

Bandura, A. "The Stormy Decade: Fact or Fiction?". In *Adolescent Behavior and Society.* Ed. R. Muuss. New York: Random House, 1980.

Bell, N.J. and A.W. Avery. "Family Structure and Parent Adolescent Relationships: Does Family Structure Really Make a Difference?" *Journal of Marriage and the Family.* May, 1985, pp. 503-508.

Bernard, H. and Huckins, W.C. *Dynamics of Personal Adjustment.* Boston: Holbrook Press, Inc., 1971.

Block, Jeanne H. *Sex Role Identity and Ego Development.* San Francisco: Jossey-Bass Inc., 1984.

Blos, P. *The Adolescent Passage.* New York: International University Press, Inc., 1979.

_____ *The Adolescent Personality: A Study of Individual Behavior.* New York: D. Appleton-Century Co., 1941.

_____ *The Young Adolescent: Clinical Studies.* New York: The Free Press, 1970.

Cambor, C.G. "Adolescent Alienation Syndrome." In *Current Issues in Psychiatry.* Ed. J.C. Schoolar. New York: Brunner Mazel, 1973.

Cantril, H. "A Fresh Look at the Human Design." *Journal of Individual Psychology,* 20(1964), pp. 129-136.

Coleman, J.C. *The Nature of Adolescence.* New York: Methuen, 1980.

Conger, J.J. *Adolescence and Youth: Psychological Development in a Changing World.* New York: Harper and Row, p. 573.

Cottle, T.J. *Time's Children, Impressions of Youth.* Boston: Littlte, Brown and Company, 1971.

Cottle, T.J. and Klineberg, S.L. *The Present of Things Future.* New York: The Free Press, 1974.

DuLit, E. "The Three Stages of Adolescence." In *The Short Course in Adolescent Psychiatry. Ed. J. Novello. New York: Bruner Mazel, 1979.*

Elkind, D. *"Egocentrism in Adolescence." Child Development.* 38 (1967), pp. 1025-1034.

_____ *The Hurried Child.* Reading, Mass.: Addison-Wesley, 1981.

Ellefson, L. "Personality and the Biological Nature of Man." In *The Study of Personality.* Ed. E. Norbeck *et al.* New York: Holt, Rinehart and Winston, 1968.

Erikson, E. "Growth and Crises of the Healthy Personality." *Psychological Issues, 1:89, (1959).*

_____ *Identity: Youth and Crisis.* New York: Norton, 1968.

_____ "A Memorandum on Identity and Negro Youth." *Journal of Social Issues,* Volume XX, No. 4 (1964), pp. 29-42.

_____ "The Problem of Ego Identity." *Psychological Issues,* Volume 1, No. 1 (1959).

_____ "The Problem of Ego-Identity." *Journal of American Psychoanalytic Association,* 4 (1959), pp. 56-121.

_____ "Youth and the Life Cycle." In *Adolescent Behavior and Society.* Ed. R. Muuss. New York: Random House, 1971.

Evans, R.I. *Dialogue with Erik Erikson.* New York: Dutton, 1969.

Farrell, C. *My Mother Said.* London: Routledge and Kegan Paul, 1978.

Feinstein, S.C., Looney, J.G. and Schwartzberg, A.Z. *Adolescent Psychiatry,* Volume IX. University of Chicago Press, 1981.

Frankl, V. *Man's Search for Meaning.* New York: Washington Square Press, 1963.

Freud, Anna. "Adolescence." In *Adolescence: Contemporary Studies.* Ed. A.E. Winder and D.L. Angus. New York: American Book Company, 1968.

_____ "The Ego and the Mechanisms of Defense," *The International Psychoanalytic Library,* No. 30 (1937), pp. 149-150.

_____ *Adolescence: Psychoanalytic Study of the Child,* 13 (1958), pp. 255-278.

Freud, S. "On Narcissism: an Introduction." In *The Major Works of Sigmund Freud,* Volume 54. Chicago: Encyclopedia Britannica, Inc., 1952.

Friedenberg, E. *The Vanishing Adolescent.* New York: Dell, 1959.

Fromm, E. *The Art of Loving,* New York: Harper and Row, 1956.

_____ *Escape from Freedom.* New York: Rinehart, 1946.

Galbo, J.J. "Adolescents Perceptions of Significant Adults: A Review of the Literature," *Adolescence,* Vol. 19, No. 76 (Winter 1984), pp. 951-970.

Gallatin, J.E. *Adolescence and Individuality.* New York: Harper and Row, 1975.

Gilbert, E.H. and R. DeBlassie. "Anorexia Nervosa: Adolescent Starvation by Choice." *Adolescence,* Vol. 19, No. 76, (Winter 1984), pp. 839-846.

Glasser, W. *Mental Health or Mental Illness?* New York: Harper and Row, 1970.

Glock, C.Y. and Wuthnow, R. *Adolescent Prejudice.* New York: Harper and Row, 1975.

Group for the Advancement of Psychiatry, Committee on Adolescence, *Normal Adolescence* (GAP Report No. 68), pp. 829-830.

Hall, G.S. *Adolescence: Its Psychology and its Relation to Physiology, Anthropoloby, Sociology, Sex, Crime, Religion and Education.* Vol. I and II. New York: D. Appleton, 1904.

Hall, C.S. *A Primer of Freudian Psychology.* New York: Mentor Books, 1979.

Haslam, M.T. *Psychiatric Illness in Adolescence.* London: Butterworths, 1975.

Haviland, L. and Scarborough, H. *Adolescent Development in Contemporary Society.* New York: D.V. Nostrand, 1981.

Hendin, H. "The New Anomie." In *Issues in Adolescent Psychology.* Ed. D. Rogers. New Jersey: Prentice-Hall, 1977.

Ishiyama, F. Ishu. "Shyness: Anxious Social Sensitivity and Self Isolating Tendency." *Adolescence,* Vol 19, No. 76 (Winter 1984), pp. 903-911.

James, W. *The Principles of Psychology.* Chicago: Britannica Great Books, Volume 53, 1952.

Jense, G.P. "Adolescent Sexuality." In *The Sexual Experience.* Ed. B. Sadock and A. Freedman. Baltimore: Williams and Wilkins, 1976, pp. 142-155.

Johnson, F.A. "The Existential Psychotherapy of Alienated Persons." In *The Narcissistic Condition.* Ed. M.C. Nelson. New York: Human Sciences Press, 1977.

Kagan, J. and Coles, R. *12 to 16: Early Adolescence.* New York: W.W. Norton, 1972.

Kelly, G.A. *The Psychology of Personal Constructs.* Volumes I and II. New York: Norton, 1955.

Kernberg, O.F. *Adolescent Psychiatry IV,* pp. 40-45, 1975.

Kimmel, D. *Adulthood and Aging: An Interdisciplinary Development View.* Toronto: John Wiley & Sons, 1974.

Konopa, G. *Young Girls: A Portrait of Adolescence.* New Jersey: Prentice-Hall, 1976.

Lasch, C. *The Culture of Narcissism.* New York: W.W. Norton, 1978.

Laufer, M. "Object Loss and Mourning During Adolescence." In *The Psychoanalytic Study of the Child.* New York: International Universitites Press, 1966.

_____ "Assessment of Adolescent Disturbances: The Application of Anna Freud's Diagnostic Profile" (1965) In *An Anthology of the Psychoanalytic Study of the Child.* New Haven: Yale University Press, 1977.

Laufer, Moses and Laufer, M. Egle. *Adolescence and Developmental Breakdown: A Psychoanalytic View.* Yale University Press, 1984.

Lewin, K. "Regression, Retrogression and Development." In *Personality.* Ed. E. Southwell and M. Merbaum. Belmont: Wadsworth Publishing Company, 1964.

Lindsay, Jeanne W. *Teens Look at Marriage: Rainbows, Roles and Reality.* Beuna Park, California: Morning Glory Press, 1985.

Lutwak, Nita. "Fear of Intimacy Among College Women." *Adolescence,* Vol. XX, No. 77, (Spring 1985), pp. 15-20.

Marini, M.M. "The Order of Events in the Transition to Adulthood." *Sociology of Education,* Vol. 57, No. 2 (April 1984), pp. 63-83.

Martin, E.C. "Reflections on the Early Adolescent in School." In *12 to 16: Early Adolescence.* Ed. Jerome Kagan and Robert Coles. New York: W.W. Norton, 1972.

Maslow, A.H., "Critique and Discussion." In *Sex Research: New Developments.* Ed. J. Money. New York: Holt, Rinehart and Winston, 1965.

_____ "A Theory of Human Motivation." *Psychological Review,* I, Volume 50, 1943.

_____ *Motivation and Personality.* New York: Harper and Row, 1970.

_____ "A Theory of Metamotivation: The Biological Rooting of the Value-Life." *Journal of Humanistic Psychology,* Volume 7, 1967.

Matteson, D.R. *Adolescence Today: Sex Roles and the Search for Identity.* Homewood, Illinois: The Dorsey Press, 1975.

May, R. *Power and Innocence.* New York: W.W. Norton, 1972.

_____ *Psychology and the Human Dilemma.* Princeton, New Jersey: D. Van Nostrand, 1967.

McBroom, William. "The Influence of Parent Status Variables on the Status Aspirations of Youths." *Adolescence,* Vol. XX. No. 77 (Spring 1985), pp. 115-128.

Mead, M. *Coming of Age in Samoa.* New York: Dell, 1928.

Michalko, Rod. "The Metaphor of Adolescence." *Journal of Phenomenolgoy & Pedagogy,* Vol. 3 (1984), pp. 296-311.

Mitchell, John J. *Adolescent Psychology.* Toronto: Holt, Rinehart and Winston, 1979.

_____ *The Adolescent Predicament.* Toronto: Holt, Rinehart and Winston, 1975.

_____ *Child Development.* Toronto: Holt, Rinehart and Winston, 1980.

_____ *Human Life: The Early Adolescent Years.* Toronto: Holt, Rinehart and Winston, 1974.

Moriarty, A.E. and Toussieng, P.W. *Adolescent Coping.* New York: Grune and Stratton, 1976.

Mussen, P., Conger, J. and Kagan, J. *Child Development and Personality.* 3rd edition. New York: Harper and Row, 1969.

Nelson, M.C., ed. *The Narcissistic Condition: A Fact of our Lives and Times.* New York: Human Sciences Press, 1977.

Newman, B.M. and Newman, P.R. *An Introduction to the Psychology of Adolescence.* Homewood, Illinois: The Dorsey Press, 1979.

Oden, T.C. *Game Free: A Guide to the Meaning of Intimacy.* New York: Harper and Row, 1974.

Offer, D. "Normal Adolescent Development." In *The Short Course in Adolescent Psychiatry.* Ed. J. Novello. New York: Brunner and Mazel, 1979.

_____ *The Psychological World of the Teenager.* New York: Basic Books, 1969.

Olson, C.F. and J. Worobey. "Perceived Mother-Daughter Relations in a Pregnant and Non-Pregnant Adolescent Sample." *Adolescence,* Vol. 19, No. 76 (Winter 1984), pp. 781-794.

Osterrieth, P.A. "Adolescence: Some Psychological Aspects." In *Adolescence: Psychosocial Perspectives.* Ed. G. Caplan and S. Lebovici.

Paine, R.W. *We never had any trouble before.* New York: Stein and Day Publishers, 1975.

Parish, Thomas, and Stanley Wigle. "A Longitudinal Study of the Impact of Parental Divorce on Adolescents' Evaluations of Self and Parents." *Adolescence,* Vol. XX, No. 77, (Spring 1985), pp. 239-244.

Paton, S., Kessler, R. and Kandel, D. "Depressive Mood & Adolescent Illicit Drug Use: A Longitudinal Analysis." *The Journal of Genetic Psychology,* Volume 131, (1977), pp. 267-289.

Piaget, J. and Inhelder, B. *The Psychology of the Child.* New York: Basic Books, 1969.

Polit-O'Hara, Denise and Kahn, Janet. "Communication and Contraceptive Practices in Adolescent Couples." *Adolescence,* Vol. XX, No. 77 (Spring 1985), pp. 33-34.

Prosen, H., Toews, L. and Martin, R. "The Life Cycle of the Family: Parental Midlife Crisis and Adolescent Rebellion." In *Adolescent Psychiatry,* Vol. IX. Ed. Feinstein, S., Looney, L., Schwartzberg, A. and Sorosky, A. Chicago: University of Chicago Press, 1981.

Rakoff, V. "A Reconciliation of Identity." In *Adolescent Psychiatry.* Ed. S.C. Feinstein *et al.* Chicago: University of Chicago Press, 1981.

Rogers, C. *Client Centered Therapy.* Boston: Houghton Mifflin, 1951, pp. 483-524.

Rogers, D. *The Psychology of Adolescence.* New Jersey: Prentice-Hall, 1977.

Rokeach, M. *The Nature of Human Values.* New York: Free Press, 1973, p. 75.

Rychlak, J. *Introduction to Personality and Psychotherapy.* Boston: Houghton Mifflin, 1973.

Sahakian, W.S., ed. *Psychology of Personality: Readings in Theory.* Chicago: Rand McNally, 1965.

Seligman, M. "Depression and Learned Helplessness." In *The Psychology of Depression.* Ed. R.J. Friedman and M. Katz. Washington, D.C.: V.H. Winston and Sons, 1974.

Shapiro, D. *Neurotic Styles.* New York: Basic Books, 1965.

Sigel, I.E. and Cocking, R.R. *Cognitive Development from Childhood to Adolescence.* New York: Holt, Rinehart and Winston, 1977.

Simkins, L. "Consequences of Teenage Pregnancy and Motherhood." *Adolescence,* Vol. 19, No. 73, (Spring 1984), pp. 39-54.

Sondheimer, A. "Anticipation and Experimentation: The Sexual Concerns of Mid Adolescence." In *Adolescent Psychiatry,* Vol. X. Ed. S.C. Feinstein *et al.* Chicago: University of Chicago Press, 1982.

Stein, L. *Effective Personality: A Humanistic Approach.* Belmont: Brooks/Cole, 1972.

Steinberg, L.D. and Hill, L.P. "Family Interaction Patterns During Early Adolescence." In *Adolescent Behavior and Society.* Ed. R. Muuss. New York: Random House, 1980.

Stevens-Long, J. and Cobb, N.J. *Adolescence and Early Adulthood.* Palo Alto: Mayfield, 1983.

Sullivan, H.S. *The Interpersonal Theory of Psychiatry.* New York: Norton, 1953.

Thornburg, H.D. *Development in Adolescence.* Monterey, California: Brooks/Cole, 1982.

Tillich, P. *The Courage to Be.* New Haven: Yale University Press, 1952, p. 150.

Toews, L., Prosen, H. and Martin, R. "The Life Cycle of the Family: The Adolescent's Sense of Time." In *Adolescent Psychiatry.* Ed. S. Feinstein *et al.* Vol. IX. Chicago: University of Chicago Press, 1981.

Van Spruiell, "Adolescent Narcissism and Group Psychotherapy." In *The Adolescent in Group and Family Therapy.* Ed. M. Sugar. New York: Brunner Mazel, 1975.

Weiner, I.B. and Del Gaudia, A.C. *Archives of General Psychiatry.* 33, (February 1976), pp. 187-193.

Winder, A.E. *Adolescence: Contemporary Studies.* New York: Van Nostrand, 1974.

Whisnant, L. and Zegans, L. *American Journal of Psychology.* 132(8), 1975, pp. 809-815.

Wolk, S. and Brandon, L. "Runaway Adolescents' Perceptions of Parents and Self." In *Adolescent Behavior and Society.* Ed. R. Muuss. New York: Random House, 1980.

Yarcheski, A. and N.E. Mahon. "Chumship Relationships, Altruistic Behavior and Loneliness in Early Adolescents." *Adolescence.* Vol. 19, No. 76, (Winter, 1984), pp. 913-924.

Zelnick, M. and Kantner, J.F. "Sexual and Contraceptive Experience of Young Unmarried Women in the United States, 1976 and 1971." *Family Planning Perspectives,* Vol. 9, No. 2, (March/April 1977).

Index

Ackerman, G. 2
Adelson, J. 100, 108, 130, 161, 164
Adler, A. 43
Adolescence as the Age of Identity 15
Adolescent Alienation 39
Adolescent Prejudice 184
Adolescent Sexuality 47
Affluence and Apathy 152
Age of Identity 16
Aimlessness 44
Aimlessness and Identity Confusion 43
Alienation 46
Alienation and Identity 38
Alienation as Disturbance 39
Alienation-as-Identity 40
Allport, G. 12, 17, 71, 72
Androgens 94
Anorexia Nervosa 85
Anthony, L. 3, 7
Apathy 152
Arbitary Rightness 85, 86
Asceticism 84, 147
Assimilative Projection 74

Bandura, A. 1, 9, 10, 11, 147
Barron, F. 11
Belonging 49, 168
Belonging Needs 169
Bell, N.J. 143
Benedict, Ruth 8
Bischof, L.J. 41
Blind Spots 82, 83, 116
Block, J.H. 18
Blos, P. 4, 27, 91, 92, 97, 112, 135
Body During Late Adolescence 160

Cambor, C.G. 40
Cantril, H. 166, 177
Coleman, J.C. 1
Companionship 136
Compartmentalization 116, 147
Compartments 83
Competence 158
Competence Roles 18

Components of Identity 15
Conger, J.J. 8
Constraints Upon Adolescent Identity 27
Continuity of Experience 16, 144
Contraceptives 107, 145
Coping strategies 133
Cottle, T.J. 28, 48, 109
Cynicism 41, 86, 87, 145

Decreased Storm and Stress 142
Defensive Devaluation 88
Defense Mechanisms 69, 70, 71,
    116, 124, 145
    asceticism 85
    identification 78
    insulation 80, 81
    projection 73
    rationalization 74
    reaction formation 76
    regression 79, 80
    repression 72, 73
Defense Mechanism During Late
    Adolescence 180
Depersonalized Sexuality 61, 145
Depersonalized Sex 61
Despair 147, 148, 149
DeVaron, M. 59
Disowning Projection 74
Distantiation 164
Dominance 50
Double Standards 103
Douvan 164
DuLit, E. 91

Early-Adolescent Period, and 93
    defense mechanisms 116, 117
    home and family 102
    identity 113, 114
    moral outlook 103, 104
    narcissism 120-125
    physical growth 94, 95, 96
    sexual curiosity 104-107
    social outlook 99, 100, 101
    storm and stress 111-113

Egocentric Syllogism 118
Egocentrism 117, 119, 120, 124, 125, 130, 142, 166
Elkind, D. 55, 82, 119
Ellefson, L. 139
Elusiveness 86, 147
Emotional Insulation 80, 81
Erikson, Erik 4, 13, 16, 20, 27, 33, 58, 60, 99, 162, 164, 166
Esteem 168
Esteem Needs 170
Estrogens 94
Evans, R.I. 21, 27
Excessive Control 84, 85

Failure of Identity 20
Family Romance 135, 136
Farrell, C. 65
Fear as a Constraint 27
Fear of Intimacy 165
Fear of Isolation 136
Fear of the Future 28
Fidelity 20, 21, 31, 114
Foreclosure 18, 113
Formal Thought 16
Freud, Anna 1, 5, 6, 8, 84, 85, 162, 163, 179
Freud, Sigmund 3, 5, 47, 71, 78
Friedenberg, E. 3, 136
Friendship 60, 101
Fromm, E. 50, 75, 170
Future in the Formation of Identity 25

Galbo, J.J. 155
Gallatin, J.E. 164
Gender Roles 18
Gessell, A. 3
Glasser, W. 70, 82, 165
Glock, C.Y. 183
Golding, W. 110
Goodall, J. 139
Goodman, P. 160
Gordon, S. 54
Growth Patterns for Adolescents 8

Hall, G. Stanley 2, 5, 8, 73, 77
Haviland, L. 131

Hendin, H. 36, 80
Hope 167
Horney, K. 72, 82
Hyperactivity 162
Hypocrisy 103, 112, 179, 180, 181, 182, 183, 184, 185

Idealism 133, 167
Identification 78, 116
Identity 15, 31, 113, 124, 167, 171
Identity and Compliance 24
Identity Confusion 36, 143, 144
Identity Crises 33, 34, 114, 147
Identity Diffusion 36, 37, 38, 41, 46, 145, 175
Identity Disorder 38, 46, 175
Identity During Late Adolescence 174
Identity Foreclosure 20
Identity Formation 15, 131, 143
Identity in Primitive Societies 29
Idolatrous Love 50
Imaginary Audience 118, 120
Independence Roles 18
Inferiority Feelings 170
Insulation 80
Integrity 167
Intellect 128
Intellect During Late Adolescence 161
Intimacy 49, 59, 67, 164, 165, 171
Intimacy and Sexuality 59
Intimacy During Late Adolescence 164
Introspection 128
Irrational Perceptions 149, 150, 152
Ishiyama, F. 57
Isolation 39

James, W. 3, 132, 158
Jense, G.P. 53, 54, 179

Kagan, J. 25, 92, 115
Keniston, 152, 159
Kiell, 96, 182
Kimmel, D. 157, 159
Konopka, G. 139

Late Adolescence, and 157
    body development 160
    defense mechanism 180
    identity 174-176
    intimacy 164-166
    intellectual development 161
    psychological makeup 161-164
    sexuality 178-180
    storm and stress 173-174
Laufer, M. 4, 6, 115, 116
Lewin, J. 176
Love Needs 168, 169
Lindsay, J.W. 146

Malmquist, B. 37
Manageable Limits 87
Manaster, J. 34
Marini, M.M. 92
Martin, E.C. 109, 115
Maslow, A.H. 11, 49, 80, 168, 169
Mass Media Sensationalism 10
Masturbation 105
May, R. 35, 62, 153, 158
Mead, M. 8, 9
Meaningful Choices 167
Meaninglessness 39, 112
Menstrual Flow 95
Mental Growth 138
Michalko, R. 7
Middle Adolescent Period, and
    body development 127-128
    defense mechanism 146-147
    identity formation 143-145
    mental growth 128-131
    sexuality 145-146
    storm and stress 141-143
Middle Adolescent Intellectualism
    129
Middle-Adolescent Personality 132
Misconceptions About Adolescent
    Sexuality 64
Mitchell, J.J. 105, 106, 138, 144,
    176
Moral Outlook 103
Moratorium 18, 19, 174
Mussen, P. 58

Narcissism 120, 123, 124
Narcissistic Personality Disorder
    121, 122
Needs of Adolescence 166
Negative Identity 34, 35, 36, 52,
    144
Newman, B.N. 6, 64, 101, 117,
    131, 160
Nihilism 40, 46
Non-Profound Stress 111
Non-Rational Beliefs 149
Normal Disturbance 38
Normal Narcissism 122, 123

Oden, T.C. 59
Offer, D. 4, 7, 102, 147, 163
Olsen, C.F. 54
Order 166
Osterrith, P.A. 93

Paine, R.W. 63
Parental Defense Mechanisms 81
Partner Availability 56, 57
Passion 51
Pathology During Middle Adoles-
    cence 137
Peer Group and Identity 23
Peer Group 22, 32, 135
Personal Fable 50, 118, 119, 120
Personality Factors in Adolescent
    Sexuality 48
Powerlessness 39
Pre-adolescence 91
Predisposition to Fidelity 21
Prejudice 180, 183, 185
Prejudiced Adolescents 185
Primary Sexual Characteristics 94
Profound Stress 111
Projection 73, 116
Propositional thought 130
Prosen, H. 4
Protective Structures 82, 147
Psychogenic Nihilism 42, 43, 45
Puberty 95, 96
Purposelessness 112

Rationalization 74, 75, 76, 116
Reaction Formation 76, 77

Rebelliousness 52
Regression 79, 80
Regressive Outbursts 116
Rejection 109, 166
Religious Belief 103
Religious Experiences 103
Repression 76
Richardson, W. 150
Role Experimentation 18, 144
Role Experimentation and Identity 17
Romantic Involvements 138, 142
Roszak, T. 44
Rousseau, J.J. 2

Scarborough, W. 131
Search for Identity 31
Secondary Sexual Characteristics 95
Security 166
Self-Control 84
Self-Doubt 134
Self-Esteem 158
Self-Fulfilling Prophecy 11
Self-Importance 21, 22, 158
Sex Differences 52
Sexual Abstinence 56, 115
Sexual Curiosity 104, 107
Sexual Desire 67, 115
Sexual Feelings 115
Sexual Intercourse 66, 145
Sexual Interests 114
Sexual Passion 65, 145
Sexuality 145
Sexuality During Late Adolescence 178
Shame 37
Shapiro, D. 123
Simkins, L. 54
Social Roles 18
Sondheimer, A. 61
Stage Theories of Development 11
Stein, L. 89, 96
Stevens-Long, J. 20, 143
Storm and Stress 1, 4, 8, 111, 141, 142, 174
Storm and Stress of Middle Age 5
Sturm and Drang 2

Submissiveness 50
Suicide 108
Sullivan, H.S. 38, 49, 61, 91
Suppression 72, 116
Symonds, D.L. 179

Thornburg, H.D. 4, 119
Tillich, P. 86
Toews, L. 4
Traumatic Experience 11

Unconscious Desire to Become Pregnant 67

Vandalism 144
Voltaire, 187

Weiner, I.B. 37
Whisnant, L. 94
White, R.W. 51, 158
Winder, A.E. 179
Woolfolk, R. 150
Worth 168, 176
Worthwhileness 176

Yarcheski, A. 98
Youth in Primitive Societies 29

Zelnick, M. 64, 65
Zongker, J. 55